"Hail to Bacchus and Eros!"

Salute!

Bruno Buti

1997
Happy
Birthday!
Richard!
Bob, Laura + Steve

RUMBLING
WINE
BARRELS

BY BRUNO BUTI

RUMBLING WINE BARRELS

Illustrations by: Dug Waggoner
Wordprocessing/Co-Editor: Marisa Murphy

For information regarding this publication, please write to the publisher:
Buti Publications, P. O. Box 304, Cloverdale, CA 95425.

ISBN 0-9648960-0-1

I

A Miracle Divine©

Cultivated and nurtured by the hand of man,
A vine comes forth through rock and sand.

Clusters of fruit hang from meandering canes,
Ripened to perfection by the sun and rain.

Crushed and pressed until its juices flow,
Turning burgundy red while fermenting slow.

Monitored constantly by the winemaker's gauge,
In barrels of oak it is allowed to age.

From the barrel a sample is finally drawn,
Awakened from its sleep to face the dawn.

What was once the fruit of a struggling vine,
Has now become a beverage divine.

Glass in hand I make the sign,
To praise the Lord for this glass of wine.

Bruno Buti

In Memory of My Parents,

Michele (Mike) and Livia

Preface

This story builds from a true wine hijacking incident involving my father Michele (Mike), a truck farmer destined to be a "Capo"; his nephew "Primo", a teamster and rascal of sorts, and his buddy Puccinelli (Pucci), a fireman seeking challenging adventure.

In telling the story, it is my intent to glorify my parents, their friends and colleagues, as well as other ethnic groups, with respect and admiration. The input from their descendants is credited to stimulating my memory and enhancing my imagination, thereby lending authenticity if not actual fact to this story. With them, however many more there may be, I share my cherished memories.

Abrupt sentences and mispronounced or Italian words are purposely omitted, because the characters depicted spoke colloquial Italian amongst themselves. When translated it would then be in common English, and so written. Therefore, the reader must depict them speaking in their native language, but in broken English when speaking to non-Italians. However, the word paesano (countryman) and its plural, paesani (countrymen), does crop up occasionally.

Profanity and sexually oriented expressions were an accepted part of their vocabulary; however, much of it has been omitted or at least toned down to an acceptable level.

A special thanks to Georgina Tognotti Seals for coming to my rescue by applying her professional expertise in the fields of English and computers; to Donald Coughlin for putting me on track to better editing, and to Raymond Burdette for volunteering to apply his 35 years' experience in the field of education to the final proofreading.

Since it was at the urging of my immediate family that this story be put in book form, I can hardly avoid expressing my gratitude for their encouragement to put pen to paper. Hopefully they, such as I expect the reader to, understand that imaginative creating has been applied to better depict the people I write about.

Since hearsay, my own childhood memories and imagination have been applied, this book must therefore be deemed a work of fiction, yet is factually based. The names, characters, places and incidents are, for the most part, either the product of my imagination or are used fictitiously, and resemblance to actual persons, living or dead, or to events or locales is entirely coincidental.

Introduction

The Prohibition Era

The beginning of World War I saw Congress pass the Act of August 10, 1917, which prohibited the manufacture of distilled spirits for beverage purposes. This was followed by passage of the Act of November 21, 1918, which now included beer and wine. This same Act now prohibited the sale of these alcohol products for beverage purposes after June 30, 1919. All of these Acts were later consolidated in Title I of the National Prohibition Act, which became effective October 28, 1919. This was the start of the Prohibition Era in the United States, which was to remain in effect until 1933.

The Eighteenth Amendment to the Constitution now also prohibited the sale, transportation, importation, and exportation of alcohol into or from the United States as well. The Amendment was to be effective one year from the date of ratification in order to allow the distillers to dispose of their products on hand, which amounted to between 58 and 60 million gallons.

The Volstead Prohibition Enforcement Act that followed set forth which Federal agencies would investigate and enforce as well as prosecute offenders. However, the passage of these acts did not dampen America's thirst for wine or, for that matter, alcohol-related beverages of whatever sort. What had once been taken for granted – wine on the table for many Italians, was now illegal to possess. But, they were determined to have their wine, regardless of Prohibition.

Obviously, the well-to-do citizenry had little problem with acquiring wine through underworld connections. But the immigrants, poor Italians especially, could ill afford to pay the exorbitant prices being asked for contraband wine. So, driven by their thirst for wine, many chose to steal it.

The fact that crooked Federal Prohibition Agents with ties to eastern gangsters were on the scene made little difference to these enterprising Italians, especially since the local law enforcement agencies were not in sympathy with Prohibition or the Federal lawmen that enforced it, thus encouraging them to flaunt the Prohibition laws rather than obey them.

Therefore, this story deals with an escalated wine hijacking endeavor by a group of Italians centered in the City and County of San Francisco, California, with headquarters in neighboring San Mateo County at San Bruno; the year – 1922, the dawn of Prohibition.

STORY POINTS OF INTEREST IN SAN FRANCISCO

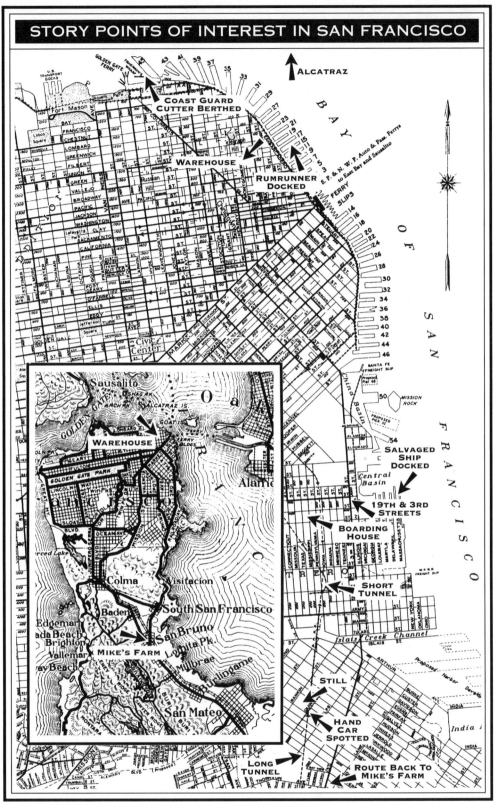

Period maps courtesy of the University of California Map Library

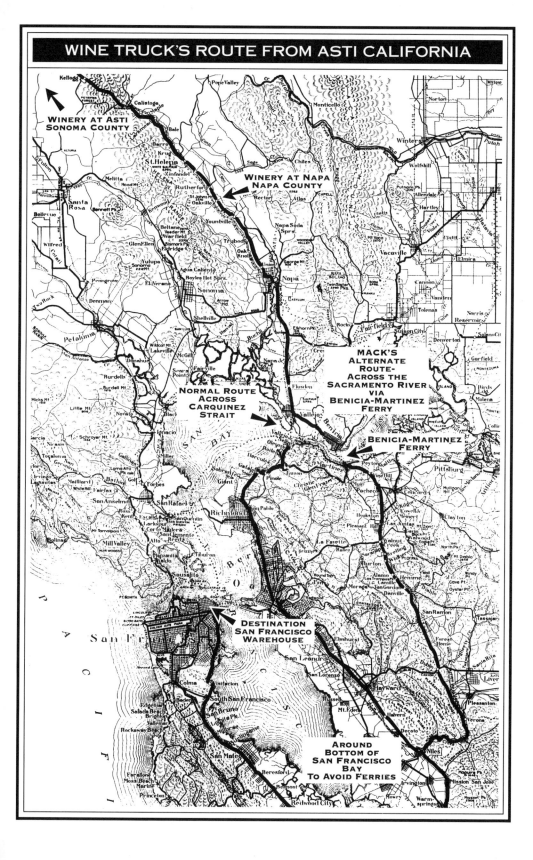

WINE TRUCK'S ROUTE FROM ASTI CALIFORNIA

WINERY AT ASTI
SONOMA COUNTY

WINERY AT NAPA
NAPA COUNTY

MACK'S
ALTERNATE
ROUTE-
ACROSS THE
SACRAMENTO RIVER
VIA
BENICIA-MARTINEZ
FERRY

NORMAL ROUTE
ACROSS
CARQUINEZ
STRAIT

BENICIA-MARTINEZ
FERRY

DESTINATION
SAN FRANCISCO
WAREHOUSE

AROUND
BOTTOM OF
SAN FRANCISCO
BAY
TO AVOID FERRIES

CHAPTER 1

"Uncle Mike, wake up! This is Primo." After rapping a couple more times on the back door, Primo called out once again: "Mike, come on, wake up!"

Livia rolled over and poked her husband in the ribs with her elbow. "Wake up," she said. "You better go to the back door and see what that mischievous nephew of yours wants. Maybe he's in some kind of trouble. You better hurry up!"

That was Primo's voice all right, and he sounded excited. After all, at this hour of the morning Mike's nephew wouldn't be interrupting his sleep for a social call. This wasn't the first time that he had been called upon to help hide stolen merchandise there at his ranch in San Bruno.

Mike made his way to the back porch switching on the outside light as he opened the door. Primo was standing there grinning from ear to ear, pleased with himself for whatever he was up to. His loaded paper company truck was parked in the back yard, creaking and crackling noisily as it cooled down from its laborious journey from San Francisco. Driving truck for the paper company was his job. However, tonight's activities were what might be referred to as "moonlighting."

"What happened? What's the matter?" asked Mike as he looked out past his nephew toward the dimly lit yard. In addition to the truck, he could also see a man he recognized as Primo's friend walking back from the edge of the shadowed yard while buttoning his fly.

"Put your pants on and come downstairs. I have something to show you," said Primo as he started back down the steps. The

1

expression on his face reflected pride, for he knew his uncle would be proud of him for what he had accomplished this night. He was the first child born to Mike's oldest sister, Rosina, a short, stocky, domineering woman who married young, thus making her son close to his uncle's age.

At the bottom of the steps, Primo's friend Pucci (short for Puccinelli), the Fire Inspector, waited to shake Mike's hand. The two men had known each other for some time. Mike knew that when this well-built, muscular, good-looking young man was teamed up with his short, slightly-built, olive-complexioned nephew at this hour of the morning, mischief was in store for sure.

These two young, unmarried friends were children when their parents first immigrated to America from Italy. They spoke common English between themselves but colloquial Italian when speaking to fellow paesani.

Unlike his nephew, Mike was light-complexioned but with the same silky, black-brownish hair. He was as tall as Pucci, but not as muscular, with a much less pronounced nose and gentler facial features.

Having completed the task of untying the truck's canvas sides, Primo called out to his uncle:

"Take a look at this, Uncle Mike," he said as he exposed the truck's cargo.

"Jesus Christ!" exclaimed Mike. "Are they all full?" he asked, hoping for a positive answer.

"All full," answered Pucci. "Twenty-seven, 50-gallon oak barrels of wine. What do you think of that?"

"That's good, but how did you get it? You know this is Prohibition. You better be careful that nobody finds out about it."

"Yes, we know, and that's why we came to you," answered Primo. "We'll talk about how we got it later. For the time being, we want to put it in your basement. Nobody'll think of looking for it here at your ranch in San Bruno." The request was granted instantly and unconditionally.

The barrels were easy to unload off the truck's low bed. In no time at all they were rolled into the basement of the two-story ranch house. Mike then put a question to his nephew:

"What do you propose to do with all this wine?"

"You just keep on growing your vegetables and say nothing

to no one. We'll check back with you in about a week or so. Then we'll talk about it."

Mike agreed. Having all that wine in his basement, even if it wasn't his, gave him a good feeling. As Primo and Pucci stepped out of the basement, Livia called from above:

"I'm making some fresh coffee; will you two — stay and have some . . .?"

The ring of resentment in the statement didn't go unnoticed. Her offer had the tone of a duty rather than a willingness. Pucci was quick to answer:

"No, thank you. I think we better get back to the City. It's getting pretty late."

Primo followed up with a broad smile and a "Good morning" as he glanced up at Livia. She was standing on the porch in her nightgown, leaning with her head out the screen door. She retreated back into the house without further comment. It was obvious; she was annoyed.

At the break of day, the Doane truck, now empty, rattled and bounced onto San Bruno Avenue (also referred to as the Bayshore Highway as it heads north to San Francisco).

Primo, at the wheel, was the first to speak. "Pucci," he said vibrantly, "did you notice how my Uncle Mike handled those barrels? He'd never roll the barrel over the bung."

"Yeah, I noticed that. Your uncle sure knows how to handle barrels all right. Where do you suppose he learned to do that?" Pucci's voice also reflected the truck's vibrations.

"In Italy," answered Primo, "working with his father when he was a kid. Over there his father is a teamster. He hauls puncheons and barrels of wine from one city to another, especially to the seaport at Livorno for export. He learned a lot about wine from his father."

"Your Aunt Livia seemed to be somewhat annoyed with this wine affair, don't you think?"

"Yeah, I'm sure she is. But, what the hell," answered Primo with a shrug.

Livia's light brown braided hair framed a soft, fair-skinned face, suggesting a Northern European heritage. The worried expression on her face, however, was unmistakenly Italian. She was upset about the whole affair. She knew this kind of conduct

3

was illegal. It put the father of her children at risk of a confrontation with authorities. Neither of them were citizens; to her, it was imperative that any illegal activities be avoided.

Mike felt just the opposite about such matters. He always felt confident about everything he did. He was delighted with the excitement this wine affair had to offer.

A week had gone by. Mike hadn't received any word from Primo. He was getting impatient. One day as he sat on a wine barrel he asked himself the question: "Wouldn't it be a mistake to keep all this wine here if it wasn't any good? Besides, what kind of wine is it?" The answer was obvious. The wine should be sampled, the sooner the better. After all, it was left in his care so it would be his responsibility to take care of the matter.

Mike selected a barrel, then firmly tapped the bung with a wooden mallet, first on one side, then the other. Out popped the bung from the barrel. He stuck his nose in the bung hole and took a sniff; no mildew or souring could be detected. The wine gave off a pleasant, inviting aroma. "Ah," he said. "This calls for drawing a sample immediately." He held the glass up to the light; the color was a clear, deep, rich red. It was no doubt made from choice, ripe grapes. He held a sip in his mouth for a second; it revealed no bad taste. Mike concluded it had been well cared for. Another sip revealed the characteristics of Burgundy, a little heavy, but good. He talked to himself: "This wine has to be at least two or three years old, just right for a good table wine." Emptying the glass, he then remarked again: "Yes, this is good wine." Drawing another glass, he added: "One will always know good wine when it beckons you to have another glass."

There was no need to continue the tasting. But, since the barrel had been opened, and it was nearing supper time, Mike drew a bottle for supper.

Livia was not convinced that this wine affair was a good idea. To make matters worse, her husband was taking liberties with Primo's wine. After supper, while they were both still seated at the dinner table, she put a direct question to him:

"What will Primo say when he finds out about you opening that barrel of wine?"

"He will say that I have done him a great service, and he should have thought about it himself," answered Mike.

4

"Did he tell you where he got it?" she asked.

"No, he didn't tell me, but listening to their conversation the morning they were here tells me something," he continued. "I have the feeling they hijacked it from a San Francisco warehouse, or at least from one of the warehouse trucks."

"You mean they stole the wine?" she asked, horrified.

"No, it's not the same as stealing; that's not what I meant," he insisted. "You see, this is Prohibition. It's illegal to have this wine, so no matter who has it, it's still illegal. The people who had it before were not supposed to have it in the first place, so if Primo and Pucci took it away from them, that's all right. You see, nothing has changed, has it?" Satisfied with his explanation, he leaned back in his chair, puffing hard on his Italian "Toscanello" cigar, trying to keep it lit.

"Michele, please listen to me," she pleaded. "Now you're stealing it from them, and you think that's all right because they stole it from somebody else. Is that what you're saying? Besides, you know how they are, they won't stop, they'll steal more."

Her last and parting words for the night were: "I think you had enough wine for tonight, you better go to bed. Don't forget, tomorrow morning you must get up early for market."

Next morning as the farm truck churned along on the way to the San Francisco produce market, Mike's mind weighed heavily on the comments made by his wife the night before. "Yes, she's right, they'll steal more, and that'll be fine." His thoughts wandered back to the days in Italy when he was a boy, riding the wagons with his father early in the mornings, hauling wine from the village of Buti to the seaport at Livorno. When the load consisted of several large puncheons of wine, it required the larger freight wagon pulled by two, huge, white oxen.

Delivering wine in this manner meant leaving long before daylight. Bracing himself in the seat enabled Mike's father to catch up on his sleep as the animals plodded along to their destination. There'd be one stop at a watering trough. While the animals watered, he'd knock the bung off each puncheon, draw off a few liters of wine, then fill them back up with fresh water. Mike's father once told him: "This wine will be shipped out of the country, no doubt to America. This is a product of Italy so a little should remain here. Italians like good wine too."

Mike recalled the time he put a question to his father:

"Papa, why do you take just a few liters? Why don't you take more?"

"I will tell you why, my son," answered his father. "You must remember that before this wine reaches America, others will be doing the same thing. So you mustn't be greedy; leave some for others as well."

Yes, thought Mike. My father taught me many worthwhile things; what good are all those lessons if they're never put to good use? His mind was made up. There was no question now. He would tap each one of the twenty-seven barrels, and draw a few gallons for himself.

He concluded that wine this heavy could easily stand to be diluted five gallons of water to each barrel and not even be noticed. Since there was no time to lose, he was determined to act at once. He would take care of this matter that day, the minute he returned from the market.

Much to the dismay of his wife, he diluted the wine. She complained furiously of his conduct, and let him know about it by saying: "To think that you are stealing wine from your nephew." She was pointing an accusing finger at him like a prosecutor at a criminal hearing as she added: "You see, you're just like your father, the teamster, a thief. No different."

Mike was not insulted; his answer was: "Why do you talk like that about my father? Your father is a teamster too. Why don't you talk about him?"

"Yes, but he doesn't steal wine like your father does," she snorted in anger.

"He doesn't steal wine because he doesn't haul wine — he hauls olive oil. So he steals olive oil instead. There's little difference."

"The difference is my father is a good businessman, and your father is a thief, just like you and your nephew." As usual, she had the last word.

The following Sunday Primo showed up with his friend Pucci. Livia prepared a superb Italian dinner and to complement the meal, Primo said to his uncle: "Draw a couple of bottles and let's see what we've got." Mike complied. But nothing was said about the fact that the wine had already been sampled.

6

After dinner the men talked about how good the wine was, and that it was time to market it in some manner or other. Primo suggested that first they should draw ten gallons from each barrel and fill them back with water. Mike protested.

"You're adding too much water," he said. "It could ruin the wine. Five gallons is the most you can cut it."

"Why do you say that, Uncle Mike? It's not unusual to cut a barrel of heavy wine with ten gallons of water." Of course he was right, but what he didn't know was that his uncle had already cut it once, and to cut it again at that suggested ratio would, indeed, ruin the wine.

After much discussion, Pucci sided with Mike. He respected his knowledge of wine. His concern for the ultimate consumer touched Pucci.

"Primo," said Pucci in extreme sincerity, "your uncle is right. It's not fair to take advantage of the consumers such as you propose. Listen to him."

They finally agreed that Mike would handle the dilution. He would also handle the sale and distribution. All proceeds after expenses would be split three ways.

Mike gave the method of distribution considerable thought. He transferred the wine from the barrels to one-gallon glass jugs which he then packed in crates along with the vegetables. The system provided protection against breakage as well as detection.

His method of sales was the same for each client. As usual, a vegetable buyer would call out:

"Mike, I need a crate of radishes this morning."

To this request, Mike typically responded: "That'll be fine, but my radishes are special this morning so I must charge you a little extra."

The customer would then respond: "What can be so special that you must charge more this morning? Radishes are radishes."

Mike would then invite the customer to take a look. He would reach in the crate, while exposing the top of the gallon jug of wine, and answer: "If it's not the best, bring it back. I guarantee my vegetables."

The Italian buyer's eyes would light up in amazement. No complaints were ever registered about paying a few dollars more for a crate of vegetables.

Business was extremely good and even though he kept raising the price with each additional batch, the demand continued to grow. The cash poured in. Mike reported back to his partners that the wine supply would soon be running out. Both Primo and Pucci assured him that they had no intention of letting that happen.

Over a cup of coffee at their favorite diner, the two buddies spent the evening pondering their next move. Their thoughts once again centered on the matter of hijacking more wine. Not whether they should or shouldn't, but rather, when and how. Pucci expressed his thoughts:

"That truck we hijacked had to be hauling wine into that warehouse across the street. Why else would it have been there if it were not?"

"Yeah, maybe you're right. It doesn't seem logical that it'd be left there by chance. But how come it was left there loaded overnight?" asked Primo.

"It wasn't left overnight. Like that first one I came across the night of the fire. The engine was still warm. If it wasn't for my being on the way back from the fire in the early morning, I'd have never come across it. Come daylight, it would have been unloaded and gone. The same goes for the one we did hijack; it, too, came in early," explained Pucci.

"If they've left two out there, don't you think they'll do it again?" asked Primo.

"Who's 'they'?"

"Whoever they are that have anything to do with that warehouse, who else?"

"Good question; who else?" answered Pucci thoughtfully before adding a concerned comment: "This is Prohibition; getting caught hijacking wine could fetch us a load of 'buckshot'. If we're not careful, we might find ourselves picking lead out of our ass."

"So, what now?"

"Keep an eye on that warehouse, and find out what we're dealing with."

CHAPTER 2

Pucci was keeping a close watch on the warehouse whose truck they had previously hijacked. It seemed there were always truckloads of wine going in and none coming out. This activity raised a question in his mind of just how much wine was stored there, its purpose, and who was behind it. He decided it was time to make an official fire inspection and see what was going on in there. He felt confident enough of his authority to make the inspection without prior consent. So he went back to the Fire Station and picked up a ring of master keys kept purposely for emergency use. He hoped the locks on the warehouse office door had not been changed recently; if not, one of his master keys should open it.

Returning to the warehouse, he parked and waited around the corner until everyone left for the day, then proceeded to try the master keys on the office door. "I'm in luck," he thought, as he felt the key easily rotate in the lock. He entered and closed the door behind him. There was still enough daylight filtering through the small barred window of the office to enable him to see some papers and documents on the desk. He shuffled through them with interest. The documents indicated there were Federal Prohibition agents involved. He replaced them in the same order that he found them.

The door from the office to the darkened warehouse was unlocked; flashlight in hand, he stepped through it.

"My God, look at that," he whispered. There, to his amazement, was a warehouse over half-full of wine barrels. Row after row, barrels were stacked neatly on pallets. He inspected the main warehouse doors and determined they could only be opened from the inside. A husky padlock secured the locking mechanism. It would be quite a chore to open the doors without the key.

He then worked his way between the rows of wine barrels towards the rear of the building. The faint beam from the small flashlight he was holding gave off barely enough light to determine that the massive front door with the internal locking device was the only practical way to gain access to the warehouse and its contents. This, he gave serious thought to as he made his way back. Careful not to disturb anything, he stepped back out the office door and locked it behind him.

As was their habit, Primo and Pucci got together for the evening. They spent this evening, however, parked across the street from the warehouse, talking about its contents. The fact that there was some possible connection between the warehouse operation and the federal government made Primo uneasy. When the two men hijacked the warehouse truck several weeks before, they had no idea of the extent of this wine operation. It appeared obvious that the loaded truck which was parked out in front of the warehouse that early morning was intended to be unloaded later that same morning.

"Apparently there are times when they arrive in the early hours of the morning," said Pucci. "When they do, they just leave the trucks parked out front for unloading first thing. When we lifted that load, it's possible that the driver didn't even bother to check with the warehousemen when he returned to pick it up."

"We sure as hell better not count on that every time," said Primo. "They'll get wise sooner or later."

"That load was peanuts compared to what we could do with proper planning," said Pucci thoughtfully.

"I hope you're not thinking of raiding that Government warehouse, for Christ sake."

"This isn't really a Government warehouse", asserted Pucci. "The way I see it, some Federal agents are in with a possible bunch of crooks, and are using their position to swing one hell of a big deal. That's why there's no Government seal on the warehouse. They're so damned confident, they don't even bother posting a guard. They're relying solely on that inside locking device and their Government status."

After giving it some thought, Primo couldn't help but agree with his buddy and he, too, thinking the Federal agents themselves were a bunch of crooks tied in with God knows whom. Encouraged

10

with their findings, they formulated a plan to hijack another truckload.

"The sooner, the better," said Pucci. "If they leave a loaded truck parked out there again tomorrow morning, that means they didn't get wise to the last one we hijacked."

At two o'clock the following morning, Pucci met Primo with his Doane truck along with a half-dozen North Beach paesani. They parked two blocks down the street from the warehouse on the dimly-lit street. They waited and watched, hoping the loaded truck would arrive early. If it didn't, the hijack would have to be aborted. They assumed the truck would be coming from a long distance; therefore, its arrival could not be accurately predicted. The paesani didn't mind waiting around for awhile since they were unemployed and eager to make a few bucks.

The night was fairly quiet with the exception of conversation between the men. Pucci, in low tones, called out to the men:

"Quiet down! Listen!"

The laboring sound of a truck could be heard several blocks away coming up from the Embarcadero. Pucci looked at his watch and said:

"Three o'clock. That must be the truck. If it is, there's still plenty of time to pull it off." Sure enough, it was. The truck was heading up the next street over from the warehouse. They watched it as it went past the side street.

"It's a Fageol, the same as the one before," commented Primo. "That's it all right."

They listened to it as it made its way up to the street above the warehouse. The truck made a right turn, then another right turn, and stopped at the curb just up from the warehouse doors. Its headlights dimmed, then went out.

Down the street the paesani waited. The Doane was parked on the opposite side facing the same direction. The canvas was pulled down on all sides; the back flap was partly open. The hijackers watched the driver step out of the Fageol. He stretched and yawned as if tired from the long night's journey, then reached in the cab for his heavy coat and tucked it under his arm. He then crossed the street at the end of the block and disappeared around the corner, walking toward California Street.

"If my guess is right, he'll hop a trolley and head home,"

said Pucci. "Come on, let's get over to California Street and see what he does."

The paesani hung on as the Doane swung around the corner to the right, made its way to California Street and stopped just short of turning the corner. They remained parked in the shadows.

"Pucci, you sure as hell guessed it right," said Primo. "That truck had to come all the way up the Peninsula. The ferries don't run at this hour. Arriving at this time of morning means he must have made his load somewhere in the northern counties or even out in the valley somewhere. They're probably intentionally avoiding the ferries and city streets during daylight hours so as not to be detected."

From the shadows they watched for the driver. After a few minutes he showed up at the corner on the next block up. The driver lit a cigarette as he waited for the trolley now coming up from the foot of California Street heading in his direction.

"Okay," said Pucci, "we know what he's going to do, so let's not waste any more time. Back up and turn around. Let's get over to that loaded truck."

The Fageol was relieved of its load of wine barrels in short order. While Primo tied down the load, others folded up the canvas, laid it neatly on the truck bed and tied it down in a manner like the driver would have done. Having finished with the transfer of barrels, the paesani headed back on foot to their usual North Beach haunts with a couple of bucks in their pockets. Pucci climbed into the cab alongside his buddy. He admired Primo's ability to handle the Doane without any lighting in the open cab. But then, there wasn't much need for light since the controls were quite simple. The truck, loaded with barrels, made its way out of the city, heading south for Mike's ranch at San Bruno.

Mike was totally surprised when Pucci and Primo arrived with their truck-load of wine. He noted that the truck bed had a sway resembling an old swayback horse. A sure sign of a heavy load. When Primo swung back the canvas exposing the load of wine barrels, Mike's eyes popped wide. For a few seconds he couldn't think of what to say. But when he did, the first words out of his mouth were:

"Jesus Christ." He had to catch his breath before continuing. "How the hell did you do that? How many are there? Is it the same wine as the load before? My God, I can't believe this!"

"Another twenty-seven barrels," Pucci answered. "No doubt the same kind of wine as before. How about that? What do you think?"

All Mike could say was, "Jesus Christ," with heavy emphasis on both words. He didn't really give a damn how or where they got it. The important thing was that they had it. After the truck was unloaded, Primo turned to Mike and instructed him:

"Now don't forget, cut it at least five gallons of water to the barrel — no less."

"Yes, of course, I'll cut it the same as the last time," answered Mike, knowing well that there would be two cuts instead of one, the extra one for himself.

Livia's call to breakfast broke up the men's conversation. As disgusted as she was with this whole affair, she still saw fit to prepare the men's breakfast. Before leaving the confines of the basement, Mike warned his nephew and his friend that Livia frowned on this sort of conduct — hijacking wine.

Again the Doane bounced and rattled down the long driveway

and onto the highway heading back to the city. In its empty state especially, the truck's massive, underslung springs and hard rubber tires were unforgiving. It didn't offer any comfort whatsoever to the two occupants of this mechanical beast of burden. Primo dared not push the old truck to its top speed of 35 miles per hour for fear of being rattled to death or suffering a fractured spine. As for conversation, that, too, was cumbersome. They had to speak in loud voices to overcome the chugging, churning and clattering. Primo was forced to keep both hands on the steering wheel. This gave Pucci the conversational edge since his hands were free to gesture. He expressed his satisfaction with the way things were going, only this time he suggested that the split should be more favorable for Primo's uncle: a full one-half of the proceeds instead of just a third.

"After all," said Pucci, "we both have good jobs with good pay while your uncle doesn't have much income from that small ranch. Besides, he has three kids to raise whereas we have none."

"I'm all for it," said Primo. "We'll tell him the next time we see him. I'm sure he'll be grateful."

These were three partners with undying loyalty and concern for each other. They were paesani working together for a common cause, to provide wine for the good of the community, to say nothing of lining their pockets as well. True American enterprise!

Livia, however, had a nagging sense of doubt about this affair. She thought surely these three men would get themselves in trouble. However, she was resigned to the fact that there was not much that she could do about it. Her husband's constant assurance did overcome most of her misgivings. Besides, thanks to the wine at dinner, their relationship was improving, although the usual trivial arguments continued: "Like our fathers back in Italy," Mike would say, "they would look upon this as good business."

Things were going great guns. For the first time in his life, Mike was making money to the extent that he decided to seek out and hire a few of his paesano friends. They, too, could share in this good fortune as well. Besides, he could use the extra help. However, once word got out that he was in the wine business, the paesani started drifting in on their own, welcomed but not invited.

Mike set out to cut the wine before his partners returned. But wait a minute! A sudden thought rushed through his mind.

"I'll take another couple of gallons more from each barrel for myself. If they say something, I'll tell them that this batch is a little bit lighter. After all, it was Primo's idea to cut it as much as ten gallons in the first place. As for the customers, they're so eager to get it, they won't notice the difference." However, his father's advice suddenly flashed in his mind: "You mustn't be greedy." He was looking up at the ceiling, pondering the thought, when Livia called down to him:

"Supper is ready. Bring up some wine." This shattered his thoughts for the moment.

When the three partners met again, Primo announced Pucci's offer of a fifty-fifty split. Mike was delighted with their generosity and gratified that his partners were so thoughtful. He was now pleased with himself for not following through with the additional watering down of the wine.

"Yes," said Pucci, as the two buddies drove off again heading back to San Francisco, "that uncle of yours is quite a guy! No wonder you're so proud of him."

They rode in silence for awhile before Pucci spoke up again. "You know, Primo, when we hijacked that first load, it was just horsing around, but this last one got me to thinking that maybe some real money can be made in this business."

"What's on your mind? Seems like something's bothering you, old buddy," Primo inquired.

"Well, that damned warehouse, for one. If they keep hauling in at the rate they're going, it won't be too long before they fill it up. They're so cocksure of themselves that I'll bet they won't notice what we're doing for quite awhile. Besides, what the hell are they going to do with all that wine? This whole damned operation really bothers me."

"Does the idea of Federal agents being involved bother you?" asked Primo.

"Well, it certainly means we better watch our step. But then, if they are crooked, and I'm sure they are, so — what the hell," said Pucci with a shrug.

"You mean — take 'em again?"

"Exactly! Let's catch up to your uncle tomorrow morning at the market. We need to talk."

CHAPTER 3

The three partners met at the only restaurant open in the produce market during early morning hours. The "Chinaman's restaurant", as it was referred to, was nothing more than a space made available among the vegetable stalls. Since it had no name or sign, you had to know exactly where it was to find it, but no matter, because the only patrons were those men who frequented the market. The menu was brief. A hardy breakfast cooked on the griddle or, in the case of vegetables, in a wok.

One could never get a couple slices of good, crunchy French or Italian bread to go with the meal, and whether you liked it or not, you always got a generous portion of rice. Mike couldn't stand rice for breakfast. Neither did he like the way this Chinese cook prepared his eggs, to say nothing of the oily vegetables. Every time they met, almost without fail, these two men of diverse ethnic origins had it out with each other.

The Chinaman, as Mike would refer to him, could speak but a few words of Italian or English, but he did know almost every Italian swear word there was, and used them generously. Mike would slam his fist down on the counter, and announce that he didn't want any rice under any circumstances. But, regardless, not only would he get a generous portion of fried rice, but he would also get a fair ration of Italian profanity with a Chinese accent along with it, all pronounced without the r's, of course.

The proximity of the market provided a variety of fresh vegetables for the restaurant. But here again, Mike would fume as he watched the cook chop up the vegetables and throw them all in the wok together. The reclaimed cooking oil, caught in the coffee

16

can hanging at the edge of the griddle, was splashed in among the vegetables as he stirred and tossed them around every which way. When the dish was finally shoved across the counter, Mike would lose his appetite completely. No matter what was in the dish, it all tasted the same. Everything smelled and tasted of reclaimed cooking oil. Mike's pleadings that the cook use fresh olive oil were completely ignored.

With all these disgruntled Italians eating in his establishment, it was no wonder that this Chinese immigrant learned to swear fluently in Italian . . . without the r's, of course. Whether you ate it or not, you didn't dare walk out without leaving the two bits on the counter. The ever-present cleaver stuck into the chopping block just opposite the cash box was a constant reminder that the bill must be paid before exiting. The parting words of these two men were always barely short of an insult:

"Even for a Chinaman, you're a lousy cook!" Mike would say in Italian. The cook wouldn't know the meaning of Mike's remark but concluded it held a latent insult. So his answer was always the same:

"Okay, Dago." This he could say without difficulty because it contained no r's.

Pucci was seated at a corner table away from earshot of the other produce men when Primo walked in with his uncle. "Good morning, Mike," volunteered Pucci. "Come on, sit down and let's order some breakfast. What shall we have?"

Mike grumbled: "We'll have exactly what that Chinaman wants us to have so don't bother ordering. Just tell him you want breakfast." He continued sarcastically, "And for God's sake if you don't like it, don't send it back because it'll only come back worse than the first time. And make sure you remember to pay him the quarter or he'll split your skull with a cleaver."

Once the matter of breakfast was settled, Pucci leaned over the table, looked straight at Mike and asked: "How much wine do you think you can sell? Do you think you could handle maybe — three or four times as much as you're selling now?" Before Mike could respond to his question, Pucci divulged their method of obtaining the wine and told him about the warehouse loaded with more wine than he could imagine. He also added the possible involvement of Federal agents.

17

Mike was flabbergasted. His eyes reflected excitement. All he could say was, "Holy smokes." He was eager to hear more. Pucci continued:

"Trucks are hauling in wine from outside the City during the early morning hours, this we know for sure. Apparently there are three trucks involved in the hauling: one each day, three consecutive days a week arriving on Wednesday, Thursday, and Friday, then again the following week. To only make a load a week means it's a long haul from somewhere; it may also mean that they're trying not to be too conspicuous as well."

"Now that you're telling me this, I can tell you that the wine comes from up north, Napa or Sonoma County. No other place do they make wine like that," said Mike excitedly.

"You're probably right," said Primo. "They're hauling all the way around the Bay from up there . . . coming up the Peninsula to purposely avoid the ferries. They're using long-haul trucks with pneumatic (air-type) tires like the Mack truck we have at the paper company."

"Say, by God!" exclaimed Mike, "I've seen those trucks. I'll bet they're the same ones that go by the ranch. I see them on the highway early in the morning on my way to market. Yes, I'm pretty sure they're the same ones."

After some discussion the three men broke up their meeting and agreed to contact each other again in a few days. Pucci volunteered to come up with some new ideas as to how they might improve their methods of acquiring more wine with less risk. Primo's parting words were:

"Hijacking the trucks in front of the warehouse is certainly asking for trouble. Besides, by now, the paesani we've been using have spread the word to others — maybe to the wrong ears, at that."

CHAPTER 4

For the next week or so, Pucci kept a close watch on the warehouse. On the pretence of inspecting other buildings in the same block, he dropped in at the warehouse office and introduced himself to the men who appeared to be associated with the operation. There were four of them, all well-dressed, as Federal agents would be expected to be.

"Good morning, gentlemen," announced Pucci.

"What can we do for you?" one of them asked, quite dryly.

The other three glanced towards the speaker as if to acknowledge his authority. The agents looked Pucci over from head to toe; this was the first time anyone in uniform had set foot in their office since the start of their operation. His fireman's cap sat straight on his head with the visor resting on the bridge of his Roman nose, shadowing his eyes and upper face. The cap's insignia indicated his position as Fire Inspector.

"Well sir," said Pucci in a very courteous, businesslike manner, "we have reason to believe that there could be some problem with arsonists in the area."

"What leads you to believe that this warehouse may be affected?" asked the senior agent.

"It's the vacant building adjacent to you that concerns us the most. For obvious reasons, these are the kind that are most likely to be torched. If a fire was to get a good start in a building like that, there'd be no way we could save any of the rest of the buildings on the block. Yours would go up as well." The Federal agents hadn't given much thought to the possibility of a warehouse fire. His statements made real sense.

"I understand. What do you suggest we do as a precautionary measure?" asked the senior agent.

"Well sir, for one thing, we'd like you to report anything of an unusual nature going on in the area. Have you noticed any suspicious activities around here lately during the night or early morning?" Pucci was fishing, but so far they said nothing that indicated any problems with their trucks being hijacked. He continued: "We're in a better position to control warehouse fires if we know what we have to deal with. Information concerning the contents of a warehouse is important to us. Do you mind if I make an inspection of the premises?"

His request made sense to the agents. This time he hit pay dirt as he watched an expression of concern crease the brow of the senior agent. The thought of a disastrous fire crossed his mind.

"As a matter of fact," he said, "we did have an incident with a truck some days back that we found to be unexplainable." After a pause, he continued: "But we are going to keep a closer watch on our trucks for a while to avoid a reoccurrence."

"Good," said Pucci. "That's the right thing to do. Please feel free to call on me if you think I can be of any help."

"Do you have the time now to make your inspection of the warehouse?", asked the senior agent. Pucci indicated that he had time and followed them into the warehouse. "You see," said the senior agent, "this is all Government property, confiscated contraband," gesturing toward the rows of wine barrels. "We must do what we can to protect it. I'm sure you understand."

You goddamned liar, thought Pucci, before saying: "Of course, but I won't be able to take the time today to make a complete inspection. However, I will come back shortly and do so." With this, he bid them all good day and departed.

Pucci came back again the following day. But before announcing his presence, he checked the exterior of the warehouse as it related to the interior. There was something about it that didn't add up. As he suspected, the exterior ran the full length of the block, whereas the interior did not.

A false wall had been built across the interior at the back end of the warehouse, constructed so that a panel on a concealed overhead track could be pushed to one side, thereby opening into a secret garage-like area that fronted on the back street. The doors which opened to the back street were locked, but by peeking through the cracks of the loosely hung doors, he was able to determine its true purpose.

In this secret garage, the agents housed a high-speed automobile which was serviced and ready to go in the event of an unexpected emergency. You might call it a getaway car, an essential precaution when dealing in such corrupt activities. The agents didn't know that Pucci had discovered it. He was keeping it to himself.

At their next meeting Pucci explained his findings to his partners. He expressed his reluctance about pulling off another hijack in the warehouse area. He outlined a new strategy for an assault on the trucks based on Mike's insistence that these were definitely the same ones going by his ranch.

"We're going to take all three trucks in succession," announced Pucci.

"All three!" exclaimed Primo in astonishment. "How the hell are we going to do that?"

Mike was all ears; while puffing furiously on his Toscanello cigar trying to keep it going, he listened. He wanted to hear every word Pucci had to say.

"It can be done, and I'll tell you how," said Pucci. "We'll start with the first one on Wednesday morning. If that goes off without a hitch, we'll take the next two in succession in the same manner. It's important that all three be taken in rapid succession within the same week. That way they won't have a chance to communicate with each other before they're all three hit." Pucci continued to outline the plan of attack: "Since these are trucks with pneumatic tires, they're vulnerable to flat tires which will stop them if deflated."

By now Mike's stogie had gone out completely. He was so intent on listening that he missed the sequence of puffing that would keep it lit. He took it out of his mouth, cursed it, then threw it on the floor in disgust. This act caught the Chinese cook's eye. Before the cigar had stopped skidding through the sawdust, he was already on his way to retrieve it. This particular Chinese had a strong passion for Italian Toscanelli cigars, pre-chewed, pre-smoked or otherwise. Besides, the constantly lit gas burners were convenient for keeping the cigars fired up. As pots and pans were simmering, with the cigar stuck in his mouth, he would bob his head from burner to burner in order to keep it lit without the use of his busy hands.

As Pucci continued to unfold the plan, his two partners injected their own ideas and expertise on how to make it work. They were in accord; the first truck to be hijacked was set for Wednesday morning. If successful, their scheme would add an additional eighty-one barrels of wine to their inventory.

Zero hour was 2:00 a.m., Wednesday morning. Pucci was parked facing north along the highway approximately one mile south of Mike's ranch at San Bruno, waiting for the first truck to pass him coming up the highway. He didn't have to wait long. He could see the head lamps of the Fageol truck coming up through his rear-view mirror. The instant it passed by, he knew it was the one. At that instant, the paesano waiting along the side of the highway just south of the ranch driveway saw Pucci's head lamps come on behind the truck. This was his signal. He scattered several handfuls of nails with large heads in the oncoming lane in the direct path of the truck and then ducked back down in the ditch out of sight. Needless to say, when the tires rolled across the scattered nails, they picked up a fair ration of them. By the time Pucci came up to assist the paesano in sweeping the remaining nails off the highway, Mike was pulling out of the ranch driveway with a load of vegetables and wine heading north to San Francisco.

Mike was taking it easy. There was no need to hurry. The idea was to come up on the Fageol stopped along the highway with flat tires and offer assistance to the driver. Sure enough, there it was stopped off the highway. Although all the tires were not completely flat, they soon would be. He pulled up behind it, stepped out of his truck and walked up to the driver, offering assistance. The driver addressed the situation with a barrage of profanity that would embarrass a madam in a whorehouse. There was only one thing the man could do, and that was to accept this helpful farmer's offer to drive him into the city. At the moment, there was no other option.

After Pucci and the paesano finished sweeping the highway lane of nails, they joined Primo back at the ranch with the Doane, along with a half-dozen paesani, who were ready to pull out.

"Well, what do you think?" asked Primo. "Did he pick up a few nails off the highway?"

"He picked up a hell of a lot more than just a few. You can

bet on that!" responded Pucci.

The Doane traveled up the highway for several miles before overtaking the stranded, deserted Fageol. By now, all the tires were flat. Primo remarked: "Hell, this is going to be easy. The truck isn't so high now. Damned good idea, Pucci."

Jabbering in low tones as they worked, the paesani proceeded to transfer the barrels onto the Doane truck. Once the job was complete, they returned to the ranch and unloaded the barrels, storing them in the barn where the paesani slept. The performance was repeated the following two mornings with the same results. Three perfectly-executed hijackings by a bunch of immigrant Italians motivated more for the challenge of the deed and the love of wine than for the revenue it produced.

Mike's imagination was now running wild. Standing in the barn looking over the stack of wine barrels was, indeed, inspiring. The place was getting crowded, though. Expansion was necessary. He was aware that the ranch next door had been foreclosed on by the Bank of Genoa, owned by an Italian named Battisoldi (meaning coin pounder), who had a reputation of being somewhat partial to Italians. Mike decided to talk to the banker and see what could be done about acquiring the adjacent ranch. The big two-story farmhouse would work out fine for the paesani. The big barn would provide double the present storage area, and the extra farm land was needed for additional vegetable production. The banker proved to be all of what was said of him. So, they struck a deal. Mike deposited his accumulated cash with the banker, and the banker loaned it back to him to buy the ranch.

The paesani could now set up housekeeping for themselves, thus taking the pressure off Livia. Nevertheless, she was skeptical of the deal with the banker. She felt that bankers had a selfish motive when it came to dealing in money, no matter how helpful they appeared.

"Why else is the banker so eager to offer you interest on your money? Isn't it obvious that he's using you and your money to serve his purpose?" she asked Mike.

"So the banker benefits, so what? There's enough for him too," countered Mike. He refused to concern himself with such trivial details. He was on a roll. Ignoring his wife's counter arguments, he concentrated strictly on Pucci's discovery: a sizeable cache of wine . . . there for the taking. There was no question in his mind that his mischievous nephew, Primo, along with his conniving fireman friend, Pucci, would soon be coming back with more wine.

Mike was giving the paesani a helping hand in getting moved out of the crowded barn when he noticed a genuine leather jacket hanging on a nail. Since none of these men could afford to buy such a garment, he asked who this expensive jacket might belong to. Without hesitation, one of the fellows stepped up and claimed it, stating that he had taken it from one of the trucks they had hijacked.

"And, what's this?" Mike asked as he pulled some folded documents out of the pocket.

"Those papers were already there. I was going to tell you about them," said the fellow Paesano. He couldn't read English, but they did look important enough not to throw away.

The documents looked important to Mike as well. The name, Italian Swiss Colony, rang a bell. He wasn't sure what the papers meant, but assuming they had something to do with the shipments of wine, he delivered them to Pucci.

The documents proved to be important indeed. The logo across the top was in bold print. It gave the name of one of the largest wineries in northern Sonoma County. The merchandise shipped was in code, but the units specified as "twenty-seven" clearly indicated that this was a "bill of lading" for the twenty-seven barrels of wine they had hijacked from one of the trucks. It was consigned to a company called West Coast Distributors of San Francisco, assumed by Pucci to be a dummy company set up by the Federal agents with the intention of keeping their operation undercover. The curious paesano who took the jacket had served the cause well.

CHAPTER 5

The discovery of the winery bill of lading created a new challenge for Pucci, the mastermind. In some way, he would have to devise a plan in order to take advantage of this newfound evidence. What he had suspected all along was finally beginning to make sense. He figured that the Federal agents were probably making deals with large wineries that, due to Prohibition, were hurting for cash. For that matter they could be blackmailing or using extortion tactics to pressure them into selling them good wine cheaply. Pucci also figured there would have to be someone bigger than these local agents involved in this scheme.

The hijacked trucks would normally not concern the agents since the wine never reached the warehouse, but you can be sure that one hell of an argument was taking place between the truckers and the winery. The truckers were caught in the middle. Pucci met with his partners again and brought them up to date concerning his thoughts.

"There's bound to be mistrust amongst the principles in schemes of this sort, you can be sure of that. Soon they'll be accusing each other of misconduct, especially in reference to the truck hijackings", he said. "And since the activities of both parties, as well as the truckers, are illegal and must be played down, everybody will keep their mouths shut, and reach some compromise in order to keep the whole affair undercover. No one will bring in the local authorities."

Pucci had no problem convincing his two partners that some day, in the near future, a ship would dock at the Embarcadero and sail off to parts unknown with all the wine in the warehouse. There was no sense in even trying to estimate the horrendous amount of money these crooks and their associates were going to reap with this caper. Satisfied of their findings, they agreed to pull off another hijack.

Pucci deemed that another fire inspection of the warehouse would be in order. He therefore made it a point to be there early the next morning, in hopes of catching them while unloading one of the trucks. But there was no truck, only the four agents at the little office. Pucci made no direct inquiry of the missing truck. His only concern appeared to be fire safety. There were numerous violations. He discussed each one thoroughly with the senior agent, emphasizing the fact that with the warehouse well over half full, trucks pulling in and out could pose a fire hazard. He also volunteered that perhaps he should check the trucks in the interest of protecting the warehouse and its contents.

The senior agent expressed his appreciation for Pucci's concern. "Mr. Puccinelli," he said in a very serious, businesslike manner, "I can't help but agree with what you're saying, and do appreciate your concerns. We did find it necessary to terminate the services of our previous truckers. Their integrity was highly questionable."

The senior agent's statement explained the absence of any current trucking activities. He went on to explain that three new independents were hired as replacements and would continue the same schedule as the previous truckers but didn't indicate where they would pick up their loads. Of course, Pucci already knew which winery it was by the bill of lading given to him by Mike. Nevertheless, he was insistent on knowing who these drivers were, since they would be entering the warehouse with motors running. He repeated his offer to inspect the trucks. The senior agent agreed. It did make really good sense.

"Yes, Mr. Puccinelli, that's a good idea. I'll give you their names, and where they may be reached," he said. "But you must contact them immediately, because they'll start hauling the first of next week."

The new drivers were satisfied with the need for this inspection. They were eager to cooperate since this was a high-paying job for them. So, each inspection was scheduled to take place at the time of their departure, at approximately 8:00 p.m. The truckers preferred to drive at night because of the absence of traffic, but they had to catch the last ferry which departed at 10:00 p.m. to take them across the bay.

Pucci went racing around town in his little Reo run-about fire truck looking for Primo. He couldn't afford to waste time; his proposed strategy was now reality. Primo advised his buddy that he was all set to go. He had no problem convincing his dispatcher that he needed to borrow the paper company's long-haul, big Mack truck for a few days. His excuse was the need to move a family member from one farm location to another. Primo explained that since there was substantial distance between the two farms, his old Doane with the hard rubber tires was impractical.

"No problem," said the dispatcher. "I'll see to it that it's checked out and ready to roll. We'll unhook the trailer and leave it right where it is. You can back up to it when you return and just leave the truck parked there."

"The trailer!" Primo gasped. He had forgotten about the trailer completely. He quickly commented: "Say, by God, the trailer might come in handy for the farm machinery. It could save me an extra trip or two," he lied.

"Fine, we'll leave it on. It's all the same to me", said the dispatcher.

As he had done on previous occasions, Primo reminded the dispatcher to check the cab of the old Doane before he left work. Leaving a case of wine lying around in a hot garage could spoil it.

On Monday evening at approximately eight o'clock, Pucci made his first truck inspection as planned. He knew damned well there was nothing wrong with it but did make a production out of it anyway. Once cleared, the driver took off. He was glad to be on his way. "This jerk is a first-class ass," he mumbled. If Pucci could have heard him say that, he would no doubt have agreed with him since the whole idea was nothing but a sham in order to disguise the real purpose behind the inspections.

At approximately the same time on Tuesday, at the predesignated location, Pucci made his second truck inspection. This one was also approved and cleared after much fanfare. This driver was no more impressed than the first one. He thought he was dealing with a first-class nitwit.

Wednesday's inspection of the third truck, however, was a

different story. At approximately the same time as the other two inspections on the two previous days, Pucci stood alongside the third truck ready for the inspection. Only this time he brought along the recruit fireman who supposedly needed training in truck inspection. The routine of fire inspecting trucks had been explained to the recruit. He must be ready and alert at all times, especially when first starting up a truck. There was always the possibility of a malfunction, and since there was gasoline involved, the danger of an explosion should not be ruled out. As anticipated, the recruit was ready. The fire truck's engine was at a fast idle; the main valve from the auxiliary water tank was wide open. The pump was engaged; pressure was up to maximum. The fire hose was swelled up, sort of slithering on the ground like a huge boa constrictor ready to strike. The recruit, with a firm grip on the nozzle, was standing by to open it up in the event of an emergency. He was ready for action.

"Shall I lift the hood?" asked the truck driver.

"No," answered Pucci. "We must start it up first just as if you were ready to leave in a normal manner."

What the driver and the recruit didn't know was that earlier in the day Pucci had paid a kid a couple of bucks to sneak up and hook up a "torpedo" smoke bomb to the truck's engine. This sort of device (about the size of a fat cigar with a couple wires sticking out of it) was quick and easy to install by connecting one wire to a spark plug wire and the other to ground. They were usually used as a practical joke, never causing any damage. What was also to come into play a little later were the two potatoes that Pucci had in his coat pocket.

"Okay," he called out. "Start 'er up." With this, the driver hit the starter, cock-sure that all was in order and no reason to believe that he wouldn't be on his way in a matter of minutes. At that instant, the torpedo under the hood took off with the damnedest screech and ear-splitting whistle one could imagine. Smoke poured out from under the hood blowing in all directions. Pucci yelled out:

"Shut 'er down." At that instant the final phase of the torpedo let out a blast that surely resembled a gasoline explosion. As Pucci stepped back to the rear of the truck, he turned and yelled again at the startled driver: "Get that hood open, quick." With this the hood was jerked open.

The recruit flew into action with a blast of water that soaked the driver as well as everything else around him. But the truth of the matter was, there was no fire. There was only smoke, and lots of it.

While the recruit and the driver were preoccupied up front, Pucci ran to the back of the truck, reached in his pocket and jammed the two potatoes as far up the exhaust pipe as he could. Only then did he give the order to shut off the water. The initial blast of water wiped out all the remnants of the torpedo with the exception of a few tell-tale wires which Pucci reached in and quickly removed. He reattached the spark plug wire, and proceeded to wipe down the engine while pretending to be checking for possible damage and the cause of the malfunction. As for the driver and the recruit, they thought that an incredible disaster had been avoided. The driver thanked God that the fire truck was on hand at this crucial moment. Pucci praised the quick action of his recruit.

"Surely he'll make a great fireman," he was telling the thoroughly soaked driver. Not only did he save the truck but also gave the driver a much-needed bath to boot.

They came to the conclusion that the carburetor float must have stuck open causing it to flood the engine with gasoline. Thus, the explosion. There was no reason why it shouldn't start right up. However, the attempt to get it going was not successful. It would take hold, run for a few seconds and then die down.

"Maybe it should be allowed to set awhile and fully dry out," suggested Pucci. The truth of the matter was, with the exhaust pipe plugged up solid with potatoes, it wouldn't allow the exhaust gases to escape so the engine couldn't run.

The driver was resolved to the fact that he would miss the last ferry out that night. His hope of getting the truck repaired for the next day was also doubtful. This meant he would be at least a couple of days late at the winery. This was exactly the strategy Pucci had planned.

While all this was going on, Primo was climbing up into the cab of the paper company's Mack truck, confident that his buddy, Pucci, would somehow disable or stall the third truck out. Needless to say, he had done just that. In the eyes of a truck driver, this monstrous machine was a beauty. Primo admired it. Settled behind the wheel, he cranked 'er over; the engine started up with a deafening roar, then once warmed up, settled down to a constant, purring, beat like a contented tiger. Pistons the size of two-pound coffee cans were sliding up and down shiny cylinder walls, pushing connecting rods the size of a man's arm down into the crankcase. It took all this little Italian could do to push down the clutch peddle, then let it out gently as he felt the chains tighten up on the sprockets. The truck started to move out like a beast from its den. The blunt, bulldog-appearing hood with its cast, polished brass emblem, loomed up and out of the shadows of the garage followed by the rest of this magnificent piece of machinery with almost as many wheels as you might count on your fingers and toes.

Traffic from all directions came to an abrupt halt as the truck moved out into the street. It was an awesome sight. It demanded the right of way. All lanes in both directions were needed in order for the trailer to clear the garage doors. The big Mack looked like it was grinning as it hogged the roadway. Selection of the "Bulldog" for the truck's symbol was appropriate. This massive machine demanded respect, and it was, indeed, the "King of the Highways." Hopefully, if all went well, Primo's would be the third truck loaded at the winery the next day instead of the intended truck that Pucci had successfully delayed.

CHAPTER 6

Early next morning, Pucci caught up to Mike at the produce market just as he was stuffing a handful of cash in his money sack. His approach was unexpected.

"Good morning, Mike," he said. "All sold out?"

Surprised, Mike tossed the money sack into the Model T and responded:

"Yes, all sold out. What brings you here? Everything alright? Did Primo get off to Sonoma County?"

"Everything worked out fine. Primo made the ferry in plenty of time. No problem."

"Will he come back the same way?"

"No, too risky–besides, it'll be late. He'll come the long way, around the peninsula. Do you have enough men to handle the unloading when he gets in?"

"More than enough–even too many."

At the ranch, Mike's main concern now was to get things set up to handle and store the anticipated new incoming load of wine. Although he had never seen the Mack truck before, he assumed it to be a good size truck, and that Primo would succeed in coming back with a full load. Needless to say, there was no shortage of helping hands. Word had gone out among some of his other unemployed paesano friends that he had an abundance of wine at his disposal. Whether he was willing to share it made no difference to them. They showed up at the ranch anyway. By now, the farm house was bursting at the seams with arm-waving, wine-drinking paesani.

Livia enjoyed their company immensely. No way would she allow her husband to put a single one of them out in the street."So

31

they drink a little wine, so what?" she would say. "You have too much of it anyway. Besides, they're happy-go-lucky. They add a spark to our lives."

Mike would grumble but he wouldn't fight it; they were his paesani, his countrymen. And since he was doing so well, it was expected that he provide them with the basic essentials of life until they were able to fend for themselves. They looked up to him as their leader — a Capo.

"But do they have to drink so much wine?" he would ask. Of course, he did make it a point to give them only watered down wine, but then they'd only drink that much more. So, either way, they did get more than a fair ration of wine. Regardless, in some way or another, he was determined to get some work out of every one of them whether they were on the payroll or not. It was imperative to keep them occupied doing something or they would spend too much time around the wine barrel — a situation unacceptable to Mike. So he assigned them duties according to their characteristics.

Contini was without question the laziest of the bunch, so he was assigned menial yard and household chores. Other than drinking wine, his pastime was to recite poetry, tell stories, and to philosophize on any and all subjects or matters regardless of whether he understood them or not.

Aldoino was the simplest of the lot but loved to sing and talk about all sorts of trivial things. He was useless in the fields, but terrific company for Livia since she loved to sing as well. Also, his childish horseplay was entertaining to the kids. So, he was assigned accordingly.

Julio was smart and the most trustworthy of the bunch. He was also a licensed driver. He intended to someday return to Italy and rejoin the family he had left behind. Mike had him assisting in distributing the wine.

Vasco was a pleasure to be around. He was a stable and sensible man with a good sense of humor. Mike appointed him as his foreman.

Scanavino was a natural for handling wine. He came from a long line of wine merchants extending back to the days of Pompeii. No doubt his family lineage was the reason for such an appropriate name which meant "to draw wine." His job was to fill jugs and prepare them for shipment.

Then there was Aquatorre. Aside from his desire to drink wine, his great love was water. His ancestral lineage went back to the days of building aqueducts. Mike assigned him to developing the irrigation systems.

Salvatore (Sal) Di Culteliari was an expert with a knife; this was understandable since his name meant "knifeman." It was said that his clan originated from a secret squad of cutthroats put together by Julius Caesar to intimidate and destroy undesirable opponents. He could cut and trim enough cauliflower to keep any three men busy packing them. However, although he was a countryman, he didn't come from the same town as Mike and most of the others. Julio had introduced him to Mike as his friend.

Sal had indicated to Julio that in time he must someday return to Italy, his beloved Sicily, but not until he had settled a score with a man he was searching for. This man had done Sal's father and family a terrible wrong back in Sicily. However, knowing better, the paesani never joked about his home town or his family. Above all, they never asked or discussed his reason for being here. Julio knew, but kept it to himself.

Funarino, meaning the "rope man", came from a long line of rope makers. It is said that his ancestors were the first to develop and put to use the block and tackle. He was called upon for anything that had to do with ropes or lifting heavy objects.

Fiasco, so named for being a flask maker, was assigned to weaving straw around bottles and inscribing the words "special reserve" on the fancy labels. Labeling the bottles as such would fetch a better price.

Taliaferro was a blacksmith and so assigned. He could repair or build anything as long as it was made of iron. Whenever a piece of machinery was beyond repair, he would shape the iron into a sword, mattock, or axe and hang it on the wall. His ancestral instincts were still with him.

Casseta was a casket maker, as his name implied. His family had a thriving casket manufacturing business back in Italy. His ambition was to someday get established in the casket business in this country. So he was assigned to repairing and assembling vegetable crates, as well as carpenter work in general.

Matteoli, Julio's first cousin, was also trustworthy and an expert at wine making. One might say he had attended the University

33

of Practical Experience. He had a keen sense of smell and taste. Cutting and blending wines was his specialty. He could also be relied upon to keep his mouth shut about illegal activities. He, too, was a great storyteller and philosophizer, but unlike Contini, he stuck to what he understood. After a few glasses of wine, Contini and Matteoli would test and challenge each other just for the sake of argument. There was considerable contrast in the features of these two men. Contini was short and somewhat plump due to lack of exercise. His balding head, owlish eyes, and bushy eyebrows lent him a scholarly appearance, whereas Matteoli was more the athletic type. Matteoli's Italian military training had taught him discipline, and developed his physique. He had handsome features, a full head of hair, and a typical pronounced Italian nose. He carried himself like a true gentlemen.

Other paesani of different characteristics that drifted in and out of the ranch were assigned menial jobs, such as cleaning up the barn and clearing a path around the chicken house for the Mack at the new ranch in preparation of storing the anticipated new load of wine.

Livia knew nothing of the new hijack scheme now in the works. However, activities next door did cause her to suspect that something out of the ordinary was afoot. Something she was not being told about. That same evening she fired a volley of questions at Mike:

"What were you doing over there–at the chicken house–the barn? Why all the running around? Why weren't the men out working in the fields?"

The questioning caught Mike off guard. He was not about to mention that another wine hijack was in the making. So he said the first thing that came to mind:

"We're building a 'Bacci' ball court–yes–that's it, a 'Bacci' ball court alongside the chicken house..."

"What! A 'Bacci' ball court alongside the chicken house? Are you out of your mind? I can't believe this!!"

Rather than get himself in an argument, annoyed, he marched out of the house. It was bad enough that he was burdened with the ordeal imposed upon Primo, let alone trying to explain it.

CHAPTER 7

The Mack pulled into the Winery at Asti early the next morning, well ahead of the day's regular work force. The night watchman was astounded at the sight of this monstrous truck, let alone being piloted by such a small man. Not having seen the truck on any previous occasion, the watchman, after wishing Primo a "Good Morning," questioned him:

"Are you sure you're in the right place?"

"Yes, I'm sure," responded Primo from within the cab. He purposely avoided a formal introduction.

"I don't know . . . I've never seen anything the likes of this before around here," stated the watchman before adding: "Who you hauling for?"

"The same warehouse company the Fageols have been hauling for . . . the San Francisco warehouse," answered Primo, a little nervously.

"Oh . . . yeah, that outfit. Well, I can't help ya there. You'll have to wait until the shipping clerk gets here. In the meantime, go ahead and park it back there," said the watchman, pointing to the rear of the office building.

"O.K., I'll do that . . . but tell me, that little church over there . . . is it Catholic?" Primo was referring to the little church that could be seen across the vineyard with its simple cross rising above the structure made up of redwood wine vat staves, and shaped accordingly.

"Yes . . . why do you ask?"

"Oh, I thought . . . just wondering . . . that's all."

In truth, as much of a rascal as Primo was, he leaned heavily

35

on the blessings of the Church. The question always lingered strongly on his mind: "How would the Church view this wine hijacking affair?"

Having parked the truck where indicated, upon disembarking he made his way through the grape-burdened vines towards the church. Hopefully, there, he might get an answer to his troublesome question. Approaching the entrance, he noted the unique church structure's name: "Madonna Del Carmine." He stepped through the unlocked door into the foyer. There, perched on a pedestal, a figurine of the Virgin Mary stared down at him. If it was the intent of the sculptor to instill a sense of remorse within the heart of its viewer, then it could be said that the figurine served its purpose. With a lump in his throat, he peered down the center aisle. Standing at the alter, with his back to him, he witnessed the parish priest, an elderly man of the cloth, mumbling in prayer as he went through the ritual of saying his early morning Mass. There were no others present. Primo quietly made his way along the side of the pews towards the alter, once again hesitating at the sight of an even larger statue of the Virgin Mary. Her eyes, expressing sympathy, seemed to follow his every move. Her right hand extended forward from draped clothing as if beckoning, while her left hand, palm facing the viewer, appeared to be pointing to a slot in the wall alongside that extended to the anti-room to the rear of the church. It was obvious; it was intended to receive donations. He got the message: "Come, let me relieve you of your burden." With a feeling of guilt, he knelt, made the sign of the cross, then reached in his billfold and slipped a $5 bill through the slot.

The rustling of the crisp bill caught the attention of the elderly priest. He cut his saying of the Mass short, glanced at Primo, then hurriedly made his way back to the anti-room. In the meantime, Primo stepped into the first pew and again knelt before the alter with hands clasped and head bowed in prayer.

In the anti-room, the priest immediately retrieved the $5 bill, snapped it several times while viewing it in disbelief. It had been some time since he'd seen a single donation of this magnitude. He pondered the questions: "Who is this man that makes such a heavy contribution, on a work day at that? Does he have a problem . . . something heavy on his mind? And, does he have more of this kind of money on his being?"

The priest answered his own questions with a simple, solid thought: "Yes, indeed, this man needs my help."

Frock flaring with every hurried step like the skirts of a Spanish Fandango dancer while going through her frenzied dance routine, the priest came up to the kneeling Primo. Interrupting his prayer, he said:

"My son, if you have the time, and you so wish, I will say a special Mass and administer Communion; that is, of course, after confession."

The statement made in heavy, broken English, with a definite Italian ring to it, made it obvious to Primo that the elderly priest would be more comfortable communicating in Italian rather than in English. Thus, Primo responded accordingly:

"Father, I appreciate your offer, but time does not permit it," he said in their native tongue.

"Ah, so you are Italian," said the priest, somewhat surprised, since again, especially from an Italian, did he ever expect such a generous contribution. The Church and its parishioners were all suffering from the effects of Prohibition in this wine-producing community, so he wasn't about to give up just yet. He was determined to know more about this generous young man now standing before him. He extended a second offer:

"But surely you will have time for confession, will you not? It will take only a few minutes, then you can be on your way with a clear conscience, and cleansed soul."

The offer was accepted. The priest, followed by Primo, walked over to the Confession Chamber, stepped into its cubicle and sat down, as did Primo in the adjoining cubicle. Instantly, the little panel between them slid open. Although dimly lit, the priest's profile could be seen through the separating screen. Following customary procedure, Primo opened the discussion:

"Bless me, Father, for I have sinned . . . "

"Yes . . . yes, go on." The priest was eager to her him out.

"Well, Father . . . I can't be sure if what I'm doing is proper. What I mean is . . . "

"Just what are you doing, my son?" interrupted the priest eagerly, trying to hurry things along.

"Dealing in contraband wine, Father," blurted Primo with a sigh of relief.

"Dealing - in - contraband - wine . . . ?" repeated the priest, in a somewhat curious and thoughtful manner.

"Yes . . . Father," came the simple answer.

"You mean you're here to steal wine . . . ?"

"Well . . . no, not exactly," stammered Primo. "It's just that . . . well . . . as you know, this is Prohibition, and the mere possession of wine is illegal, and . . . "

The priest cut him off again, then explained to Primo that Prohibition laws were made by men . . . not God. Without bothering to go into great detail, he explained the difference between man's laws and God's laws, and that God's laws pre-empt the field, especially when it pertains to wine. After much back and forth discussion on the subject, Primo, now pressed for time, interrupted the babbling, elderly priest with a direct request:

"Father," he said, "I beg forgiveness of my sins . . . "

"Ah . . . yes, your sins. But, in the eyes of the Church, one who applies himself to the benefit of 'Mankind,' and 'Shares' his 'Fortune' with the needy, especially through the 'Church,' is looked upon as a 'Savior,' not a 'Sinner.' Therefore, since it is obvious that you intend to 'Share,' through the 'Church' (an assumption on his part), that in itself can serve as penance. But, to be sure, kneel before the Virgin Mary, heed the direction she points, and your burden shall be lifted."

The elderly priest had made his final pitch. Primo, uncomfortable about this whole affair of confession and penance, promptly exited the confession cubicle. While wiping the beads of sweat off his brow, he hurried to the slot next to the Virgin Mary, slipped a couple of $20 bills through it, knelt, glanced up at her, made a quick sign of the cross, then made a bee-line for the door.

Once the attentive Priest heard the creaking front door slam shut, he quickly exited the confession cubicle, hurried past the Virgin Mary, glanced in her direction, gave the sign of the cross while maintaining a brisk gait, rounded the alter, and dashed into the anti-room to evaluate his efforts. He peered into the collection box with anticipation: "Yes, he had scored." Shoving the twenties into a pocket within the folds of his frock, he rushed out the door in time to see Primo heading across the vineyard towards the Mack. Scampering up on a mound of dirt in order to get an unobstructed view, he proceeded to chant 'Blessings' directed at both man and machine. But, hopefully, all would benefit by this day's endeavor.

The shipping clerk, now at his post, was just as astounded as the night watchman at the sight of this monstrous machine, the Mack. The third truck of the week was expected at the winery all right, but certainly nothing like this truck with a trailer coupled to it. Primo explained that he was hired out at the last minute to make the third load because the regularly scheduled truck was having engine trouble that might require extensive repairs. Since the original truck might not even be ready the following week, they hired him with the added trailer. With this arrangement, he could then haul the following week's load ahead of schedule if it was agreeable to them. This did sound perfectly logical. It made real sense to the shipping clerk.

"At last, someone down there is thinking," he said. "How many barrels can you haul?"

Since the newsprint rolls and wine barrels were about the same size and weight, Primo was quick to answer.

"Three rows on end, on each rig, ten-deep: sixty barrels. Two tiers high makes it a full load." Obviously, he was pushing for all he could get. He felt sure the truck could handle it.

"Okay, so it's 120 barrels. I'll make up the bill of lading while it's being loaded," said the clerk.

Care was exercised during the loading operation. Nothing was left to chance. The barrels were nestled and stacked perfectly tight; a shifting load could cause a disaster — lose the load, wreck the truck. First, the barrels were tied down and lashed together firmly, then the heavy tarps were stretched out over the top and down the sides and secured to the truck bed with strapping. Heavy ropes were then tightened across the entire load for additional protection against shifting.

By now, an audience made up of winery employees had gathered around to watch this monstrous machine, its snout resembling a mean "Bulldog," pull out of the yard with the equivalent of four normal truck-loads of wine barrels. This was a sight they had never seen before, and for that matter, a new experience for the driver as well. Primo looked the tires over carefully. They were without a doubt being stretched to their capacity. But, being new, and traveling in the cool of night, would help. As he climbed up into the cab, a silence fell over the crowd. He cranked the engine over. It responded with a roar as a blast of black smoke shot out the exhaust pipe. The truck idled briskly, excess fuel burned itself out of the cylinders. The exhaust was now clear. Primo was working shift levers while searching through the transmission and special gear reduction box for the lowest possible gear he could find. He made the selection. The truck was now ready to roll out. He took a deep breath as he tried to calm his feeling of nervousness. Although confident that the truck could handle the load, he was almost afraid to let the clutch out. Unpleasant thoughts crossed his mind. "Suppose I rip out the rear end or maybe break an axle, or break a drive chain? I would be stuck here and this hijacking scheme would be exposed for sure." His thoughts now turned to an audible whisper: "One hundred twenty barrels. Wine and barrels combined, sixty thousand pounds. Holy Christ! Thirty tons." His moist hands reached for his handkerchief. He wiped the sweat off his face. It was a warm, late afternoon, but it was the nervousness more than the warmth that caused the sweat.

There was no turning back now. The truck was starting off level; this would help. As Primo gently let the clutch out, he could feel the drive chains tightening up as they were picking up the load. The truck should start to move, but it wasn't. He continued to release the clutch as he fed more fuel to the engine. "What the hell," he mumbled. The engine was definitely picking up the load, but the truck wasn't budging. The truck's front end rose up as if about to pounce on the people standing around. There were doubts among the audience as to whether the truck would budge the load or not.

Finally, with a hefty grunt from the engine, the big Mack started to move forward. The gear boxes moaned and groaned. Gear teeth gnashed at each other as it inched along, picking up speed. Primo let in the clutch. The whole front end eased down to its normal position. He then picked off the next highest gear. Again the front end rose in response to the surge of power to the drive train. The Mack picked up more speed. Once around the office building, he shifted into the next highest gear. The deafening roar of the engine caught the attention of the priest across the vineyard. He had another blessing to offer: "Do what you must, my son; God will surely understand — and hurry back."

Breathing somewhat easier, and as if responding to the blessing, Primo said: "We have to be careful. We have to get out of this yard and clear out of this winery no matter what." He had no intention of taking the risk of trying to get into a higher gear while pulling out of the uphill driveway. The flag man at the highway was waving him on; Primo poured more fuel to the Mack. It swung out onto Highway 101 heading south. As the truck picked up speed in the next selected gear, he reached down with his left hand, grasped the exhaust horn ring and let out several loud blasts to let the cheering crowd know that he was on his way.

For the next several miles the Mack kept climbing out of low gears into higher gears until it reached cruising speed. Primo took a deep breath and sighed. "Well, we got out of that one, but Mack, it's still one hell of a long way home. Just take it easy and we'll make it."

All through the night Primo endured the roar of the laboring engine, and the rumble of wine barrels. Now and then the babbling of the elderly priest popped into his mind. But what really haunted him most was the fixed stare of the Virgin Mary; it seemed to be radiating a form of message: "God is within you. Seek his guidance."

It was early and dark the following morning as the Mack approached the ranch at San Bruno. Primo went through the gears to slow the truck down. The engine backfire was spurting orange flame out the exhaust pipe as the powerful engine let up at each shift of gears. He swung the truck out wide to make the right turn into the driveway of the recently acquired ranch. The Mack moved slowly down the rough driveway, creaking and crackling as it rumbled along like some prehistoric monster. The big headlights lit up the entire farmhouse, yard, and barn to the rear. The paesani were still asleep.

The prearranged plan was to go through the yard past the sheds, clear the chicken house, and swing around to the right and park alongside the rear of the big barn. This would have been fine without the trailer, but with the trailer there just wasn't enough room to clear all the buildings without swinging out wide into the celery patch to the left. Primo couldn't see in the dark well enough to judge his clearance for the trailer through the rear view mirror. However, realizing the area was tight, he swung out wide to the left, wiping out the first dozen rows of celery along the driveway. Irrigation pipe got caught up under the undercarriage of the truck. Not realizing this, Primo was now dragging several hundred feet of four-inch irrigation pipe along with him. Nevertheless, he cut the turn shorter to the right hoping to ruin less celery. In doing so, the trailer swung in tighter to the right side grabbing up chicken wire as it moved along. Thinking he was in the clear, he continued slowly in a right turn. By now, it was obvious that the chicken house was also going to go along for the ride. That powerful beast of a truck never as much as lurched, giving no indication at all of what it was dragging along with it.

The clatter and rumbling of wine barrels aroused the sleeping paesani in the big farmhouse. They poured out the back door in their underwear, running through the darkness, and in a state of panic were yelling instructions. In their half asleep and confused state, their first thought was that the train had left the tracks and wiped out the chicken house as it charged headlong through the yard. The fastest runner of the group went charging through the darkness to carry the news to Mike next door. The celery stalks didn't seem to slow him down much as he raced through the patch in his bare feet. Minutes later, Mike appeared on the scene. He, too, was attired in his long johns. He viewed the disaster in amazement. The truck was parked where it was supposed to be but so was the crumbled remains of the chicken house with chickens cackling and squawking in a complete state of confusion. They were all over the truck, flying and scrambling in all directions, flying into the lanterns like moths attracted to light.

For all practical purposes, you could say that the trailer was neatly wrapped in chicken wire with boards and debris strewn along the way. The irrigation pipe was twisted and wrapped throughout the undercarriage of both truck and trailer, with one end sticking up high in the air in a long bend, swinging gently back and forth between the truck and trailer like a giant python snake.

Primo was tired and exhausted from the long night on the road. He scrambled down from the cab wondering what the hell all the excitement was about. He was instantly confronted by all these paesani talking at the same time in their native tongue. Debris and cackling chickens were scattered all over the place. The situation was so confusing that for an instant he, too, thought he had barely missed the train charging through the henhouse.

The paesani circled the truck and trailer in the semi-darkness. It did, indeed, look like a train. They gazed at the load of barrels in absolute disbelief. Not one of them (not even Mike) had ever seen

or heard of such a huge truck with, or without, a load of wine barrels.

The chickens became annoying. They flocked around the lanterns, following whomever was carrying them, so in order to get them out from under foot, the paesani herded them into the barn where they were to remain until daylight. Being unprepared to start the unloading, the men drifted back to their quarters. Seeing how beat Primo was, Mike said to him:

"Come on. Let's get some breakfast. After that, I'll drive you home so you can get to bed and get some rest. Don't worry about the truck. The men can unload it later in the day. Leave everything as it is."

By the time the two men reached the house, Livia was up making coffee and preparing breakfast as she normally did on Mike's market days. They all sat down at the table. It was obvious that Primo had gone through quite a strain. He was beat. Livia, sensing this, didn't give either man a chance to start a conversation before she had her say.

"You two, and your friend Pucci, are crazy." This was said loud and clear. "What was all that noise about over at the paesani's house? They sound like a bunch of crazy guys, too."

"That was nothing," answered Mike. "They were just excited seeing Primo's big truck and trailer."

"Oh, no," she said. "Don't tell me that, because I heard a big noise and all the chickens acted like they were scared to death. Primo, you tell me," she demanded.

"Aunt Livia, it was all my fault. I knocked down the chicken house but none of the chickens got hurt. They'll settle down and so will the paesani."

"Thank God for that. But tell me, what did you bring this time that you needed such a big truck?" she demanded to know.

"One hundred twenty barrels of wine," answered Primo grinning with pride. Mike also chuckled in an expression of pride for his nephew's performance in the feat.

"For the love of God," she said in despair. "How could you do such a thing? You'll all go to jail for sure. You must stop this!" She clasped her hands in prayer as she pleaded with God to intervene and bring these men back to their senses.

Before starting for home, Primo assured Livia, or at least he thought he did, that there was no great need to worry. But, as he said this, visions of the 'Virgin Mary' kept popping up in his mind. As for Mike, the vision popping into his mind was of the horrendous profits the newly-acquired load of wine would fetch. Needless to say, the two men left the ranch satisfied with themselves and their achievements.

When they stopped in front of Primo's house in the City on Lombard Street, they were in for another scolding. Only this time it was from Primo's mother, Mike's oldest sister. Italian women (mothers, wives, and sisters alike) have a strange way of handling a situation like this. They sit up worrying night and day for their loved ones. They pray for your safe return. They ask God to watch over you. They beg him to please bring you back to their loving arms. When you do show up and all their prayers are answered, they are overwhelmed with joy. But this only lasts for a few seconds. When they suddenly realize that no harm has come to you, they set out to do to you the very thing that they had prayed wouldn't happen. A good Italian sees this conduct as true undying love.

It was late morning when Mike returned from the market and pulled in at the ranch. As usual, his pockets were bulging with cash. The Model-T Ford truck was loaded with returned empty crates and jugs. He was anxious to walk over to the paesani's ranch and take another good look at the big Mack loaded with barrels before having his lunch and afternoon siesta. As he made his way to the adjoining ranch, he couldn't help but notice the unusual gathering of men in a tight circle. "Now what do you suppose they're doing?," he thought. "They certainly are not doing their chores standing around like that in the yard. It was understood that they'd wait for my return before unloading the Mack, but why the tight circle?"

As he approached the group of men, it now appeared that they were engaged in some sort of gambling sport. This didn't bother Mike except for the fact that none of them had any money to gamble with. Whatever it was they were up to must be investigated. As he drew closer, occasional puffs of dust could be seen drifting up from the center of the circle. Maybe they're watching a wrestling match, he thought. But who are the participants in the match? None of them would roll in the dust just to entertain others. He pushed his way into the circle.

There, before his eyes, sketched out on the smoothed-over dust, was the complete layout of the yard area showing the position of the buildings. Two blocks of wood were used to represent the big Mack truck and trailer. The men standing in the circle were observing a strategic dispute between Contini and Matteoli. With sticks in hand, they were calculating distances and scratching the figures in the dirt. They would move the wood blocks around in different positions like two disagreeing admirals planning a naval maneuver. Each time one or the other would move the imaginary truck and trailer, a howl of disapproval could be heard above the constant chatter, to the delight of his opponent. It was obvious that the men standing around had chosen sides and expressed their opinions in the form of hoots and hollers as they watched the two men trying to outmaneuver each other. To listen to them argue the issue, there would have been no question, had they been at the wheel that morning, the destruction would not have taken place for they would have first mapped out their strategy complete with mathematical calculations beforehand. It wasn't easy for Mike to bring the situation under control, but he did manage to quiet them down long enough to hear him out.

Once he had their attention, he directed his comments to the two great strategists still kneeling on the ground but now focusing on him looking down at them.

"Yes," Mike said as if agreeing with their strategy. "But if you two were in command of the truck, before you would arrive at a conclusion as to the final manner to proceed and what route to take, the wine would have spoiled from the many days it would remain in the sun. So I think it was better to lose the chicken house and save the wine."

With this, a howl of approval from the observers signified they were in agreement. The two kneeling men got up off their knees and joined the others as they marched towards the truck to tackle the task of unloading.

CHAPTER 8

It always seems that the best time for argument between Italian husbands and wives is right after supper when the wine bottle is empty or, at least, close to it. This night was to be no exception at the Buti residence. It started off with Livia putting a question bluntly to Mike:

"What will Mr. Battisoldi say when he finds out that you and that fool nephew of yours knocked down the chicken house the other morning?"

"He'll say nothing because he is a good friend of mine and because he don't give a damn about chickens and neither do I," he answered firmly.

"Tell me, Mr. Buti," responded Livia with a question and kind of formal like, "the chickens, where are they sleeping these nights? Please tell me that." He knew that being addressed so formally meant she was annoyed beyond reproach. There were other things on her mind besides the chickens. Mike resolved to have it out with her and get it over with.

"They're sleeping in the barn on top of the wine barrels and the hell with the chickens and all the eggs they lay that are falling down between the barrels!" he answered angrily.

"So you're a smart one. Just wait until Mr. Battisoldi finds this out. He'll throw you and all your paesani out in the street. You'll see what kind of friend he is."

"I already told you that he don't care. All he cares about is money and charging everybody interest. That's all he ever talks about — how much interest you pay him and how much interest he pays you. Nothing else. Besides, he understands these things. He treats me good, like a businessman."

Livia was not about to back off just yet. "So, he likes you, does he? He treats you real good. So tell me, how much interest does he pay you for the money you put in his bank?"

"He pays me three percent. We're making money," answered Mike with an air of genius.

"Oh, so you're making money. Now tell me, how much interest do you pay him on the mortgage for the ranch?"

"Ten percent!" he blurted out in anger.

"So he pays you three percent for your money, then lends it back to you at ten percent. And you call him your friend — a good, honest businessman? Bah! He's a crook. Not a little crook but a big one. Like the knot you're going to get on top of your head if you don't shut up!"

She had him this time for sure and he knew it. Besides, he wouldn't put it past her to carry out her threat since she was capable of doing just what she said she might do. He wasn't about to turn his back to her for fear of getting hit on the head with a cast iron skillet, nor would he continue the discussion any further. Besides, it was time to leave the table since the wine bottle was now empty anyway. He grumbled as he picked his hat off the nail on the wall and started out the door. He paused for a moment, searched around in his vest pocket and came up with a half- smoked stogie. He struck a match on the wall, fired up the cigar, and started down the back steps shaking the match back and forth to extinguish it as he descended.

It was still daylight as he walked slowly across the celery patch towards the new ranch next door. His paesani would certainly offer him some of their quota of wine. They don't have a woman running their household over there, he thought. They can drink all the wine they want, providing, of course, I give it to them. They work for me, but in some ways, they're better off. "Yes, I believe they are," he said to himself.

The banker, Battisoldi, crossed his mind again. "That bugger is making a fortune off these poor Italians he befriends. At this rate, he will someday own the biggest bank in the state," he grumbled to himself.

Mike continued walking toward the farmhouse puffing hard on his cigar. The continuous puffing was essential in order to keep it lit. If you stopped even for a few seconds, the cigar would immediately extinguish itself as if it had a built-in safety feature. You would then have to go through the whole process of lighting up again with a match the size of a small torch.

"These damned Toscanelli cigars look like tule roots and taste even worse yet. How can the Italians make such a bad cigar? They must do it on purpose," he mumbled.

He kept thinking about the poor Italians. What a beating they take in the business world. No wonder God shaped Italy like a boot. It was certainly appropriate since these poor souls were constantly being booted in the ass by men like this banker. So, why not shape their country, Italy, in the form of a boot?

He wasn't sure whether he was glad or mad when his thoughts were interrupted by the paesani rushing out in the yard to greet him waving bottles of wine like there was no tomorrow. One swallow of their wine convinced Mike without a doubt that this bunch of drunken paesani of his had tapped one of the newly acquired wine barrels on their own.

"You damned idiots!" he shouted. "You're drinking uncut wine. No wonder you're all drunk. This is costing us money. What the hell's going on here?" The way they were staggering to and from the barn, it looked like a bucket brigade at one of Pucci's downtown fires.

As much as he hated to, he tossed his cigar off to one side cursing the day they were born, including the ship that carried them to this country in the first place. He ran up and down the line snatching the bottles away from them until he had an armful.

This delighted the paesani no end for they thought he wanted to drink with them and was trying to make up for lost time. So they rushed back to the barn for more wine. The laughter and senseless chatter completely drowned out Mike's complaints. There was no point in fighting it any longer, so he joined in with another big draw from one of the bottles he was carrying. "Damn, that's good wine," he said, while pursing his lips. "Why go home now?" Under the circumstances, he was better off there than at home where he would be getting a kick in the ass by his outraged wife. "Let her cool off," he thought.

The party ended when no one was able to stand on their feet long enough to reach the barn. Even then, some diehards were still trying to make it on their hands and knees. What with the shattered chicken house, twisted irrigation pipe, chicken wire, boards, and debris scattered around among the bodies lying around here and there, one would think it was a war zone.

The next day Mike organized the men into a cleanup and repair crew. Surprisingly, they were in pretty good shape considering the amount of wine they had consumed the night before. This was attributed to the good quality of the wine.

Rebuilding the chicken house was the first priority. Chickens roosting on the barrels was not acceptable. Above all, it was messy. Besides, it was extremely difficult to gather eggs among the barrels.

As the men busied themselves with the chore of rebuilding, Mike stood in front of the stack of barrels sizing up the situation. This was really the first chance he had to take a good look at this newly acquired inventory. "Jesus Christ!" he whispered to himself. "One hundred twenty barrels all in one pile. Well, after last night, maybe one less." He grinned as the thought crossed his mind of last night's party. As he studied the stack of barrels, he noted that the barrels appeared to be shaped somewhat differently than the previous ones. As a matter of fact, they appeared to be larger and made of heavier wood. Something stamped in small print on the end of each barrel caught his eye. He looked closer.

"Holy Christ!" he murmured. "French oak barrels. What do you know about that?" He continued to talk in pleasant surprise. "No wonder it was so good. But that's not all." He scrambled among the rows looking to see how many carried the same stamp. "All of them. Every last one. Incredible," he thought. "Not American, but French oak barrels." Mike knew that the French didn't measure their barrels in gallons but in liters. Normally, their barrels were bigger. Not so much that the average person might notice, but to a European wine man like himself, it would be noticed. He swirled the half empty barrel up on end, moved it closer to the door to get a better look at the emblem stamped on the barrel head. It was burned in a manner as you would brand a cow. The emblem designated the French maker of the barrel. Along the lower edge of the brand in very small neatly stamped letters, were the numbers 230-L. He knew in an instant its significance.

"Oh! Jesus Christ!" he burst out in excitement then straightened out stiff as a plank while slapping his hand over the brand as if trying to shield it from view. "My God," he said. "Two hundred thirty liters. These barrels contain almost 59 gallons per barrel, not 50 as others might think." He looked around hoping that he had not attracted the attention of the others working nearby. He stood there facing the barrel, head raised toward heaven, his right hand still firmly pressing on the stamp and barrel end. He looked like a statue. No, better yet, he looked like King Arthur about to ordain a knight to the Round Table.

In his calculations, Mike discounted the half-empty barrel that had been consumed the night before. One hundred nineteen barrels times an extra nine gallons per barrel equaled 1,071 gallons of extra wine that only he knew about. He snapped back to his senses, slammed the barn door shut, picked up a hammer and a handful of nails, and proceeded to nail a good husky plank across the door. The work crew stood at attention as he announced:

"From now on, no one but me or whoever I designate enters this barn — regardless of the circumstances! All of you obtain your wine supply from the stock on hand at my residence."

To cut the paesani completely off or restrict them from their wine was unthinkable, because it was the endless supply of wine more than anything else that kept them on the job. But it didn't have to be choice wines aged in French oak barrels. After Mike made his announcement, he turned and departed, walking back to his place thinking of his great discovery and good fortune.

"No wonder that freight train of a truck ripped the hell out of the ranch the other morning", he mumbled. "That truck carried ten thousand extra pounds of weight. How the hell Primo ever got here with it is a miracle for sure."

In order to keep his personal sales separate from partnership sales, Mike devised a bookkeeping system that would be envied by the most brilliant professors of accounting and mathematics. He positioned the figures so that columns of numbers would always add up equal no matter which way you held the paper in your hand. Under normal circumstances, you would think he would keep two sets of books: one for himself (unknown to his partners) and one set for the partnership. However, with his system, two sets of books were not necessary because of his employment of figures in such a manner that when the subtotal in one column was carried across to the grand total column, a series of dots and dashes were used to appear like your eye should follow them across to that figure. They were, in fact, his code to determine the percentage that was discounted for his benefit. He, therefore, had a constant record of both accounts on one sheet of paper. On the same sheet he also kept figures in columns for his personal vegetable sales, so that in the event something didn't add up right, he could shift figures from vegetables to wine and vice versa. No way would he ever be suspected of maintaining questionable accounts, because only he could decipher them. He once went through the trouble of trying to give an accounting to his two partners, but they just simply faked their understanding so as not to appear ignorant of sound accounting practices.

With Mike, it was more a force of habit that was the contributing factor to this sort of conduct. With Primo and Pucci, it was the challenge and excitement that urged them on. On several occasions both his partners had offered him a greater share of the profits, but he had refused. He liked to get it this way better. The old-fashioned way.

CHAPTER 9

The news of the hijacked premium wine caused a furious argument between the Federal agents and the winery. The agents were seething. They swore and cursed in loud voices that echoed throughout the warehouse. They could possibly tolerate or, at least, explain to their supervisors the small loads that were previously hijacked. Some of this could be expected in this unholy business. However, this latest 120-barrel hijack incident that involved a monstrous truck, the Mack, was another matter. The senior agent smashed his fist on the desk and screamed:

"Impossible! It didn't happen! Those goddamned dagos at the winery are all a bunch of liars. They didn't witness nothing of the kind. There's no truck in the whole state of California that can carry off a load like that. It would collapse in the yard before it could move an inch. They're liars! Just plain liars! All of them! No independent trucker owns such a truck. Where the hell did it come from, and where the hell did it go with 120 barrels of wine? Those goddamned dagos up there have screwed us again, and you can be sure they had something to do with the other hijacking down the peninsula as well!"

The senior agent was in a fit of rage, taking it out on his three cohorts as he stomped around the desk pounding his fists. "Those bastards up there are the only ones besides ourselves that know anything about schedules or anything else about this operation!" He insisted over and over again that the winery was giving them a screwing.

The agents were in trouble all right, and they knew it. They would have to pay for the stolen wine. The winery had a signed receipt for the wine. If the signature could not be traced because it was a fake, that was just too bad for the agents and of no concern to the winery.

The new deal (since the last three trucks were hijacked) was that the agents pick up the wine at the winery and pay on demand. And that's exactly what the winery was asking them to do. Pay up.

The agents had established a code system for telegraphing information to their confederates back East in Washington, D.C., and their Sicilian associates, "the Mob", in New Jersey. Since the agents were never really too sure of the first two hijackings that took place on the street in front of the warehouse, they didn't say anything about them, nor did they mention anything about the peninsula hijacking. However, they did not dare keep them in the dark on this latest event, regardless of the consequences. Their confederates and associates back East had to be advised immediately of the loss of 120 barrels of wine.

However, the Sicilian Mob back in New Jersey were not people to screw around with. They meant business and the agents knew this. The Federal agents and their crooked supervisors in Washington had aligned themselves with an organization that didn't play games. Asking these Sicilians for money again without being able to deliver the goods could be hazardous to their health.

There were several things you had to be careful about in dealing with Sicilians. The first was to never, under any circumstances, fool around with their women. In their society, there is no such thing as a love triangle. The only triangle would be the scar left after they removed your "joys" permanently.

The second was never go back on your word regardless of the reason, justifiable or not. Because to do so meant you would have your tongue neatly sliced, marinated, and served to you on a silver platter.

Third, but not least, was never screw them in a business deal unless you wanted a tonsillectomy the hard way: without the need to open your mouth.

As for collections, they had developed the most practical and successful method known in the industry. It never failed. It was so good that you could never refuse the terms of settlement.

However, if you dealt with a Sicilian in an honorable manner, and he was to befriend you, then God help those who would as much as harm a hair on your head. They were just as trustworthy as they were tough, providing you held up your end. A pleasure to do business with if your intentions were good.

The agents were fully aware of these Sicilian traits, nevertheless, they had to take their chances. And so the telegram went out in brief and in code. It read as follows:

HI, JOHN — STOP. MACK STRIKES OUT 120 — STOP. ITCH BAD, NEEDS SCRATCH — STOP.

Well, when their merciless associates back in New Jersey received the telegram, they wasted no time in dispatching a coded telegram back to San Francisco. It read as follows:

SHOVE SCRATCH — STOP. NORTH DAKOTA — STOP.

The agents were sitting in their little office at the warehouse when the telegram arrived. They couldn't decipher the code because the words "North Dakota" had not been used in their code plan. They only knew that "scratch" meant "money," but how do you apply it to North Dakota?

It so happened that Pucci arrived at the warehouse on the pretense of checking if all was well with the agents' fire prevention procedures. He pretended not to notice their obviously extreme concern as he wished them a cheerful good morning. By now, they were comfortable with Pucci and felt that as a fire inspector, he was always trying to do the right thing. He was always very concerned about protecting government property. At least they thought he knew nothing else. In their minds, he was just a simple-minded city employee. How wrong they were.

The agents figured that because Pucci was Italian (such as the people they were dealing with), the words "North Dakota" might mean something to him other than what it meant to them. Hopefully, he could help them decipher the code. They saw no harm in confiding in him because whatever it meant, it could surely be passed off as more government code without divulging the true meaning of the correspondence or the true identity of the sender. So they asked for his assistance and showed him the telegram. They waited anxiously for his opinion.

Pucci looked the telegram over briefly, then set it down on the desk, and announced that this was a very simple matter. "You see," he said, "North Dakota among Italians means," he hesitated a minute, then wrote the words out on a piece of scratch paper as the four agents moved in closer for a better look. The letters in bold print read: "UPPER-U.S."

They stared at the words momentarily and then glanced up at Pucci, trying not to show ignorance on their part. They were no further along now than before. But it did make sense because North Dakota is in the upper U.S.

"Surely," said the senior agent, "there must be something else to that as well. Isn't there?" he asked.

"Yes," answered Pucci, "there is." The agents were confident that now they were going to score. He continued: "You see, if you pronounce these words in the true Italian dialect," he hesitated again as if thinking this highly technical matter out.

"Yes — yes, go on," they urged. "Tell us."

"Well, it's pronounced, UP-AH-YOU-ASS. And so, what they are telling you in this telegram is that whatever the word 'scratch' means, for you to shove it up your ass. That's all I can tell you gentlemen." With that he bid them good day and departed, leaving them standing there staring at each other.

"Oh, Jesus Christ!" said the senior agent as he slumped down in his chair. "Are we ever in trouble! They're not going to send us the money for sure. Those Italians at the winery up north are not going to sit still forever. They're liable to blow the whistle on us. We have to find that wine somehow or God only knows the consequences."

The hauling of wine from the winery to the warehouse with the small Fageol trucks continued on a cash basis as the agents searched the city for the missing 120 barrels. The search went on for days to no avail. They talked to everyone who could possibly give them a lead to its whereabouts. They found nothing, absolutely nothing. No one would tell them anything. Nobody would have anything to do with them. They dared not go to the Mayor or, especially, the Police Chief. However, one of the agents did come up with a worthwhile idea:

"How about this Fire Inspector, Mr. Puccinelli? Maybe he could be of help. After all, he did decipher the telegram code for us. Why not ask him?"

"Say, that's not a bad idea." admitted the senior agent. "As a fire inspector, he's able to get into warehouses and buildings of all sorts. Somewhere out there that wine is in storage awaiting distribution. Yes, maybe he can help us."

They agreed to contact the Fire Inspector immediately. The call went out right then and there. They wasted no time in placing the call directly to Pucci's firehouse. When the call came through, the dispatcher at the firehouse listened to the Federal agent's urgent request:

"We need the assistance of Mr. Puccinelli, the Fire Inspector, here at the Government warehouse immediately. Will you please relay the message to him posthaste? This is an emergency!"

Well, the firehouse dispatcher had no idea of the purpose of this urgent call. As far as he was concerned, this meant there was a fire at the warehouse and to get equipment down there immediately. This is what he was trained to do. There was no time to contact Pucci. He would be informed as soon as possible, but in the meantime, they must report to the call.

The blast from the alarm jolted the fire crew to attention. Cards and poker chips scattered to the floor as they bolted for their gear and slid down the pole from the upper floor and onto the trucks. They took off from the firehouse with every piece of equipment they had, including the hook and aerial ladder truck, complete with tiller. What the fire engines in the lead would miss, the hook and ladder truck with tiller out back was sure to hit. It would clear a swath down Market Street from curb to curb. Taking corners at high speed with this thing was a real challenge.

The tillerman on the tiller had no idea what the hell the driver up front had in mind. The poor bugger was strictly on his own. On a left turn, he would jump the corner curb on the left, scattering pedestrians — if not running over their toes. Then he would overshoot coming out of the turn, jump the curb on the right side, and race down the sidewalk wiping out newsstands and waste cans along the way. Yes, you better believe it was no easy chore for the tillerman of a hook-and-ladder truck. To make matters even worse, he was always the last one to reach the fire. In most cases, the long extension ladders were not needed in the first place. So the front tractor section would reach the corner and stop just short of the fire, waiting further instructions while this poor bugger steering the tiller was still around the corner, never even getting to see the fire.

The guys in the lead on the fire engines were obviously always the first ones to arrive at the scene. Their objective was to beat the fire captain to the fire so that they could have some fun with their fire axes before they could be stopped. However, this time when they arrived at the scene, Pucci was already there. It so happened that when the call went out, he was parked up the street keeping an eye on movements in and out of the warehouse. He did hear the fire engines coming but had no idea that the warehouse was their target until the first unit pulled up in front of the big wooden doors.

From where he was parked, it only took him a few seconds to reach the big doors ahead of them. Experience had taught him that these eager, young firemen would attack the doors first with their axes, not bothering to see if they were locked or not, which it so happens, they were not.

He reached the doors ahead of the crew, took a position facing them with his arms outstretched, and demanded they all back off.

"There is no fire! It's a false alarm! All a mistake!" shouted Pucci. He was pleading to the captain to call them back when someone standing on top of a fire engine threw his axe. It sailed through the air and sunk its blade handle deep into the door just above his head.

"You damned idiot!" screamed Pucci at the top of his voice as he reached up to pry the axe out of the door.

These firemen were gamblers as well. Back at the firehouse, they had a pool which paid off in stages, such as: first prize for the one who could sink his axe in the door first. The so-called idiot instantly announced his victory. He was the undisputed winner of the pool. With this, the rest of them turned towards the axe throwing Indian.

Axe in hand, Pucci also faced this character in a threatening manner. He knew in an instant that it was the Indian fireman, because to throw an axe like that would be a talent that one would have to acquire from axe-throwing ancestors. Also, the way he scrambled off that engine and took refuge in the hook and ladder truck, was a sure indication that he knew what it might feel like to be scalped with an axe. The urgency to chop the doors down was now over. Thank God for that, thought Pucci. The last thing on earth he wanted was to have the contents of the warehouse exposed. It was indeed a close call.

The captain organized his men instantly, and headed back to the firehouse with sirens blowing and bells ringing at the same

59

breakneck speed in which they had arrived, for there was a master pool the captain participated in as well. He was paying more attention to his stopwatch than where his lead driver was going. Timing was all important.

Pucci was relieved to see the tiller apparatus of the hook-and-ladder truck finally disappear around the corner with the Indian hanging on for dear life. He addressed him once again:

"Hang on, you axe-throwing jackass!" he yelled out while standing there axe in hand.

The horrified Federal agents were huddled together at the office door as these few minutes of assault took place. They had realized their mistake in placing the call in the manner such as they had done. Their actions could very well have exposed their entire operation. They rushed up and shook Pucci's hand vigorously. They were extremely grateful to this true patriot. He was, without question, their man. They could now take him in their complete confidence. They befriended him. As a matter of fact, if he was to be considered their friend, it would be the only one they had.

Pucci was quick to respond to their grateful gestures. He hammed it up as he stood there. His left hand resting on the end of the axe handle as if using it for a walking cane, standing straight, chest out, chin in, his fireman's cap pulled down with the visor shading his eyes. His beautiful Roman nose was still pointing in the direction of the departed fire engines, but his black eyes were penetrating the phoniness of these crooked bastards pumping his right hand. He followed them in to the little office. The senior agent sat down behind the desk. The others leaned back against the wall with their hands in their pockets. Pucci leaned the fire axe back against the wall. Too bad that Indian hadn't sunk it into the skull of one of these shitheads, he thought as he turned to face the senior agent.

The senior agent laid his cards on the table and proceeded to explain the missing 120 barrels of wine and how it supposedly came about. "Do you think this mysterious 'Mack' truck — that can haul the equivalent of four normal truckloads — exists?" he asked.

"I don't believe it does," lied Pucci. He explained that he inspected most trucks in the city and that so far as he knew, there was no truck described as such. However, if he was to come across it, he would cite the owner for not having a truck inspection before leaving the city.

They guessed right, so they thought.

"We knew we could rely on you, Mr. Puccinelli. Now, would you be kind enough to do us a favor, within reason of course?" asked the senior agent.

"Yes, of course. Name it," said Pucci.

"Would you inspect any building large enough to hold 120 barrels, and/or any other buildings that look suspicious, in the event the load has been split up?" the senior agent asked. "Or perhaps, investigate any alcohol-related activity which you become aware of, that might help us determine the whereabouts of the stolen wine, or who might be involved."

Pucci agreed to do his best to help them out. He picked up his axe and bid them good day as he swung it over his shoulder and walked off in the direction of his little Reo fire truck. No sooner out of earshot, he mumbled: "Screw you, Mr. Federal Agent. I'll bring you a report all right but not the kind you're thinking of, you crooked bunch of rabid hyenas."

CHAPTER 10

Pucci pretended to comply with their request. Over the following several weeks he fed the agents bits and pieces of information that he had supposedly gathered up in checking out every suspicious event going on in town. He finally concocted a list for them to review, but pointed out that it would be up to them to decide which ones they should raid. It was understood that there were no guarantees as to the productivity of any raids they might choose to undertake.

The agents eagerly poured over the list, going through a process of elimination until they had picked out several that they targeted for a raid. Of course, what they didn't know was that Pucci (with the help of his many friends and people he knew) had purposely set them up for a ridiculous roller coaster ride that would produce nothing.

According to the report, every Tuesday at 2:00 p.m. sharp, a Model-T Ford farm truck pulls up to the loading platform of the slaughterhouse down on Third Street and hauls away six full, fifty-gallon wine barrels of an unknown substance. The truck then hastily departs for parts unknown. The agents wholeheartedly agreed that this was, indeed, suspicious in nature.

"What do wine barrels have to do with a slaughterhouse operation? Quite suspicious, wouldn't you say?" inquired the senior agent of Pucci.

"I agree," said Pucci. "If they're wine barrels, you must assume they contain wine. The slaughterhouse should be the first target on the list."

"Fine," said the senior agent eagerly. "I'm glad you agree.

We'll set up a raid immediately."

On the following Tuesday, shortly before 2:00 p.m., the agents arrived at the slaughterhouse. They parked across the street and waited. The four Federal agents had a grim task ahead but they were ready, come what may.

They were not to wait very long before Mike came chugging along in his Model-T Ford truck. He swung out in an arc, then backed up to the loading platform in preparation to load the supposed six barrels of wine. These were wine barrels all right, but that's not what was in them now. Mike and two of his paesani had filled them with cow dung the week before. Using a big funnel and buckets, they dipped into the cistern alongside the slaughterhouse and filled the barrels. The barrels were now full of this awful-smelling cow dung washed out of the slaughterhouse. The bungs had been hammered in good and tight. They had purposely left the barrels sitting out in the sun on the back platform for the past week to allow the stuff to ferment.

Mike stepped down from the Model-T and walked up the steps onto the loading platform and over to the closed door. He cautiously looked around before rapping on the door several times and muttered some secret password in Italian.

"Look at that," said the senior agent to his cohorts sitting in the big sedan. "This is it all right. They're a bunch of Italians. That guy's our man," he said, referring to Mike. "We'll get him and the rest of those dagos in there."

As previously planned, two paesani, dressed as butchers in bloody white aprons, stuck their heads out the door, looked around, then slammed it shut again.

"Did you see that?" said the senior agent excitedly.

"We'll get those two and whoever else is in there that's involved in this hijacking business," he announced. "Stay down. Don't let them see us just yet," he added.

The two paesani went out back and rolled the six barrels through the slaughterhouse and out the front to the loading platform. The two men handled the barrels very carefully since the barrels were under extreme pressure as a result of being left fermenting in the sun during the previous week.

In the meantime, Primo was running late. He wanted to be there to witness the event that was about to take place. He raced up

Third Street with throttle wide open. His old Doane was bouncing and rattling over patches of cobblestones with canvas sailing in the wind like a schooner in a gale. His right hand clutched the vibrating steering wheel while the index finger of his left hand pulled hard on the exhaust whistle ring which protruded up through the floorboards. The whistle blasted away in a continuous loud "quok-ah, quok-ah, quok-ah, quok-ah." Primo pulled up to the slaughterhouse just as the agents had swung their big, black sedan across the street trapping the Model-T in its loading position.

Pucci was at an open window in a warehouse across the street. He stood back in the shadows and watched without being seen. He wanted to study the action. If mistakes were made, he wanted to know about them so he could change his tactics in some future campaign. Napoleon, watching a battle from a hilltop, could not have been more interested in the scene about to unfold below than this great strategist.

The agents, guns drawn, piled out of the sedan as the senior agent yelled out, "Hold it! Get your hands up! Quick now!"

Mike had quickly made his way back down the steps and away from the barrels that had been rolled out on the platform. He didn't want to be near them.

"You, there," pointing his gun at Mike. "Back against that truck. Come on! Up with your hands!"

Mike had already taken a leaning, somewhat half-sitting position against the front fender of the Ford. How much farther back could he go?

"You two up there, get back up against that wall. Be quick about it!" commanded the senior agent, while waving his gun at the two paesani.

They couldn't understand too much English but they knew what the man waving the gun in their direction wanted. They were eager to comply. They had backed up against the wall the minute they saw the guns. Now they were looking around for another wall to back up to. They were scared as hell and not about to disobey. By now, heads were poking out of windows. The butchers didn't want to miss out on this raid of a century. If asked, they would have gladly stepped out if for no other reason than to just get a better view of the action about to take place.

Like a pack of rats, the agents marched up the steps in single file, guns ready, strutting across the loading platform towards the neat row of barrels. The last three men stopped abruptly as if on cue. One spun around facing Mike, who was still leaning against the fender of the Model-T down below. With his gun ready and his legs spread out as if ready to gun down an opponent in a gun battle, the agent kept Mike covered. The other two also spun around with their legs outstretched and faced the two horrified paesani frozen against the wall. They wouldn't have to be shot. They were about to die of fright anyway.

The senior agent never broke stride until he reached the far end of the row of barrels he had just passed. He stopped, turned sharply, then started back slowly while holding his pistol loosely in his right hand, pointing at the barrels with the gun in a manner such as you would point your index finger. He started to count as he walked along slowly. He flipped the gun barrel down and aimed at each barrel as he went along counting.

"One, two, three, four, five, and six. So, we have six barrels here," he announced.

Any moron could have told you there were six barrels with just a casual glance from fifty feet away. But no, this jerk had to point at each one with the gun barrel to count them out. Now that he had established the unmistakable fact that there were six barrels out there, he faced the two paesani from across the platform, using his gun to point and gesture in order to better emphasize what he was saying.

"How many more barrels of wine are there in there?" he demanded to know. Before they could answer, he reminded them of the severe consequences of dealing in contraband.

The one most knowledgeable shook his head and answered: "No wine."

"Is that so? I want a hell of a lot better explanation than that, you damned dago," insisted the senior agent.

As he opened his mouth to speak, the paesano started to lower his hands.

"Keep your hands up!" shouted the senior agent. "Don't you dare lower your hands. Come on, explain this right now!"

Again the paesano started to lower his hands as he opened his mouth to speak.

"I said keep your hands up, goddamn it!"

Well, what this asshole didn't know was that it's impossible for an Italian to explain anything unless he uses his hands. As a matter of fact, the hand gesture is much more important than the spoken word. If you were to watch two Italians discussing a subject, you would note that there could be three-to-four times more hand gestures than spoken words. The words, for the most part, are merely incidental to the conversation of the hands.

Since the paesani were not allowed to lower their hands to answer the question, the senior agent got nowhere with his interrogation so it was necessary to shift to a different tactic.

He now asked direct questions that required only a "yes" or "no" answer:

"This wine belong to you?"

Answer: head shake, "No."

"Do you work here?"

Another head shake, "No."

"Any more barrels of wine in there?"

Answer: head shake, "No."

"Who is the owner of this place?"

Answer: A facial expression with a sharp upward thrust of the shoulders while exposing his palms. (Meaning: "Don't know.")

The senior agent was really frustrated but, nevertheless, he was getting some answers from these two scared-stiff Italians. They were not about to lie to him. He continued his interrogation getting madder by the minute.

"Do these damned barrels contain wine or not?"

Answer: head shake, "No."

"Do they contain whiskey?"

Answer: head shake, "No."

"Do they contain brandy?"

Answer: head shake, "No."

The agent blew his stack. He was in a rage. "God-damn it! What the hell is it then!? Vodka!?"

Both the paesani shook their heads violently up and down in unison like a couple of yo-yos. The answer was a definite "yes." These poor souls had never heard of the word "vodka" spoken before. To them, it sounded like their native word "vaca", meaning "cow", so they answered with a definite "yes" because the closest thing you could relate the barrel contents to was a "vaca" (cow). They had answered truthfully.

"Well, well. What do you know about that? Vodka! How nice, bootleggers. So we didn't get wine but at least we're not empty-handed." The senior agent continued to chat with his cohorts. "Relax, fellows, they're not going anywhere. We have them dead to rights."

While the interrogation was going on, Mike had long since lowered his hands. Having scratched around in his vest pocket, he came up with a half-smoked stogie which he puffed, while resting on the fender with his arms crossed. He was not about to keep his hands in the air for the likes of these four jerks up on the loading platform. All he was waiting around for was to get those barrels of cow dung loaded — along with the two paesani — and get home so he could fertilize his vegetables.

The senior agent ordered the two paesani to stand the barrels on end. He intended to bust up each barrel and destroy the supposedly illegal alcohol that he had just confiscated. The two paesani were relieved to lower their hands and arms, responding immediately to his request. They then moved back against the wall. The senior agent jammed the gun back in its holster, reached up on the wall and removed the full-size fire axe off its brackets and leaned it against the first upright barrel. He took off his hat, coat, and tie, and handed them to one of the other assholes standing close by. The butchers pulled their heads back in from the windows like turtles seeking to protect their heads from predators. They knew all about cow dung and its fermentation properties.

Mike knew what was coming as well. He moved slowly away from the Model-T, while still puffing on his stogie. He wanted to be in the clear so that he could run in any direction. There was no telling where that stuff might end up.

The paesani couldn't understand or speak much English but they did know that cow dung is cow dung whether it's in Italy or America. It was all the same stuff. They were inching their way along the wall, putting as much distance as they could between themselves and the barrels without making it appear like they were trying to escape.

The senior agent picked up the axe, took a position on top of the next closest barrel to get more leverage, spread out his feet for balance, then raised the axe high up over his head.

What a beautiful axe, thought Pucci, watching from across the street. It had a big, shiny wide blade on one end with a long pick-like, slightly curved point on the other end. Except for the cutting blade, the head was painted fire engine red, including a portion of the strong hickory handle. What a shame that such a beautiful axe as that should have to be christened in a barrel of cow dung, thought Pucci.

Primo was sitting in the open cab of the old Doane watching his uncle slowly moving away from the dock. His ever-present grin was almost as wide as he was tall. He knew how meticulous Mike was. Guns or no guns, they would have their hands full if they were to slop that cow dung on him. He was chuckling out loud at the thought of it.

The blade end of the axe came down with all the force this asshole could muster. It sunk deep into the end of the barrel. The tough oak didn't split but the shock jarred the barrel end loose. The extreme pressure created by the fermentation did the rest.

With a loud "vrroomph," the lid flew straight up, cartwheeling as it sailed through the air. Mike kept a close watch on it. He had

no intention of being hit on the head with the point end of that axe with the blade still firmly embedded in the cartwheeling lid. It was bad enough being hit occasionally with a cast iron skillet, let alone the point end of a fire axe. However, he was in no danger. He watched it come down, flipping end over end until the pick end of the axe (with the lid still firmly attached to it) buried itself deep in the roof of the agents' sedan.

The upward surge of cow dung caught the axe-wielding agent with full force and with his mouth wide open. The smug look on his face suddenly changed to a look of complete horror. He coughed violently as he came tumbling down from the barrel he was standing on. The other three agents were missed as the dung surged upward. But what goes up must come down. The other three agents were also christened with a shower of cow dung. All four government men left the scene thoroughly saturated with cow dung, retrieved from the cistern of a slaughterhouse by the willing and helpful hands of these immigrant Italians.

Pucci stood at the window like a general viewing a battle scene. His left hand with palm open was slung across his midsection supporting his right elbow while he stroked his chin with his right hand as if in deep thought. His magnificent nose with its keen sense of smell had picked up the aroma of the fermented cow dung drifting his way. Pucci was satisfied, but he could see where there might have been some room for improvement in his strategy. If there was, only he could see it.

As for Primo, he no longer sat upright in the cab of the Doane. He was stretched out and rolling around across the seat, roaring with laughter. The sight of the Hudson as it passed him, with the axe and lid embedded in the roof with the handle extending forward like an ornament, sent him into hilarious convulsions.

Mike wasn't amused. His truck was thoroughly splattered from radiator to tailgate, which of course amused the paesani no end. Discarding his stogie, he skirted the stinky mess while shouting orders up to the chuckling paesani:

"Get those barrels on the truck — including the broken one, and you two ride back there with them, understand!"

They understood all right, but they weren't too happy with the idea.

CHAPTER 11

Why is it that Italian wives inevitably end up having the last word, along with winning all arguments regardless of certified documentation that could prove them wrong? Mike was tapping his fingers on the dinner table while pondering this question when it all started.

Livia, still annoyed about his dealings with the banker, was not about to let up on him. The interrogation began as the wine bottle was emptied of its last drop of nectar.

"Did you go to the bank this morning?" she asked rather casually.

"Yes, I went to the bank. Why do you ask?" he answered, still tapping his fingers.

"Did you deposit some cash with your good friend, Mr. Battisoldi, the great, honest, banker?"

"Yes, I deposited a bunch of cash with that guy, Battisoldi. And if you must know, he makes me sick," he answered in disgust.

"Well, then," she pressed, "that's good. You give him a bunch of cash, and he will pay you three percent."

At this point, he cut her short. He had heard this before. After what he had been through at the slaughterhouse earlier in the day, Mike was not about to sit there and try to match wits with his wife. He snapped back:

"Damn it! I've had enough of that lousy banker, stupid Federal agents, cow manure, and your smart remarks."

Jumping up from his sitting position, he marched out of the house and down the back stairs leaving his hat behind.

She followed along, gently lifted his hat off the nail on the wall, swung the screen door open, and threw it down in the dust in front of him as she addressed him in a firm tone:

"You stink of cow manure. Don't come back in this house until you've taken a bath. Do you understand me?" With these parting words, she flung her head up and back, held her nose high in a manner as if she couldn't stand the smell in the air, turned and slammed the door behind her.

Mike didn't bother to comment. He picked up his hat, dusted it off, placed it on his head, lit up a fresh Toscanello cigar, and started out in a slow, casual walk in the direction of the big farmhouse across the celery patch. His wife's constant needling about this Battisoldi affair really bugged him. "That big-shot banker," he grumbled to himself. "Someday, he'll be in for a big surprise. Every time he sees me, he wants to shake my hand. He reminds me of the pickpockets back in Italy. They shake your hand while they pick your pocket. He thinks he's fooling me, but he needs my cash. Pretty soon I'll have so much cash in his bank that I'll take it all out in one day and put him out of business. Then I'll start my own bank. I'll call it the 'Bank of Buti.' I'll show Mr. Battisoldi how to run a bank." The idea delighted him no end.

He was working his way through the celery patch while puffing vigorously on his cigar, spitting occasionally between the celery rows. The music and singing coming from the big house caught his attention. "Well, at least my paesani are happy tonight," he thought. He could also detect the stomping of feet along with the music. It was coming from the basement.

"Ah, that's how life should be," he said, talking to himself. "It reminds me of the 'old country' during grape harvest with everybody dancing around while they stomp the grapes with their feet, drinking lots of wine in their festive mood."

"Drinking lots of wine!?" he exclaimed. The thought of the paesani drinking wine caused him to stop dead in his tracks. He was, for a moment, staring in the direction of the house, then he shifted his gaze towards the barn. "Are they drinking uncut wine? No, they can't be. But then, again, they could be. I better make sure," he said to himself.

He hurried along. The more he thought about it, the more convinced he was. He reached the edge of the yard, hesitated a second looking to his left towards the house. "They're not just happy, what the hell — they're having an all-out party!" Instead of heading directly towards the house, he swung to the right and hurried along in a fast trot in the direction of the barn. As he suspected, they had taken one of the new barrels of wine. The plank that had been nailed across the barn door had been ripped off and was now lying to one side. The door stood ajar. Mike swore, clenched his fist, and waved it in a threatening manner in the direction of the frolicking paesani in the basement of the farmhouse. They'd be punished–you can be sure he'd see to that!

The footprints on the soft ground, along with the wide markings of a rolled barrel, were apparent. This evidence would negate the need to inspect the barn itself for the missing barrel. Although he knew damned well where the barrel had gone, Mike proceeded to follow the path left by the rolled barrel through the soft dust. The path led him around the barn past the end of the hen house and sheds. At this point, the imprints of feet and barrel in the dust indicated that the barrel had been given a sharp jerk to the left, thereby setting it on course in a straight line that would put it through the basement door, dead center.

He was straddling the barrel's path, walking along at a fast gait, crouching, leaning forward as if stalking, his feet angled outward like a duck; the typical Italian walk. His shoes were slapping the dust like a beaver tail. He had his quarry cornered. It was now a matter of pouncing on his prey, wrestling it away from its captors, rolling it back to the barn, and restoring it where it originally came from, or so he thought.

Looking back over the dusty trail imprinted across the yard, a person would have to have been informed otherwise not to assume that a large, pregnant seal had dragged and rolled her body across the yard followed closely by a flock of large ducks.

Mike jerked the basement door open and quickly stepped inside simultaneously announcing the termination of their employment and that they, to the last man, vacate the premises immediately — posthaste. He was bound and determined to retrieve the barrel regardless of the consequences, even if it meant running them all off the ranch.

Well, the termination of their employment would be an easy matter since most of them were not really employees in the first place. All they were was a gang of paesano friends of his that were hanging around because of the unlimited supply of wine, watered down or otherwise.

Vacating the premises was another matter more complicated, indeed. Livia would never permit it. Besides, how do you get rid of a horde of wine gnats swarming around a wine vat? They certainly are not about to leave on their own accord. You would have to exterminate them, and that would be unthinkable considering these were men he was dealing with, not gnats. Nevertheless, Mike gave it another try by shouting:

"You're fired, all of you! Get out! Pack your stuff and get out this instant!" But nobody paid any attention to him. Frustrated, he stood there studying the situation; somehow he must get their attention.

Julio and Aldoino (in his soprano voice) had formed a duet, singing old Italian folk songs as the accordion player churned them out. There was no need to interrupt them. To do so would alert the others and eliminate the element of surprise.

Contini and Matteoli, the great philosophers, were engaged in philosophizing the importance of wine to an Italian's mental stability. To disturb them could mean getting himself embroiled in a useless counterproductive argument.

In the center of the room, the rest of the men were holding hands, stomping their feet, dancing around in a circle, shouting and singing while kicking their heels towards the center of the circle where sat that magnificent, French Oak wine barrel minus the bung. Judging by their actions, it was obvious that at least a good portion of the contents had already been consumed.

Mike wasn't amused one little bit with their conduct. He didn't care about their having some fun, but the barrel of uncut wine was another matter. This really infuriated him. He was determined to retrieve it and return it to the barn whence it came. While puffing hard on his cigar he approached the dancing men, stopping just short of the circle. To get any closer would surely result in skinned shins. He started to raise his hands in a gesture intended to get their attention and break up the dancing circle. He would attempt another announcement. It was only then that anyone realized his presence. Without missing a step or breaking rhythm, the circle temporarily split. The breach in the circle came around and, as it did, each man at the breach grasped Mike's hands. He was now a part of the dancing circle.

Mike's options were limited. Either he would dance or get trampled to death in the stampede. So, obviously, he exercised the one option that would result in the least bodily injury. He was trapped. So, around and around they danced. It would now be impossible for him to make the announcement since his hands were not free to make gestures. The swirling draft of air fanned the cigar clenched in his teeth. A heavy ring of smoke formed above the dancers heads like a big halo, as if they had just been ordained into sainthood by God himself. And rightfully so, for it was God's will that these paesani put this wine to the use it was intended.

"God's presence and guidance is never to be questioned. This is an omen," said Contini to Matteoli as the two men viewed the halo rising up towards the heavens.

"Let us rise to this occasion," answered Matteoli as both men staggered to their feet supporting each other while holding their hats in clasped hands as if praying.

So it was throughout the rest of the night as this bunch of God-fearing paesani continued to drain the barrel daring not to disobey the wishes of the ancient Roman Gods of Nectar.

CHAPTER 12

Several days passed before Pucci made it a point to again visit the agents at the warehouse. To his surprise, they were not upset with him at all. As a matter of fact, they mentioned very little about the slaughterhouse incident and, no doubt, for good reasons. One was their obvious embarrassment and the other being that they should have been less eager and used a little more common sense. Nevertheless, they were contemplating another raid. Only this time, as suggested by Pucci, they were going to approach the problem cautiously.

Pucci flattered the agents by telling them how he admired the meticulous manner of their operations and how much it meant to him to work with them. He offered to assist them in their next raid. His offer excited the agents. They now had an ally they could rely on and could utilize his talents, as well as his connections with the fire department.

They now plotted to raid the big, old, two-story mansion on the edge of the industrial area on the outskirts of the City just off Third Street. Relying on Pucci's original report, there was sufficient reason to believe that this raid would produce results. Besides, they had cased the place several nights in a row and their observations verified Pucci's findings. Also, as per his recommendation, the raid should be carried out at night with a couple of extra men if available. It was therefore agreed that Pucci would participate along with the new, young recruit he was training.

The plan of attack was finalized. The date and hour was set for nine o'clock sharp the following Saturday evening. The agents would leave the warehouse, stake out the mansion, and wait for

Pucci and his assistant to arrive before commencing the raid.

The three partners wasted no time in getting their own plan formalized. It was to coincide with the agents' mansion raid; sort of a "double header," so to speak.

"You mean we're going to hijack the warehouse?" asked Primo in a questioning manner.

"Yes, that's exactly what we're going to do," answered Pucci. "These assholes are so completely involved in the matter of the missing load that they're leaving themselves wide open. Now's the time to hit them again while they're vulnerable."

Mike was all enthused and excited about the whole affair. He and his paesani would participate directly in the hijack. As far as he was concerned, he would go for the idea of cleaning out the entire warehouse if it could be done.

It was all set. Each man knew what to do. However, they did agree to meet once again the following day to work out minor details. Timing would be very critical to avoid crossing paths. Delays of any sort could not be tolerated.

On the Friday morning prior to the planned Saturday evening raid, Primo once again pulled out of the Paper Company garage with the big Mack. It was beautiful to say the least. Painted silver grey, decorative striping along the edges of the open cab, shaded in darker tones at points to highlight some of its outstanding features, including the wheels. It was as shiny as a newly-minted silver dollar. The mechanics at the company garage were proud of this machine. They kept it in mint condition and ready to roll upon a minute's notice. They, too, enjoyed the good wine that Primo was so generous in handing out.

They watched the big Mack depart hogging the entire street until it straightened out. The undisputed "King of the Road." There was no other like it; at least, not in this area. It headed down to Third Street then turned south. Its destination was the ranch at San Bruno. Primo was to park it there and leave it overnight, then pick it up again on Saturday evening fully loaded with 120 barrels half full of water. The water had been left in them so they would not dry out and fall apart in handling, and to also muffle the hollow sound if knuckle tapped. Mike would take care of the loading as well as having already prepared the loading ramps that would be needed to reload full barrels from the warehouse they intended to raid.

Pucci informed the Fire Chief that since it was the 4th of July weekend, it was imperative that all leave should be suspended for the fire crews, especially the station at the foot of Market Street. He pointed out that the anticipated fireworks activity in the area of the sparsely populated warehouse district, especially, could get out of hand. The Chief agreed wholeheartedly and so ordered.

Pucci then paid a visit to Chinatown, shopped around for the smokiest, most brilliant, sparkling fireworks he could find. There was no problem acquiring a case of them along with two of the most powerful skyrockets he could find with particular patterns to suit his needs.

It was now Saturday night. Things were about to happen. With the exception of what the Federal agents and the paesani had planned for this night, you might say things were somewhat normal in the City considering it was the Fourth of July.

The City of San Francisco was being tucked in for the night. A low, overcast fog bank was rolling in from the Pacific Ocean. The lamplighters had completed their rounds wherever gas lights still existed. Fireworks activity was starting to escalate in the Chinatown district.

The Fire Chief, Police Chief, and Mayor, along with their wives, were sitting in the Mayor's living room overlooking the city. They had just enjoyed a fine dinner, complete with a good wine, thanks to Pucci and the paesani. Fine people, these Italians, the men would remind each other as they sipped wine while puffing on cigars. They had a pretty good idea where the wine was coming from but not much as to how it was being obtained.

Sometime earlier the big Mack, with its load of rumbling barrels, had pulled out of the ranch driveway at San Bruno with Primo at the wheel and Vasco sitting alongside riding with him. Tarps were pulled down tight giving no indication of its cargo.

Following close behind was Julio at the wheel of the Graham flatbed truck loaded with preconstructed loading ramps. Cassetta, the carpenter, was riding with him since he built the ramps, and it was appropriate that he also supervise the handling of them.

Taking up the rear of this mismatched caravan of trucks was Mike, in his Model-T Ford, loaded with the rest of the paesani. Matteoli and Funarino were riding up front with him. Between them rested the two-foot long rocket that Primo had handed him before pulling out with instructions as to how and when to use it. The caravan headed north towards the city. Their destination was the so-called government warehouse stored with the biggest single concentration of wine in the whole State of California. As rag-tag as they appeared, these paesani were now transformed into sophisticated, well-equipped, cunning rascals who were as determined as the tides to reach their objective.

Pucci was squatted down in a phone booth within sight of the warehouse, watching the agents standing around in front of the little office. His little Reo run-about fire truck was parked around the corner out of sight. The agents would leave in the opposite direction and, therefore, avoid seeing him or intercepting the caravan. He had insisted that they follow an exact route. He would also follow the same route when supposedly leaving the firehouse to join them. In this manner, he could catch up to them along the way. The agents thought this to be a good idea. They would comply.

The senior agent was holding his gold watch in his hand with the snap-lid open watching the second hand coming around. The other three agents were slipping their automatics in and out of their shoulder holsters, checking the guns as they did so. Surely, they would get to use them this night.

He snapped the watch shut, swung it across his vest and dropped it in its appropriate pocket, then signaled his men to move out. They piled in the big, black Hudson sedan. It was already facing the right direction. They took off right on schedule heading for the big mansion.

At Firehouse Number One, the firemen were discussing their chances of winning the master pool between stations so, obviously, strategies were being worked out. The time it took to arrive at the fire, put it out and return to the station is how they earned their merits. There was also the individual station pool among themselves. On this pool, the first engine to reach the fire and come to a dead stop was the winner. So it hinged strictly on the ability of the drivers as to which crew took that prize. There was also a prize for the first axe sunk into the burning building — generally the doors.

The City of San Francisco was now about to be jerked out of its doldrums. Pucci picked up the phone, called his station Number One and reported seeing smoke sifting through the doors of the warehouse which they had responded to once before. They should hurry. However, there would be no need for the hook-and-ladder truck. He didn't want that damned thing cluttering things up. All he needed to screw things up would be to have the ladder truck, while tagging along with the tiller out back, come swinging around a corner and slicing through Primo's caravan of mismatched trucks that were about to converge on the warehouse. No way, timing was all too critical; once their job was done, he wanted those fire trucks out of the way, fast. "Make it snappy!" were his parting words.

The dispatcher leaned on the alarm as he simultaneously raised up from his chair. He was going out on this one as well. Firemen were scrambling for equipment as the drivers started their engines keeping them at a fast idle. There would be no time to warm them up. The tillerman was pushing the doors open as the dispatcher yelled out to him:

"We're not taking the hook and ladder. We'll call you if we need you!"

The tillerman yelled back: "Screw you, prick! I'm not going to miss this one!" With those parting words he jumped on Engine Number Two, as did the dispatcher. The dispatcher yelled again:

"Where's the Captain?"

"Damned if I know!" yelled the driver of Engine Number One, then added: "We ain't wait'n!"

At the coffee shop a few yards up the street, the Captain saw the red light flash out front of the firehouse at the same instant the siren started its long, drawn-out wail. He set his coffee cup down and dashed out the door too late to make it to the firehouse. His Engine Number One was already on its way, about to go past him. Running as fast as he could in the same direction, he was grabbing at the back end of the fire engine as it picked up speed. The driver had no intention of backing off to let him on. Fortunately, hanging on across the back closest to the Captain, one hell of a husky fireman reached out, grabbed a handful of coat collar, jerked the Captain off his feet, swung him around and across the back and into the waiting arms of the others. They, in turn, pushed him up on top of the fire engine.

He quickly regained his sense of direction, crawled along the top of the fire engine as it roared on picking up speed. He moved past the Indian lying flat down among the neatly folded hoses, blending in with the surroundings, and hanging onto the ladder with

79

one hand, and grasping the handle of his axe with the other. He was holding the blade flat down as if to avoid reflection of light that might warn an enemy of his presence. His inherent traits were being displayed in his every action. Once past the Indian, the Captain dropped down into the open cockpit and sat down alongside the driver where he should have been before the fire engine left the firehouse.

"Where the hell did you come from?" inquired the driver.

"For all you give a damn, you asshole!" answered the Captain in a contemptuous manner, then asked his own question: "Where the hell are we going?"

"To the government warehouse."

"That again?"

Pucci set the long rocket well off to one side and ripped the lid of the case of assorted shooting sparklers. They were all facing straight up in firing position. He set the case against and in the center of the two, big, wooden warehouse doors just under the locking device. He struck a match, torching the fuse on the center sparkler, then stepped back out of the way. The front of the warehouse reflected the brilliant red-colored flashes as the various fireworks flared up.

By now the agents were well across Market Street on their way to the old mansion following the exact route laid out by Pucci. There was no deviation. They would arrive on schedule, park in the shadows close by, keep an eye on the entrance of the mansion, and wait for Pucci's arrival.

Primo was now on the Embarcadero. He checked his timing. They were coming in a little early; the clock tower at the Ferry Building up ahead to the right was coming into view. He would have to be alert at this hour of the night because there would be cross traffic at this point. He dropped the Mack down a couple of gears; it breathed easier. Not that the load was heavy, mind you. It was more of a release-of-tension sort of sound, almost human. He was keeping a sharp eye over the top of the buildings ahead and to the left toward Telegraph Hill.

The two fire engines had by now made their right turn off Market Street. Once across California Street, they opened 'em up. They were heading toward the warehouse on the cross street wide open. They would have to make a left a couple blocks up ahead.

The warehouse would be on the right near the far end of the block. They could now see the glare and rising cloud of smoke from the assorted fireworks as they reached their peak of brilliance.

"Holy smokes! Look at that! We've got a hot one here tonight," yelled the Captain. "Come on, pour it on. Give it all you got. Put it to the floor board."

The glare was lighting up the cloud cover making it look several times as bad as it really was. The pool was one thing, but now it was their duty to do their job that would dominate their concerns. The fire engines were no longer following each other. They were coming in, side by side, at full throttle. The men hanging on were yelling encouragement to the drivers. They had two objectives: the fire and the pool.

The Captain was leaning forward into the wind, cussing the driver of Number Two Engine coming up alongside to the right, with the intention of passing.

"Where the hell's he getting the extra power?" he yelled out as he glanced over in surprise to see the tillerman. "What the hell's he doing there? Where's the ladder truck?"

"It ain't coming."

"By whose order?"

"Inspector Puccinelli, Sir."

"Did he call it in?"

"Yes, Sir."

"Well, I'll be . . . , Puccinelli? And that government warehouse again?"

They'd now have to make a sharp, hard left or miss the corner completely. It wasn't until then that Pucci got the first look at this seemingly Roman chariot race. It was apparent that these young drivers could very well be San Francisco's first generation-born Italians. Pucci swore:

"Damn fools — imbeciles, they're going to overshoot the corner sure as hell."

Not so. Engine Number One, coming in on the left, swung into the street hugging the curb to its left; Engine Number Two also swung in as tight as it could almost to the point of collision. It was obvious, the winning of the pool was influencing his driving. The Captain turned his head and addressed the driver of Number Two Engine with a volley of profanity. Tires screaming their defiance to the pavement, the fire engines came roaring down the street, weaving from side to side.

Pucci watched them in disbelief. Like an audience watching a chariot race at the Coliseum in the ancient City of Rome, he was being taken in by the whole affair. He swore again:

"Those stupid idiots are coming in too fast!" He ran into the street to wave them down, then back up on the sidewalk again for fear of being run over. The Captain had now shifted to a vocabulary that resembled nothing like the English language. Profanity would be a mild description. Amidst a screeching of tires, they stopped directly in front of the two big doors.

Nobody waited around for instructions. They knew what they must do. Regardless of their being on fire, the wooden doors must be demolished first. The crews (axe in hand) charged the burning doors, while the Captain shouted instructions to the men stretching out hoses. Number Two, being closest to the doors, gave its axe-wielding crew a little of a head start.

The axe-throwing Indian having come in on Engine Number One immediately concluded that no way could he get ahead of the other crew members. His ancestral instincts flashed in his mind. They would come into play. One long stride catapulted him in the air setting him on course to land feet first on Engine Number Two. In this split second, in his mind, he was an Indian warrior searching through the thick smoke for his target. It was important to judge the exact distance between him and the target. He swung his long-handled axe in a forward motion, while still in mid-air, a fierce scream emitted from his lips. The muscles and cords of his neck reflected the strain that produced the blood-curdling sound. The blade was coming down and around past his ankle, then back over his head. His feet landed squarely on the neatly-stacked and folded hoses of Engine Number Two. At this precise instant, he let the axe fly. It sailed through the air above the heads of his comrades who were rushing forward to take on the burning doors looming up before them. His axe was flying through the air in graceful swooshing cartwheels. It was on course. It would sink its blade dead center of its target. The thought that held him in this trance vanished from his mind as fast as it had come. He was now back to reality.

Pucci was standing there horrified at the thought of what that flying axe might do if that over-eager Indian was to misjudge his target and hit a fellow fireman in the back instead. The savage look that flashed across this man's face sent chills up and down his spine as he muttered: "What the hell — that guy's cracking up. He's going bananas."

By now the others were racing up the ramp. In a matter of seconds they would reach the doors. However, their intention to take their station's prize for the first axe buried in the door would be to no avail. For sailing over their heads, the blade of the Indian's axe embedded itself into the thick wooden doors with a loud "ka-chunk." The handle, vibrating like a tuning fork, was sending out a constant hum as if casually announcing its victory.

Above the din of battle, the Captain could be heard calling for high pressure water.

"Get those hoses coupled to the booster pumps! Driver, engage your power takeoff! Wind 'er up!"

The pump tender, at his station at the side of the fire engine, studied gauges while ready to jerk valves open that would send high pressure water surging through the hose being held at ready directly behind the axe wielders. As the pressure gauges so indicated, valves were jerked open. The high-pitched whine of the fire truck's engine suddenly changed to a constant laboring roar. The two men at the nozzle had all they could do to control the whip-lashing effect of the high pressure hose. The blast of water directed over the heads of the axe wielders raked across the face of the building sending water cascading down onto the men as they proceeded to demolish the doors. Regardless of the drenching, within minutes the doors were completely demolished.

Pucci was the first one through the opening. He turned and yelled at the top of his voice while waving his hands desperately:

"Back off! Back off! It's over! It's over!" he pleaded. "Captain," he yelled, "stop them! Pull them back!"

The Captain couldn't see Pucci through the lingering smoke and vapors emitting from smoldering debris, but he could distinguish his pleas rising above the din of the campaign.

The ladder truck matter still on his mind, he picked his way through men and debris to get to Pucci. In a serious, no-nonsense manner, he addressed him accordingly:

"What the hell's the idea of calling off the ladder truck?"

"I didn't think you'd need it," answered Pucci.

"You must be crazy. On a warehouse fire, the ladder truck always goes out. You know that!"

"All right, so I goofed. It won't happen again."

"It damned well better not! By the way, what's in this place anyway?" inquired the Captain in a somewhat calmer tone.

Exposing the contents of the warehouse was the very thing Pucci was trying to avoid.

"Molasses, just plain molasses," he lied.

"Damned good thing, or this thing could have gotten out of hand, sure as hell."

"Captain, I hope you're not forgetting the pool. We've got a pretty good shot at it," said Pucci in a tone of urgency. "Maybe you should get your men back to the station; I'll stay and clean up the mess." At Pucci's urging, the Captain was persuaded to pursue the matter no further. He wasted no time whatsoever in getting the situation under control.

"All right, men, pick up your gear and let's get back to the station," he ordered. "Come on! Move it! On the double! Let's get back on the engines."

The drivers hit the fire engines first. The Captain by now was where he was supposed to be. He was not about to be left behind this time. As for the others, they too felt the same way. They threw their equipment aboard and hung on as both fire engines took off with a roar.

Pucci had a firm grip on the young recruit restraining him from climbing aboard. "You're coming with me," he said. "Get your ass around the corner and bring my truck around here, pronto! Right now!"

As the recruit departed at a dead run, Pucci reached around the corner of the warehouse doorway and threw the main light switch. The entire warehouse was illuminated along with the loading ramp. He now listened tentatively for Primo's signal for if he's on schedule, it would be about time.

Primo looked at his watch again. His timing now looked to be about right. The Ferry Building and Market Street were now behind them. He was going over the route he must take, rehearsing it in his mind. He was to turn off the Embarcadero one block this side of the warehouse, then up to the street above it; turn right; then one block and turn right again; swing wide; stay on the left side of the street; and park in front of the doors along the left curb. This would put the Mack facing downhill in full view of the Bay and the dismal lights of Alcatraz. He would be coming in fast; if he was to miss it, he would then have to go completely around the block and repeat the approach, wasting valuable time they could not afford. He was now increasing the engine RPMs. He wanted more exhaust pressure at the exhaust horn. He was ready to announce his position. Within seconds, throughout the canyons of San Francisco, echoed the huge exhaust horn of the Mack: "Quok-ah! Quok-ah! Quok-ah! Quok-ah!" This told Pucci that the Mack was close by and ready to move in. The long rocket was already set up in firing position. He struck a match and touched off the fuse. At that instant, the recruit pulled up with the Reo run-about truck.

"Move over. I'll drive," commanded Pucci. At that instant, the rocket shot straight up in a shower of sparks trailing smoke as it climbed toward the low overcast. The recruit was understandably startled.

"What the hell was that about?" he inquired.

"Something to let the citizens of San Francisco know that they have a Fire Department comparable to none other," answered Pucci proudly.

With this, they pulled away from the warehouse scene heading for the mansion on the outskirts of the city. There was something about the hard, determined look on his supervisor's face that told the young recruit not to ask too many questions.

CHAPTER 13

The Mayor and his guests were enjoying their glasses of wine when the rocket's first phase exploded with a booming "ka-pow" high above the fog cover. The wide plate-glass window of the Nob Hill mansion commanded an excellent view of the exploding rocket as it unfolded.

"Look at that, will you!" exclaimed the Mayor pointing in the direction of the thundering explosion.

As they rose from their chairs and rushed to the window, the second phase let go followed immediately by the third phase. The booming echoes blended into one thunderous roar. Following the third phase, a section of color shot even higher, up and out, in a "poof", while the final phase ended in two soft "pow-pows" completely lighting up the sky above the city. The group at the window were awestruck.

"My God! I have never seen anything like that before," said the Mayor's wife.

"Beautiful! Absolutely beautiful! The Statue of Liberty in red, white and blue," said the Mayor. "Look at the size of it, will you? It looks like she's standing on the clouds." The Mayor then raised his wine glass high and said: "To the ethnic groups that make up this great city — and to you, the Chinese who invented fireworks — and also to you, the Italians, who provide us with these fine wines, I thank you for your gracious unselfish generosity in sharing it with us. 'Salute!'"

The "Amens" were in unison. They all emptied their wine glasses as the Statue of Liberty faded in the darkness. They had no idea of the rocket's true purpose.

The Mayor and his guests were not the only ones to witness this spectacle. Although he couldn't make out the spectacular display from below the cloud cover, Primo knew what the flash of color was all about, only he saw it from a different perspective and meaning. This was the signal he was waiting and watching for.

"Vasco, hang on," said Primo. "We're going for one hell of a ride." The Mack responded instantly. From a slow-cruising speed it lurched forward with the force of a determined bulldog. Primo's eyes were glued to the tachometer as he shifted into higher gears with precision.

The big Mack, with its load of rumbling wine barrels, raced up the Embarcadero. The many rail tracks, patches of asphalt and cobblestones coming in contact with the numerous tires, were adding a heavy washboard sound effect accentuating the rumble. Primo had a firm grip on the vibrating steering wheel with his left hand, while his right hand was busy working the shift levers. The Mack responded accordingly, surging forward, picking up speed. Primo leaned into the left turn. The Mack was now into the side street, an uphill climb.

The canyons of San Francisco were echoing with the rumbling of barrels and rattling noises being emitted by this caravan of mismatched trucks and their cargos. Speed had to be maintained in order to negotiate the uphill grade.

The Mack was now approaching the cross street where it would make a right turn. It was still traveling uncomfortably fast as it was about to level off at the cross street. The heavy bumper, crankcase, and bulldog snout loomed up over the rise like a battle tank about to come crashing down across trenches. The truck rocked over the hump as it started the right turn. Primo was forced to let up some on the throttle. The front wheels vibrating over the cobblestones made steering difficult. Coming out of the turn, weaving, vibrations reflected on the dimly-lit gas lanterns.

Vasco was doing his damnedest to stay in the open cab. There was no steering wheel to hang on to on his side. He was no longer thrilled or excited. He was just plain scared as hell.

Primo swung the Mack out wide, raced down along the left-hand curb like a runaway locomotive, then abruptly let up on the throttle. The back-firing exhaust added to the Fourth of July explosions of Chinatown. The next right was coming up fast. Leaning forward searching for the trailer's brake lever, he dared not take his eyes off the road. There was no way of knowing who or what might be out in front of the warehouse. Grasping the brake lever, he gave it a firm tug. The trailer brakes locked up instantly. Smoke from burning rubber boiled up off the pavement as the Mack swung out wide and into the right-hand turn dragging the trailer along on locked-up wheels. It straightened out tight along the left curb while still rolling in fast. It was only now that Primo dared apply the brakes to the Mack itself.

The big truck wheels locked up instantly. Rubber clawed at asphalt emitting a horrendous, deafening roar that pounded the eardrums. Sickening acrid smoke engulfed both truck and trailer as the undercarriage finally stopped its forward motion. But inertia continued to push the rest of the truck forward to a point of extreme resistance. Spring shackles were stressed to breaking point before the whole mass of iron rocked back abruptly, then forward again until it finally settled down.

Primo sat there a few seconds hollow eyed, mouth open, gripping the wheel with sweaty hands. "Vasco, are you all right?" he inquired of his co-pilot who was still hanging on in a state of shock, and with trembling hands searching for his hat down somewhere on the floorboards. For an instant, he couldn't seem to get himself together.

Julio came in next with the Graham truck. He was relieved to see the Mack now motionless; he moved past it, pulled in, then out again, before backing up to the curb just in front of it.

The cricket-like sound of Mike's Model-T could be heard coming around the corner. Puffs of steam vapor were emitting from around the radiator cap as it pulled in behind the Mack and stopped in the midst of the still-lingering smoke. The hinges of the big doors were all that were left of the framed opening. The still-lingering rocket smoke indicated that there had been very little time lost in getting the caravan to the scene. Debris was scattered over the entire area of the ramp.

Vasco had pulled himself together and was now working along his side of the truck untying canvas and loosening ropes as he went along. Primo was doing likewise on the opposite side until he was relieved by Funarino and Matteoli. Julio and Casseta were untying and placing the wooden ramps in preparation for both the unloading and reloading procedure.

The rest of the paesani scrambled off the back end of the Model-T. They marched down the sidewalk like soldiers with Mike in command. He ordered the group to halt, then stepped to one side, raised his arm and proceeded to address this bunch of rag-tag men dressed in baggy pants, clown-like shoes, collarless shirts, and hats sitting on their heads at cockeyed angles. Pointing across the Bay towards the dismal lights of Alcatraz glittering through the dark, he said:

"You see that? That's Alcatraz, a Federal prison. You drag your feet tonight, and that's where you will be tomorrow. And remember, they serve no wine at Alcatraz."

Needless to say, there was no need to say more. Every man knew exactly what he was there for and what must be done. Before

the smoke cleared, Primo had already scrambled up on top of the cab. He faced the rear of the Mack straddle-legged, pointing and shouting instructions as tarps were folded back rapidly. At the instant the first tier of barrels were exposed, a prefabricated ramp was in place. Half-empty barrels of water with bungs tightly secured were now rolling off and into the far end of the warehouse. The instant the unloading ramp was moved along toward the rear to intercept the next row, the loading ramp dropped into place. Now full barrels that were being rolled out of the warehouse were being restacked in place of the empties under Primo's watchful eye.

Mike was in the warehouse directing things there. As was his habit under stressful working conditions, he was shouting instructions to the men. A generous use of profanity in his native tongue emphasized each order. They worked like hell and kept their mouths shut, or heaven help them if they didn't. They knew that among other things he was now making them pay for disobeying his orders back at the ranch. He wanted every ounce of that unauthorized wine they had taken liberties with back in blood, and that's what he was getting — bloodied wine barrels from work-scuffed hands.

He pointed out the stacks they must take. All French oak barrels with 230-liter capacity were selected. They knew better than to complain about the extra work handling them. There were two lines of continuous rumbling barrels: one to the left rolling into the warehouse with water; the others coming out to the right rolling in the opposite direction with wine. Unloading and loading was being done simultaneously. Prefabricated ramps were moving along for pulling down stacks of full barrels, while other ramps would follow along restacking empties in their place making it appear that the stacks were never touched in the first place.

This was a "no-nonsense" operation. It had to be done efficiently and quickly for fear of being discovered by the crooked Federal agents, or their gangster collegues, whoever they may be, who were no doubt armed with guns. The paesani were not armed whatsoever.

The truck was fully loaded in record time. Primo now pulled the rig up placing the trailer in position for unloading and reloading with full barrels. While this was in progress, Funarino (the rope man) and Matteoli were tying down the truck and replacing the heavy tarps. At best, the ramps were especially dangerous to work around. Aside from skinned and bleeding knuckles, the operation moved along without serious injury.

Casseta (the carpenter), assisted by Taliaferro, and under Julio's direction, was now dismantling the excess ramps and preparing the planks that would be used to board up the warehouse opening in place of the demolished doors.

Mike now held his hand on the last barrel. "That's it! No more!" he yelled out.

The last barrel went into place none too soon because the dismantlers were already pulling the nails out of the last ramp before it was fully cleared. As planks were being nailed in place, debris was being swept up and loaded on the Graham along with unneeded ramps, planks, and timber as ropes were cinched and tarps stretched.

Funarino and Matteoli stepped aside as Primo, along with Vasco, climbed up and aboard the fully-loaded Mack, and cranked 'er over. A charge of black smoke spewed out the exhaust pipe. The whole front end danced like a heavy-weight prize fighter coming out of his corner, then settled down to a constant tiger-like purr. It was now ready to roll out.

Primo now spoke his first and only words to his uncle during this entire operation: "Uncle Mike, don't forget to pull the main light switch before they get too high up with those planks."

Mike responded with a nod.

Primo added: "And don't forget the rocket. I'll see you back at the ranch."

"Primo, be careful. Take it easy," advised Mike.

With these parting words, the truck and trailer rumbled off down the street with the biggest little man in San Francisco at the controls and with a still shaky Vasco as co-pilot. They were on their way home with 120 barrels of Sonoma County's finest wine. The best that could be had at any price, however acquired at the right price: a little blood letting, and a lot of sweat.

Before the Mack was out of sight, the lights were out, the door opening completely boarded up, and the excess debris picked up. The Graham pulled out first. Then the Model-T with Mike at the wheel and his relieved but fatigued paesani. The last sound leaving the scene was the "chit, chit, chit" of the Model-T.

CHAPTER 14

Pucci was convinced that all was going well back at the warehouse. The plan was that if they had trouble and could not pull off the hijacking for whatever reason, Mike would fire off the second rocket from somewhere along the Embarcadero. Not having seen it since he left the warehouse was an indication that the hijacking was in progress.

They were now at the mansion. The recruit was standing by the idling Reo run-about fire truck parked a few yards behind the black Hudson sedan. His orders were to be alert and ready, but to keep the nozzle out of sight. He was told by Pucci that these men in the car were suspected of arson. They, no doubt, are the ones who tried to burn down the warehouse. These could be dangerous men he was about to question, and if it appeared to him that something of a suspicious nature was about to happen, especially if he saw guns flash in their hands, he was to use the fire hose on them with full force and at his discretion, and not worry about his getting soaked as well.

As Pucci walked up to the Sedan, the agents stepped out in the semi-darkness. They were talking in low tones which were inaudible to the recruit. He had the makings of a good fireman, and he had studied the book of rules carefully, but there was nothing in the book he had studied that made mention of a situation like this. After much discussion among the men, Pucci made his way back to the fire truck while the four agents walked off in the direction of the mansion. His objective was to stall them as long as possible.

Upon approaching the fire truck, he advised the recruit to shut the pump and truck down. Everything was under control.

"However," he said, "I'm not too sure about these guys. Maybe we should stick around awhile and keep an eye on them. That is, of course, if you're not in a hurry to get back to the station."

The recruit knew damned well that this comment was only a matter of being courteous. Therefore, he obviously agreed with his superior. But he did ask the question:

"What's the deal with that old mansion, and why are those men going in there?"

"Well, that place is where a man can go in a virgin and come out a veteran, all in the same night," he answered. "As to why they're going in there, let's just say that some men get turned on by the excitement of the unexpected."

The agents had now reached the front door. It was locked. The senior agent rapped on it while the others stood by to break it down if need be.

They were somewhat surprised when the door opened wide and there, standing before them with the light to her back, was a charming, gracious, less-than-middle-aged woman, clad in a negligee that was purposely designed to reveal her perfectly proportioned body. The four men were experiencing warm tingling feelings surging through their bodies as they stood there, in the cool of the night, staring in disbelief at this stimulating sight: a sexually radiant woman expressing warmth. Their hands moved away from their shoulder holsters. There would be no need for guns here, at least not for the moment.

"Good evening, gentlemen. Won't you come in," the woman purred in a manner which could not be refused.

As far as they were concerned, they wouldn't have minded standing out there a little longer. They were having difficulty getting their line of sight above her belly button.

She stepped graciously to one side as she repeated her offer. "Please come in," she pleaded softly.

All four men tried to squeeze through the door at the same time as her right leg exposed itself through the slit negligee. These men were unquestionably hard and tough, but they were not made of iron. The torch they were being confronted with was putting their hardness to the test.

The two firemen outside had crossed the street as the door opened. From that distance, the thin negligee was not visible at all.

What they thought they were looking at was the naked form of a beautiful woman standing inside the doorway.

"Holy cow!" exclaimed the recruit. "Look at that, will you!"

As preoccupied as he was about the hijacking in progress back at the warehouse, Pucci couldn't help but answer the recruit. With flared nostrils, he snorted in a bull-like fashion:

"You better believe I see that, kid. I guess this is what you might refer to as being on the outside looking in."

The door closed behind the agents. The bolt could be heard sliding into its locked position. The four men's gaze worked its way up to the gardenia pinned on the lady's negligee. Its fresh, perfumed scent accented the warm sexual feelings radiating from this "goddess of temptation."

From the spacious entry hall, they heard voices, along with other varied sounds, coming from behind a pair of closed double doors which, they thought, no doubt opened into a large gaming room complete with a bar well-stocked with alcohol and wine. They were satisfied. Unlike the previous slaughter-house raid, they surely would not be wasting their time on this one.

While talking, the senior agent and the others, as well, were carefully looking over this gracious creature trying desperately not to let their emotions de-rail their intended mission. They must not succumb to nature's sexual driving forces within them. They must stand fast and not give ground. However, aside from all else, they at least could have removed their hats while in the presence of a lady, especially having been invited in such as they were. But these men, while attending the training academy for their profession, had fallen asleep when the subject of courtesy and manners were being taught. So they graduated with the notion that the gun and badge were all that were important while upholding the laws of the land, and in carrying out their duties as Federal agents.

She, in turn, was carefully studying them as they were standing there before her trying desperately, without success, to keep their sexual ambitions in check. Experience had taught her long ago that these men had not had a good woman in one hell of a long time. They were ripe. No way could they hide their sexual feelings from her keen senses.

The senior agent, without divulging the true purpose for having come to this establishment in the first place, asked:

"Do you mind if we take a look around? I mean — the premises — of course."

"Don't mind at all. Please do," was her response. She saw no reason whatever to refuse this sort of request. All her customers (the "Johns") would, for the most part, want to carefully look over the "Girls" before making their selection as to which one they would choose for the night. She glided past and just ahead of the senior agent. Her graceful stride accentuated her smooth, firm, body curvatures. Eyes glued to her synchronized hip movements, the senior agent all but ran into her as they approached the doors. He could now detect the presence of a variety of peculiar perfumed odors sifting through the doors. A surge of thoughts rushed to mind. Through tight lips, he whispered to his cohorts:

"We have, no doubt, uncovered a narcotics operation as well. Those women's voices coming from behind those closed doors are, no doubt, packaging the stuff for distribution. After all, we did see several men entering through the front door, then leaving out the back door, during our stakeout; narcotics peddlers, on a routine pickup–for sure."

Now they could understand what Pucci's report was trying to tell them. This is why he had personally warned them to use extreme caution. "Take it easy and measure your ground. Hold your staff firm. Be prepared for the unexpected. You may not have control of the inevitable. Ride with the punches." They thought this was very good advice on Pucci's part.

The Madam reached for the doorknob and in doing so, she noticed a badge as she brushed by the senior agent. A careful glance also disclosed the bulge under his left arm. No doubt a gun, she concluded. However, this didn't bother her much. After all, half her clientele were policemen: both when off duty or on duty, with or without uniforms, individually or in groups. Sometimes gentle, and sometimes acting like wild beasts. So, why should it be of concern to her now? Her "Girls" knew how to handle them. They loved it. It put more zest in their lives. It made the affair all the more exciting, and so they performed better.

The senior agent reached out beating her to the doorknob. "Wait a minute; let me do this for you, if you don't mind?"

The Madam stopped dead in her tracks, surprised at this gallant gesture. Their eyes met not more than inches apart. She was pleased with his gracious offer. She liked this in a man. "Maybe I'll just take this one on myself," she thought. Signs of excitement and nervousness were beginning to show, and were difficult to conceal. Pleasant thoughts were now floating through her mind. He in turn watched her closely. He had been trained to spot this kind of nervous reaction in suspects, a sure sign of guilt. No question about it now, they were on the right track, and were ready to spring like cats at the first quick movement they saw. He rudely brushed her aside as he grabbed at the door handles with both hands. She responded excitedly:

"God damn you're feisty! I like that in a man." Unable to hold back her sexual emotions any longer, she raised her arms with fists clenched above her head, whirled her hips in a rotating, forward thrust as she let out a sexually actuated scream:

"Here they come, Girls!"

"Damn it! That's an alarm signal!" cursed the leader. "We'll have to move fast." As he held onto the doorknobs, he swung his body to the left in order to clear the path for his men to charge to the right the instant he pushed the doors open. This maneuver placed him directly in front of the over-sexed Madam who was in the same forward-leaning position that he was. His split coat-tails framed his butt in an inviting manner; at least, inviting to the Madam in her present frame of mind.

At the instant he yelled out to his men: "Now! Let's go in and get them!" she moved up close behind him and with a quick, firm motion of her hips, slammed him in the butt with her crotch, knocking him off balance and sending him clear through the doors. The others, eager to participate, rushed in with their guns drawn and ready for action.

Well, the Girls inside heard the Madam yell out, "Here they come!" To them that meant that the fare had been paid and the men were coming in ready for action.

These jerks had no sooner cleared the doorway when this swarm of skimpy-clad Girls came rushing at them.

The agents were caught with their pants down so to speak. Pucci's advice flashed across their minds like the past of a dying man. There was no longer any need to measure their ground now; but by the look in this horny Madam's eye, the senior agent damned well better get a firm grip on his staff and prepare himself for the

96

inevitable. They suddenly realized that this old mansion was in fact an Armenian whorehouse. But it was too late to look back now. Realizing his predicament, the senior agent yelled out another order:

"Keep cool men! Take defensive measures!"

How the hell are you going to keep cool when you are thrown into a red-hot furnace? Defend yourself, how? As for measuring their ground, these olive-skinned girls with big black eyes and jet black, ponytailed hair had already measured whatever there was to measure. Their belly buttons were quivering with excitement.

Business hadn't been all that good. These girls were hell bent for enjoying their work as much as their clients. Surely they would be glad to work for nothing rather than lose a customer. If they had any idea that there were two more men standing around outside the mansion, you can be sure that several of them would have been sent out to run them down and drag them in as well, regardless of pay.

They made short work of the men's clothing, guns, holsters, hats, underwear, shoes, etc. Everything ended up in the corner in a rather disorderly pile. The only thing they didn't peel off these startled lawmen were the horrified expressions on their faces.

The four men backed into each other hoping to ward off the second attack. They were holding their staffs firmly all right. They were indeed preparing themselves for the inevitable. Since rape was apparent, they might just as well sit still and enjoy it.

The Madam was no longer gentle and suave. Surging with excitement, she was now extremely aggressive, like a female tiger clawing at her mate demanding his attention. They were in for a session of sex therapy whether they wanted it or not. The men were now standing there in the middle of this large living room naked and in a complete state of shock.

The "Girls" were now holding hands and dancing around them just as children dance around a maypole. Their chubby, sexy, little bodies were bouncing around resembling a litter of little pigs holding hooves while they danced upright around and around. As a matter of fact, when this sex orgy subsided several hours later, the whole place did, indeed, resemble a pig pen.

As the circle of girls danced around, the Madam broke into the line throwing off her negligee high over their heads. It floated toward the center of the room and snagged on the chandelier just over the men's heads. It was now hanging lazily, waving gently against their faces, giving off an incredibly sensational perfume which was driving them mad.

The senior agent had by now lost all self-control, therefore allowing his emotions to dictate his physical appearance. The Madam saw this change come over her quarry, her eyes drifted from eye level to the lower portion of his body. She saw what she had hoped for. "Oh, God!" she exclaimed. And with that, she broke ranks and charged at him, grabbed his staff firmly, and led him off into a side bedroom while the other girls literally carried the other three men off in different directions. These men were about to be introduced to gypsy sex therapy. Survival would depend entirely on their physical conditions. To be sure, this sort of thing was not for weaklings.

While all this was going on in the whorehouse, the young recruit was watching Pucci as he moved about nervously. At times he'd be with his foot propped up on the fire hydrant, then he'd walk over and lean on the telephone pole. It was obvious that something was bothering his superior. He had no idea what was going on nor could he understand why they just didn't leave. It was boring and uncomfortable standing around in the cold doing nothing, especially now that the various tones of squealing were no longer emitting from the mansion.

Pucci struck a match and looked at his watch. It was already past 11:30 p.m. They should have been out of there by now, he thought, referring to the warehouse raid. He addressed the recruit:

"Let's get over to the fire truck. We'll give it a few more minutes, then we'll get our butts out of here."

What Pucci was waiting and hoping for was about to happen. From somewhere along Bayshore Highway, Mike torched the powerful rocket that would signify that all went well with the warehouse raid.

The Mayor and his guests were bidding each other good night when the brilliant flash of the exploding rocket lit up the sky like a giant outdoor stadium. The booming, thundering sounds from the explosion followed each other within seconds, echoing across the city and blending into one continuous rumble. Colors unfolded high up in the sky to form a spectacular display of a huge Golden Chalice with red wine cascading over its rim. The Mayor and his guests were speechless as they kept their eyes glued to the spectacle until it faded from view. There was a moment of silence. Then the Mayor softly asked the question:

"Now what do you suppose this is all about? Do you suppose

this could be some sort of omen?" He continued, "Two spectacular displays in one night, miles apart and hours apart. Only that? Nothing more?"

The other two men simply confirmed the Mayor's comments.

"What does it all mean?" he asked again. "First a spectacular 'Statue of Liberty', then a beautiful 'Golden Chalice flowing over with wine'." He paused for a moment, then again spoke softly: "Yes, I think I have it now," then proceeded to interpret the two spectacular displays: "We have freedom. For our cup runneth over with wine. I would hope so my fellow San Franciscans. Yes, I would hope so." With this, he turned to his friends as they were about to depart and said: "Good night, and please thank our Italian friends for this wonderful gift of such fine wine."

Mike was still standing at the spot where he had just launched the Chalice rocket; he scratched a second match, torched his cigar, puffed hard to get it going, then looked at his watch. It was a quarter of midnight. With a ring of pride in his voice, he announced:

"Tomorrow morning we unload the truck. When the job is finished, we'll open up one of the barrels and we'll see what we have. Come on, let's be on our way."

Pucci and his recruit saw the flash from below the fog blanket. He turned to his recruit who was standing there with his mouth open, more confused now than ever before, and said:

"Okay, kid. Come on, let's go. We're going home."

The recruit addressed his senior in the appropriate formal manner: "Sir, what do you suppose that was all about?" he asked.

"Well, kid, since you asked, I'll tell you. The Italian translation of that message is 'All is well so I bid you good night, my fellow paesano'." He paused for a few seconds, then added:

"Good night, Mike. Good night, Primo."

"What's a paesano? And who are they, Sir?"

"Some day I'll tell you, but not tonight." With this the two men left the scene and the four Federal agents to their destinies.

CHAPTER 15

While all this was going on, there was an aching heart within the breast of a woman who only God could have created at the height of his finest hour. Livia, with her hands clasped in a sign of prayer, was sitting in her favorite chair at the window of the ranch house. This was not the rocking chair that she normally used when rocking her newborn son to sleep. This was just a plain cushioned chair, a part of the living room furniture setting alongside the front window.

With the curtains pulled back, the window commanded a view across the countryside and main highway leading north around the base of the San Bruno mountains that separated the City and County of San Francisco from the rest of the peninsula.

Her three children were fast asleep, thank God, and were not aware of the drama that was unfolding in the city to the north. Nor did they know that their father was a principal actor performing and acting out his part to the best of his ability in this theater of realty.

She sat there absorbed in thought. Staring out the window, watching for some sign or evidence that all had gone well with whatever her husband and his friends were doing, there was no choice but to wait and pray. Not only within her heart, but with the spoken words as well. Her fingers were fondling the Rosary. She was asking God over and over again to please look after her Michele, the husband she pledged to honor and obey, to love and to cherish until death do they part.

In her prayers, she was, in fact, offering the Lord her life for the well-being of the father of her children, her beloved husband; and if this be his decision, then she would give her life for his. She was now whispering a prayer:

"Please, oh, Lord, I beg you to spare him and forgive his mistakes. To look after my three children for they are innocent of any wrongdoing. They need their father as much as they need me. If there is in your mind the feeling that a wrong has been committed, then I, alone, stand before you to accept the full responsibility for the act. I, therefore, throw myself at your feet and beg for your forgiveness. Amen."

Her earlier concerns had now turned to nervous worry. It was getting late. Mike had assured her that by the hour of twelve, they would be home for sure. It was now a quarter of twelve. She was now standing shadowing the window. The dim light from the adjacent kitchen was behind her; she was holding the curtains back looking north. Her eyes were fixed on the base of the mountains hoping to see headlights coming down the highway. She had no idea that a rocket would be fired into the sky at the very location she was so intensely watching.

The flash of the rocket was in full view of the window. The distance muffled the rumble of the explosions. She stood there staring in disbelief at the "Golden Chalice" as it unfolded in the distant sky. The sight of this spectacular display had a different meaning to her than to the others who witnessed it. In her mind, this was a miracle, an answer to her prayers. The Lord had sent down his message from the heavens above. She whispered softly, "Thank you, oh Lord. But what does it all mean? Is this in response to my prayers? If so, tell me. Is he already in your care? Were my prayers too late, or are you telling me to banish my fears for he's on his way home?" Livia chose to believe the latter.

The big headlights illuminating the highway were unmistakable. It was the Mack. The backfire as its engine let up to allow the selection of lower gears verified it. Some distance behind, two other sets of headlights could be seen coming down the highway. A sigh of relief was followed with tears of joy.

Primo was now swinging the Mack into the driveway illuminating the entire house. The rumbling sound of wine barrels was now music to her ears. The last of the three trucks pulled into the yard with all her beloved paesani accounted for. Tears streaming down her face, she scrambled down the back stairs and into the dimly lit yard to embrace the paesani as they stepped down from the trucks. They looked brutally tired and smelled strongly of sweat, but their warm greetings and friendly smiles overpowered all else. The last to be greeted were Mike and Primo for they had wandered off in the direction of where the big Mack was parked and were now walking back to join the others.

Primo hurried forward to greet Aunt Livia with a respectful embrace. His assurances and genuine smile were always welcome even though she knew he was as mischievous as they come. As for her husband, she showed her true love and respect for him in a manner typical of Italian wives, by scolding him soundly, especially for having abused her beloved paesani.

"Look at them," she said. "They're bleeding. What did you do to them? Beat them like animals? Look at poor Vasco. He looks like he's been scared to death. Are you crazy? What did you do to him?"

Mike interrupted her with a grin. "Yes, he was scared to death all right. But that's because he rode with Primo. He's to blame for his condition, not me."

Vasco, now sporting a big grin, joined in the fracas. "Livia," he said, "they're both crazy. One, because he's the uncle of his nephew; and the other, because he's the nephew of his uncle. So you see, there's no hope." This comment brought on laughter as well as a round of comments from the others verifying the appraisal of these two respected, admirable rascals.

In the midst of the laughter, Mike made a suggestion which could be interpreted as an order: "You'd better break this up and get to bed unless, of course, you would rather work the rest of the night unloading." This comment, although presented in a joking manner sent them all scrambling across the celery patch. They knew damned well that he was capable of imposing such an unreasonable task on them.

As they hurdled the rows of celery, they could hear Livia scolding Mike again for having commented as he did, and they could hear Primo laughing uncontrollably in the background. No matter how tired they were or what the circumstances might be, these paesani would always end up in good spirits. Clowning around, laughing, and enjoying life were their best traits.

CHAPTER 16

Pucci showed up the following morning eager to evaluate the results of the night's endeavor. Compared to the campaign the night before, the unloading was a breeze. The unloading complete, Primo pulled out with the empty Mack. Pucci followed. His thoughts were on the warehouse and the Federal agents who would certainly have something to say about the raid at the mansion. He chuckled as he imagined the results of their encounter with that over-sexed group of whores. But what weighed heavily on his mind was whether or not they had discovered the hijack switch that took place at the warehouse. As for the demolished doors, now that they had seen the boarded-up entrance, hopefully they accepted the explanation given to them at the mansion at the time of the Saturday night raid. Pucci had explained to them that there had been a minor incident right after they left the warehouse which was brought about by the careless use of fireworks by some unknown person. It would need some attention upon their return but, certainly, not such a problem that should cause them to abort the raid. After some thought as to what kind of answers or excuses he might be able to come up with, he decided to face them immediately this day and hope for the best.

The senior agent had been giving a great deal of thought to the events of the Saturday night mansion raid as well. However, from a different perspective. How were they to know the old mansion was, in fact, an Armenian whorehouse? After all, the report certainly coincided with the conditions as they appeared from outside the mansion. The advice that Pucci had given them was certainly on target. Situations did, in fact, arise which required implementation of his suggestions. No question about that.

To Pucci's satisfaction, all went well at the warehouse. They had not noticed the switching of barrels that had taken place. They couldn't possibly imagine that anyone would dare hijack a government warehouse, especially to be brazen enough to haul a load of barrels in, then take a load back out. As for the boarded-up entrance, they were thankful that the Fire Department's policy was to always leave a building well-secured as part of their cleanup operation. Since the entrance was well-secured, they would not concern themselves with new doors at this time.

They now took Pucci in their deepest, strictest confidence. Now that the warehouse was practically full to capacity, they had received orders from Washington, D.C., to load the contents of the warehouse onto an inbound ship scheduled to arrive soon. However, they must still account for the one hundred and twenty missing barrels of wine.

"Mr. Puccinelli," said the senior agent, "time is running out. I doubt that the missing wine can be found in time to meet the ship. Surely you can see the embarrassment this could be to a Federal agency to have to account for missing confiscated evidence. Therefore, in some manner or other, it must be replaced — devise a plan — make a deal of sorts."

The statement caught Pucci by surprise. "Did I hear you right, sir? Replace the missing wine — devise a plan— make a deal. In what way, sir?"

"Well, you being Italian with influential friends, you could pass the word around amongst — the Italians that we need — you know — a favor of sorts."

"A favor, sir, from Italians?"

"Well, I don't mean a favor without — reciprocating. Needless to say, we are in a position to help a person out of a tight spot, if the need was justified, or help in some way to achieve their objective. Surely you can understand that, can't you?"

Pucci's head was swimming. For an instant his thoughts were running wild. This son-of-a-bitch thinks all Italians are gangsters, crooks like themselves. In exchange for 120 barrels of wine or its equivalent in cash, he'd let you hijack the mint. He snapped back to his senses.

"Sir," said Pucci, "I believe I do understand, and I must say your proposal has merit."

"Fine. I knew we could depend on you to come up with — shall we say — an idea." The grin on his face was that of a hyena more than a human.

"Yes, of course. I'll check back with you in a few days." With that, Pucci politely excused himself and stepped out of the little office bidding them all good day.

The thought of this whole affair was now heavy on his mind. "Holy Christ, these bastards are bigger crooks than I thought. To think," he mumbled, "while poor, hungry immigrants are being thrown in jail (their only crime having been to steal a loaf of bread to feed their hungry children), these filthy bastards get away with shaking down legitimate wine makers, and now they propose to go even further than that."

"Not so, you sons of bitches!" Pucci swore out loud, "I'll sink that goddamned ship personally if I have to, but that wine will not leave San Francisco under these circumstances! You can bet on that, Mr. Federal Agent!"

As thoughts crashed through his mind, Pucci raced towards the paper company. He had to find Primo. This latest development was an entirely new ballgame. The thought of what could be accomplished under these circumstances was indeed staggering. Some of the ideas that crossed his mind caused him to shudder.

Having caught up to Primo, the next step was to catch up to Mike. They made it a point to be at the market early the following morning. As usual, Mike was battling the commission merchants, thieves themselves.

"Mike, let's get breakfast. We have to talk," said Pucci.

"All right. You go on ahead to the Chinaman's. I'll be along in a few minutes."

Taking their usual table, the two buddies talked while waiting for Mike. In a matter of minutes he, too, showed up to the delight of the Chinese proprietor. His morning had started off a little dull; surely it would now be livened up.

Mike listened to what Pucci had to say, then commented, "You guys better not get any wild ideas. If they're that crooked, they can't be trusted. There are crooks, then there are even bigger crooks. When it becomes convenient, they'll double cross you."

Primo was pleased with his uncle's comment. No way was he interested in expanding their hijacking activities beyond stealing wine. Being a devout Catholic, he had no problem in dealing in wine, legal or otherwise. Prohibition was an unjust, unwarranted and bad law at best, especially as it applied to wine, the symbol of blood among Christians. It is a healthy beverage, not only for the body which needs its nutrients, and not only for the mind that needs tranquility, but also for the soul itself. More good friends have been made and ethnic groups brought together in peace over a glass of good wine than any other single thing or act on earth. It was indeed appropriate that a chalice of wine should be set on the table of the Last Supper. Yes, Primo was comfortable with hijacking wine.

Pucci, too, felt the need to approach the Federal agents' offer with caution. He considered it not only risky, but also an affront to the San Francisco Italian community as a whole. There may be some rascals among them, but certainly not outright gangsters. He had a thought to share:

"I go along with you guys, but that doesn't mean that the agents won't pursue the matter. What we have here now is a mild situation compared with what the City will be faced with if they seek help from the outside. The way I see it, the City of San Francisco needs our help."

The others agreed wholeheartedly. They had taken an about face, from rascals to saints. Of course that didn't mean they'd pass up the opportunity to steal more wine.

Pucci was indeed furious. This now was to be an obsession with him. But to really get to them, it was obvious others would have to be called upon for favors. Hopefully this could be done without divulging their own previous wine hijacking or their own questionable activities. He must seek the help of others from certain select, ethnic groups to join hands with his fellow Italians. Once it was explained to them, they too would see the need to eradicate these jackals from their midst. These others would not be called upon to take part in or to act as vigilantes. For the most part, all they had to do was to give these Italians the right of way, so to speak. Even clear the track, if necessary, so they could then get a better swing at these intruders. Without the help of others, it might not be done. They must all pitch in and do the job themselves because it would be absurd to take the problem to higher-ups in the Federal Government because they, too, were obviously involved. But not so at the local level.

Pucci discussed the matter to some extent with his Fire Chief who understood the need only too well. It was, therefore, agreed he would be given a free hand for the sake of the community. However, the Chief did warn him, any real rough stuff would make it extremely difficult, if not impossible, to square it up with his good friend, Police Chief O'Shaughnessy. He reminded him that the Police Chief was above all a "no-nonsense" cop. He was, indeed, fair and didn't like unfair or unjust laws any more than anyone else.

"Now, remember," said the Chief, "you're a fireman, not a cop. Chief O'Shaughnessy may not like what you're doing. He is obligated to uphold the law. He may look the other way when he feels that moral law and domestic tranquility should prevail. But he won't tolerate rough stuff," he warned. "Don't forget, Police Chief O'Shaughnessy is one tough Irishman." Pucci promised that in no way, whatsoever, would he put anyone in an embarrassing or difficult position.

In the meantime, Mike had made friends with Sheriff Kelly, of San Mateo County. He was, without question, the best lawman that any community could want or hope to expect. He refused to concern himself with the so-called problems that confronted the Treasury Department of the United States. As far as he was concerned, Washington, D.C., was a long way from San Mateo County. They could go fly a kite.

His county was, for the most part, made up of truck farms producing vegetables. The people who made up their farms were mostly immigrant Italians who worked their fields from morning till night. His job was to see that no one interfered with them. They were good people who worked hard, played hard, and loved just as intensely as they worshipped God. He was quite adamant about maintaining the domestic tranquility of his community, and seeing that it was not preyed upon by anyone. And when he could help it, not even the Federal Government.

These people, in turn, worshipped this lawman. He visited them often at their ranches. He seldom carried a gun or, for the most part, exposed his badge. No one, not even he, could visit and leave these ranches without enjoying a good lunch along with a glass of wine and a crate of vegetables to take home. To refuse the host would be an insult. He knew their traditions well and respected them accordingly regardless of their "rag tag" manner of dress. To these kinds of friends, Mike always served his best uncut wine. His philosophy was: "If you're going to raise a glass to your lips in the spirit of true understanding and friendship, especially with a man who comes from a different ethnic background, and expect this friendship to weld into an everlasting union, then you must give it your best shot the first time, because you may never have a chance to do so again."

The two wives were also fast becoming good friends. Livia introduced Mrs. Kelly to homemade pasta and ravioli and, in turn, she introduced Livia to corned beef and cabbage.

The paper company that Primo worked for was also realizing benefits from these wine related activities; therefore, Primo would have no trouble in acquiring the use of the Mack. There was better cooperation and performance not only among the top echelon of the company but also among employees at all levels as well. This was attributed to Primo's generosity with wine. An occasional glass of wine with their evening meals helped relieve tension. Their dinners were more enjoyable. Production at the plant was at an all-time high. A bronze plaque displayed on the bulletin board signified that this branch had been awarded top recognition by the main Corporate Office. The Chairman of the Board of Directors, along with other prominent corporate officers, had personally signed it.

Yes, indeed, the directive that came down from the main office giving Primo special privileges lay face up at all times on the dispatcher's desk. The old Doane and the new, long-haul Mack were now being kept parked, side by side, facing the garage doors like two battlewagons ready to be launched into battle by this little Italian commander. To the eyes, ears, and nose of an experienced mechanic, the Mack had already experienced and withstood the riggers of battle.

One exceptional mechanic was a young Italian by the name of "Ercole Giovanetti," but called "Al," short for Albert, his middle name. His new bride was Livia's cousin which, of course, would bring him and Mike together socially. Although the younger of the two and was born here in America, they had much in common since he spoke Italian, as well as English. Primo was aware of this relationship. Likewise, Al was aware of Primo's relationship with Mike. The Italian grapevine, and being assigned to the maintenance of the big Mack, led him to believe that there was a definite tie-in between uncle and nephew, and that they were using the Mack to hijack wine.

Al was aggressive and always eager for adventure. He was not about to pass up any opportunity for excitement. So he put it to Primo point blank:

"How about taking me along with you on your next trip out? How about it?" he asked in an honest, pleading manner.

Primo thought for a moment before answering. He liked this stocky, young Italian who was built like a middleweight prize fighter, but there was Pucci and Mike's opinions to be considered before granting his request.

"Al, I like the idea, but there are others that will want a say about it."

"You mean your Uncle Mike?"

"Yeah, for one."

"You mind if I ask him?"

"Not yet. He's not the one that bothers me. Let me see what I can do first. I'll get back to you."

Although not having met Pucci, Al knew of him, and figured he was the other person involved.

CHAPTER 17

Pucci was now making it a point to meet with the agents at the warehouse on a regular basis. Somehow he must take advantage of the tough position they were in and to use their desire to make a "deal" against them. The more often they met, the more they listened to his suggestions therefore enabling him to inject an idea into their minds, and making it appear to be theirs rather than his. He kept implanting the idea in their minds that the missing wine might be difficult to locate because, without a doubt, their superiors, the Washington agents, had something to do with its disappearance. They, in fact, had been screwed by their own people. So, why not screw them back. They were buying the idea and, in so doing, started to formulate a scheme to even the score. Pucci reported back to Primo and Mike:

"I'm sure they'll go for it," said Pucci. "We'd better get busy."

"Sounds confusing to me," responded Primo thoughtfully. "They con their people to buy more wine—we con them by hijacking it—they'll get off the hook on the missing load; how the hell are we going to pull 'that' off??"

"First, by locating the wine, then offer your services— supposedly as an out-of-town trucker—the only person with a truck big enough—they don't know you..."

"How about the cash—the payment—won't they be there?"

"We'll figure out something, in the meantime—first things first—find the wine while I work on the agents."

For obvious reasons, Primo ruled out the winery at Asti, as did Mike, only for different reasons. He knew the tough, no-nonsense manager of the Italian Swiss Colony from prior years. He ran his winery much the same way as an army colonel runs his command, complete with leather leggings and a military mentality. Surely, the manager would remember him from a few years earlier when he worked at the winery and got fired for shooting his mouth off. Mike's questioning of orders and accompanying smart remarks were not appreciated or tolerated. The dismissal incident had taken place at the winery's cookhouse where the field hands slept and boarded.

On this particular morning before daylight, the manager walked into the cookhouse in the usual manner. As usual the workers stood at attention much like soldiers about to be briefed. Strutting like a colonel, he went down the line giving each employee his work schedule for the day, until he got to Mike. Standing directly in front of him with legs spread out and leaning slightly forward, he barked the short, to the point, message:

"As for you, Mike, here is your pay. You're fired!"

But, Sonoma County was not ruled out entirely. Matteoli knew of a winery on the outskirts of Cloverdale on the east side of the Russian River that was bursting at the seams with wine. A logical prospect—they'd hit that one first.

"All right, we'll pay them a visit," said Mike, inferring that Matteoli would come along to help swing the deal.

"But I only know of the wine. I hardly know the person or if he'd even sell it," stated Matteoli.

"Do you know his name?"

"Yes...Mister Black, but I don't think he speaks Italian."

"That's all right, Primo can interpret, you come along."

The three men made the trip to Cloverdale and sure enough, the wine was there. One hundred thousand gallons of it. But, Mr. L.S. Black, a staunch believer in obeying the laws of the land— good or bad, was cool to their proposal. Interpreting, Primo pressed the issue:

"We'll pay you $1.00 per gallon for a load of your wine."

This was indeed a good offer that could hardly be refused. Mr. Black responded: "I'm afraid I cannot accept that—it's illegal."

"Christ, what's with this guy?" thought Primo, then went into a huddle with his two cohorts. After some discussion, they came back with another offer: "We'll take it all—name your price."

This second offer rocked Mr. Black back on his heels, but the answer was the same: "No, it's illegal."

Primo thought for a moment, then proposed an unorthodox proposal to get around his argument: "We can handle this...illegal matter, at no risk to you. We'll come up with the money up front. You and your family leave the state—vacation—whatever, while we 'hijack' the wine. You see, you're not selling it—the wine was stolen..."

The idea went over like a lead balloon. The answer was a final, to-the-point "No!"

Disgruntled but not discouraged, the trio left. However, instead of heading straight home, at Matteoli's suggestion, they cut across to Napa Valley. He knew of a winery there, owned and operated by a religious order badly in need of money such as most religious orders are. Sure enough, they connected. The winery jumped at the deal.

Now it was up to Pucci. Could he 'con' the Federal agents? "Yes," they had now taken the initiative. They would outline the details to him, punctuating the highlights and fine points. Pucci would stand straight and stiff as a grape stake while they explained it. He looked like a Marine standing at attention; always looking straight ahead at the blank wall behind the senior agent sitting behind his battered desk. The senior agent would stand up, strut back and forth, slip back his coat with his left hand at the instant he plunged it into his pocket, like a pool player sinking a ball without the benefit of the cue stick. In so doing, his badge would flash momentarily. He would then lean forward with his right hand flat on the top of the desk in order to support his weight. His eyes would roll upward, his line of sight barely clearing the brim of his fedora, his eyes ever-searching Pucci for a favorable response to his ingenious comments.

Pucci wouldn't move a muscle. Every time the senior agent would direct a sharp comment toward him, he would jerk up tight as if he had just been jabbed in the ass with a hat pin. His fireman's cap would be pulled down to eye level with the shade almost resting on the ridge of that beautiful Roman nose. Each time he answered, he would first tighten up his face muscles emphasizing his heavy muscular features. He would also flare his nostrils to give more meaning to his favorable comments.

"Yes, Sir. Brilliant strategy, Sir. May I make a suggestion, Sir?" he'd say as if addressing a military supervisor. He would then leave the little office, pull the door closed behind him, walk up the sidewalk past the loading ramp, and glance at the entry which was still boarded up. A big grin would break out across his face. His mind would wander back to the events of the "super hijack of the century" which they had pulled off a few weeks before. With one foot on the running board of his Reo run-about he would look back and address a comment in the direction of the warehouse office: "We're not through with you bastards yet!" With this, he would take off giving them "the finger" as he rounded the corner out of sight.

The plan was finally formulated in detail. The first step was to extract from their superiors double the amount of cash needed to pay for the acquisition of 120 extra barrels of supposedly extra-fine wine from a new source. Hopefully their superiors would buy the proposal. The telegraph wires were hot with coded messages going back and forth: San Francisco to Washington, D.C.; then to New Jersey; back to Washington; then to San Francisco; so forth, and so on. The proposal was being considered.

Finally, the Washington agents were convinced that maybe the idea had merit even though they had supposedly already fulfilled their contract with the Mob. Why not buy the extra quality wine as proposed? This would give them all a handsome profit. No need to steal it all by blackmail and extortion as they were doing (which would push the price down to hardly nothing). The wine was purported to be choice, so they pay the somewhat going price for a batch; the demand was there. The ship could handle the extra amount. So why not?

The Washington agents were now working on the Mob in New Jersey to come up with the cash needed to swing the deal, but the Mob was suspicious. Their coded telegram to the agents would always end with the words "North Dakota". While negotiations were going on, the winery up in northern Sonoma County was being held at bay with promises of payment.

Finally, the Mob agreed to ante up the additional cash and therefore get into the deal. However, on the condition that the Washington agents guarantee the delivery of not only the wine as per the original contract, but also the extra 120 barrels. If the agents in San Francisco were not aware of New Jersey Sicilian business tactics, their superiors in Washington sure as hell were. They were somewhat cautious about making guarantees to the Mob. Nevertheless, the deal was made.

Arrangements had been made for the transfer of the money. It was presently in the hands of the agents in San Francisco. The plan could now be executed. They had collected double the amount that was needed to pay for the new batch of wine. They had intentions of using the extra cash to pay for the missing wine. But now that they had the cash in hand, other thoughts came to mind. If they could stall the Sonoma County winery until the ship was loaded, they would then pocket the extra cash and leave their superiors holding the bag for the missing amount.

However, unbeknownst to these Federal agents, the Mob back in New Jersey was also making plans. They didn't trust any of these untrustworthy Federal agents whether it be San Francisco or Washington. They therefore dispatched three of their toughest "hit men" to San Francisco. They would drive cross-country by limousine scheduled to arrive well ahead of the ship that was also on its way. These three men would see to it that the wine would be loaded and shipped as per agreement, and accompany the cargo back to New Jersey. They were also instructed to settle the account with the four agents before leaving the West Coast. Depending on circumstances, they were to use their discretion as to whether they should be paid in money, or in the form of lead.

Needless to say, Pucci was pleased with the way things were turning out. But he had no idea that he'd eventually have to deal with notorious gangsters even though he was convinced of their close association with the agents. He couldn't possibly have envisioned the possibility of getting caught up in the middle of a gun battle between them. Besides, there was still the matter of how to divert the extra load of wine from Napa to San Bruno. This detail was yet to be worked out. That in itself could tip his hand as being the mastermind behind these hijackings. No pleasant thought, considering his adversaries were both armed to the teeth. One with the authority to shoot to kill, and the other with a mentality to kill and the hell with authority.

CHAPTER 18

At the ranch there was much to be done. Certain preparations had to be made well in advance because once the word was received which would put Pucci's plan in action, there wouldn't be time. So, needless to say, there was a great deal of activity going on at the ranch. The equivalent of a full load of 120 barrels had to be made ready. The previous warehouse hijack switch just about cleaned out the supply of empty barrels. Nevertheless, they would be made available on schedule. Mike would see to that.

First, he had Scanavino transfer wine from barrels to whatever jugs were available. He then instructed Julio to gather up as many empty barrels he could from customers.

The next step was to empty his large redwood water storage tank on the paesani's ranch (as it was now referred to). This tank was used for domestic water as well as irrigation. A simple plumbing arrangement could divert water from the tank to the ranch house or to the vegetable irrigation system. Water could also be supplied from the pump to the main house directly without first entering the storage tank at all.

Once the tank was emptied of water, wine was pumped from barrels into the tank for storage in order to create more empty barrels. Once there were enough to make a load, they were refilled with water and stored on racks in the barn in a manner so they could easily and quickly be transferred to the truck. The horse path between the two barns was cleared of vegetables in order to accommodate the Mack. The plan was to unload the incoming wine barrels at Mike's barn, then move the truck and trailer over to the paesani's barn, and reload it with water-filled barrels.

It was now Saturday evening. All preparations were complete. Pressure was off. The paesani could now relax, have an extra glass of wine, and enjoy the evening. As usual, Livia prepared a superb dinner to Mike's liking. She was careful not to offend his delicate taste buds. Regardless, there was always the discussion as to whether the wine complemented the dinner or the dinner complemented the wine. It was an argument that could never be settled. But for some reason or other, the discussion drifted into familiar territory with Livia instigating an agitating subject — "banking."

"Well, when will you see Mr. Battisoldi, your big shot banker, again?" she inquired.

"For your information, I will see him Monday morning at ten o'clock," he answered.

"Oh, and what business do you have with him at that precise time of the morning?"

"Well, I'll tell you," he answered trying to be calm. "I'm to meet Pucci at the bank with a good friend of his who needs some help to save his boat from the claws of that drooling, buzzard, Mr. Battisoldi."

"A boat!" she snorted. "What kind of boat? And what business is it of yours?" she demanded to know.

"This is a big tugboat. The kind that pushes big ships around in the harbor," he answered. "And it seems my lousy, greedy friend, the banker, wants to take it away from this friend of Pucci's called 'Sven.' He's a Norwegian with a wife and three little kids like ours. And if he loses the tugboat, the family will lose their house and just about everything else as well."

"What?" she said quite loud. "Lose the house! You mean, the little kids will not have a home? No roof over their little heads? Can that happen?"

"That's right. Yes it can. Unless I help him save the boat."

"You listen to me, Michele!" she snorted. "You make sure that you're at the bank on time. And you tell that banker, Mr. Battisoldi, that if that man, Sven, loses his house, I'll hit him on the head with my biggest cast iron skillet. Do you understand me?" It was apparent that the thought of kids being homeless really threw her out of gear.

For once they were in accord. Mike assured her that he would not let that happen. Once the matter had been settled, he politely

117

excused himself and said:

"I'm going over to the paesani's. The water system to the house should be all right, but I better check it out. We can't have the water mixing with the wine. I won't be long," he assured her.

He picked his way across the vegetable patch, delighted with Livia's reaction to the tugboat matter. The thought made him feel good. As he approached the edge of the yard, he could hear the usual loud discussions and arguments coupled with music and song coming from the upstairs portion of the farmhouse.

"The paesani are in a good mood tonight," he said to himself. "That's just fine. First I'll check the water system, then I'll join them for a glass of wine."

Mike reached down and turned on the faucet. There should be water pressure, he thought. And, in fact, water did gush out for a few seconds.

"How nice to have water so convenient," he said to himself. However, in an instant, his look of pleasure changed to an expression of horror as wine, instead of water, came pouring out of the faucet.

"Jesus Christ!" he exclaimed. "We must have hooked the pipes up wrong." Mumbling to himself, he hightailed it over to the tank and pump house.

The maze of pipes were studied carefully. "Now, let's see, this pipe comes from the well. This one comes from the tank. This one goes to the house and yard. Now then, this valve from the pump should be open in order to feed water direct to the house. But, no, it's closed. That's not right. This valve from the tank should be closed. But, no, it's open. So that's what happened! The buggers have diverted the wine to the house plumbing system on purpose." He turned toward the house with his fist raised in a threatening manner. "You damned bunch of idiots!" he swore. "Sons of dogs! Fools! Ignorant jackasses! What did those double-crossers in Italy do? Send all their imbeciles to America? Didn't they keep any for themselves?" he snorted in disgust.

This outburst of profanity dominated his vocabulary as he ran up to the house still waving his fist high above his head. As he reached the top of the back stairs, the noise coming from the vicinity of the front portion made it apparent that his suspicions were borne out. They had, indeed, diverted the wine into the household water system, and uncut at that. How can men with such ingenious minds as this be called fools?

Mike's outburst of profanity echoed throughout the house as he made a headlong dash past the kitchen, through the dining room, and into the living room.

There were several men in the living room, one pumping his accordion while Julio and Aldoino sang at the top of their voices. The two men faced each other as they sang out the part of an opera as if on the stage of "La Scala" in Milano, Italy. The rest of the men could be seen and heard shouting through the archway which opened into the wide hallway connecting the bedrooms. Mike dashed in among them yelling:

"I demand to know who is responsible for this act of deliberate disobedience!" Completely ignored, he yelled louder, then the singing got louder, then the chatter got louder, so he yelled louder. Finally the whole house became a bedlam of yelling and singing. There was no way that he could get his message across.

Those who were not in line working their way in and out of the spacious bathroom, were in the adjoining bedrooms arguing about all sorts of trivial matters. For the most part, they were in groups of two or three. Those who were right-handed, tilted their hats to the right and pointed with their right index fingers. Those who were left-handed, tilted their hats to the left side of their heads and pointed with their left index fingers. Their free hands were clutching quart fruit jars of wine. They swung them out and up in wide gestures in order to better emphasize their points of argument.

Mike worked his way to the crowded bathroom where there appeared to be the most activity, but less noise. However, they wouldn't allow him to crash the line. He must work his way in along with the rest. In his fit of rage, it didn't occur to him that those in the line moving in were holding empty jars, while those in the line moving out were holding full jars. Again his pleadings were being completely ignored. At one point, someone slapped an empty jar in his hand and asked him to keep the line moving. "Moving to where? For what?"

"What the hell is this?" he demanded to know.

"Hey, calm down. You'll get your turn. Be patient," called out a slurred voice from up front.

He didn't have to wait long to find out what was going on as he watched the man in front of him step to the left as he stooped simultaneously and came up with a partially-filled jar of wine. For the first time since he had entered the house, he stopped yelling as he stared at the sight before him.

It took a few seconds to fully comprehend the scene. There, before his eyes, was a bathtub full of uncut, rich, red wine. He was standing there dumbfounded as the man behind him grabbed his now limp, left arm, plunging hand and jar into the wine, then asking him to keep moving along.

"Huh? Move to where? What are you talking about?" questioned Mike while looking over his shoulder.

"To the next station–over there."

He was then nudged to the next station which put him in front of the washbasin. He stared in disbelief as if in a state of shock as the man in charge here asked: "How do you want it, Mike? Hot or cold?" His job was to temper the wine to the pleasure of each individual's taste buds. Since Mike didn't answer, he assumed it was just right as it was.

"Come on, Mike. Move on," he commanded in a half-drunken manner. "We don't have all day."

The next cog in the invisible chain that was moving men along like robots placed him in front of the toilet. The lid was off the storage tank which was fastened above and against the wall. At this point, he was instructed to hold his jar out and over one end of the storage tank while the operator dipped a soup ladle into the tank and topped off the jar to the point of overflow. Excess wine cascaded back in the tank. No spilling. Nothing wasted. The automatic action of the tank valve kept the wine at the desired level for easy dipping and scooping.

It was apparent that these men had spent a lot of time in the soup kitchens of the local charities. How else could they have gained such ingenious knowledge and experience in the matter of mass dispensing?

Mike was finally nudged out through the bathroom door. He looked back at the ingenious wine dispensary in amazement. The ordeal had left his mouth dry. God, he was thirsty. Instinct caused him to raise the jar gently to his lips drawing several long swallows. He really needed this. It was good. He drank again. Lowering the jar, he asked himself: "Why is this wine smoother than the previous batch they had bottled just days before?" He tilted it back as if to read the nonexistent label. While in deep concentration, he pondered the question and no longer concerned himself with the events surrounding him.

Matteoli was standing nearby watching him as he studied the wine. "Mike, do you notice how much smoother this wine is tonight?" he asked.

"Yes, I do. And by the sound of your comment, I assume you have given some thought as to why as well."

"The answer is in the working of the wine," he proceeded to explain. "You see, Mike, pumping the wine from the barrels to the raised redwood tank, then dispensing it in a release of pressure in such a manner, serves as a means of de-gassing it. This, therefore, smooths it out like decanting from a bottle to a carafe a half hour or so before serving."

"Yes, I believe you're right," answered Mike. "Now would be the time to put it in jugs. It would fetch a much higher price." At the moment he was standing at the bedroom window checking the color when the words parted from his lips. "You see," he said, "some good comes of everything. Even the actions of this bunch of nitwits in their half-drunken stupor have produced something worthwhile."

With this comment, Contini jumped into the conversation with gusto, for if there was to be a discussion relating to philosophy or of a technical nature, he would participate. He was met head-on by Matteoli. As usual, the two engaged in an argument over technical matters which were of no interest to the others who were engaged in their own arguments escalating beyond control.

From the front porch of her house next door, Livia could hear the shouting rising above the music and singing. An occasional hat would fly out a window and sail out into the celery patch, adding to her concern. She took off in a fast walk, holding her long skirt above her knees as she hurdled the rows of celery. Her approach to the battleground was with determination. There would be a stop put to this nonsense. Pronto.

She hurried up the front stairs, marched across the wide front porch, pushed the front door open, and stepped abruptly into the living room. Standing there before her, engrossed in song, were her two favorite men singing the final role of her favorite opera, "L'Aida." She had entered as if on cue.

Aldoino turned, now facing her, singing out in a pleading high soprano voice as Julio was now fading his part out in a sympathetic, soft, low voice. Aldoino was playing his part with real feeling as tears welled in his eyes. His powerful voice was escalating and wavering in a sign of despair because (as portrayed in the original opera) there stood this one woman before him whom he loved but could not have, for destiny had given her hand in marriage to another. Livia was entranced—she'd join in.

Julio gave her the nod to step in as the accordion pounded out the part which she must now play. With this, she burst out in song begging him to forgive her; to please understand. She walked slowly toward Aldoino, hands clasped before her as if in prayer.

Her voice was strong. She was now playing out her part of the drama unfolding on this imaginary stage of "La Scala." The performance continued without interruption as the rest of the men, having heard Livia's voice above the din of chatter, worked their way into the living room in silence. Hats in hand, they listened intensely to these brilliant performers who were acting out the final phase of this opera in song and music. They were the audience, standing and ready to give an ovation to the players in this spectacular performance.

There were no apologies for the tears of joy that streaked down these men's cheeks as the performers lowered their heads and took a bow. At this point, all hell broke loose. Hats flew into the air as the crowd gave forth with a thunderous applause.

"Bravo! Bravo! Magnificent. More! More!"

Now, almost as if on cue, the accordion pumped out the tune of one of the all-time favorite Italian folk songs to fit this glorious occasion. As expected, and in unison, they all raised their jars high and started to sing:

"Our fathers drank wine, and our mothers did too.

We are their children, so this we must also do.

Drink up. Drink up. Hold your glass high.

For today there is life, but tomorrow may die."

This is the way life was with these carefree paesani of Italy as they sang and frolicked late into this Saturday night.

Sunday morning Mike looked out his kitchen window toward the paesani's house. There seemed to be a considerable amount of activity in the yard area of the redwood tank and pump house.

"Those damned fools," he mumbled. "They didn't have enough last night. There they are again drawing the wine right from the tank. They can't wait for it to reach the house through the pipes. I'll fix those jackasses right now!" With this, he charged down the back steps, grabbed a big pipe wrench as he hurried across the yard, hurdling the rows of celery like an athlete taking the hurdles in a track meet.

The first to greet him was Matteoli. "Good morning, Mike. There's no need for the pipe wrench. We already have the bottling under way."

"The bottling!" exclaimed Mike in a somewhat startled expression.

"Yes. Scanavino and I decided the wine should be bottled

immediately. And since Fiasco had a good supply of two-liter magnums all made up woven in straw, this seemed the right thing to do, don't you think?"

"Oh, yes. Of course. That was good thinking. I was coming over purposely to give you a hand." He lied like hell, for his true intention was to crack their skulls with that pipe wrench.

All the men were there to give a hand with the bottling except one. Contini was not among them, and for good reason. It seems that Matteoli bested him the night before in the argument and discussion involving the technicalities of de-gassing wine and its affect on its everlasting quality.

Contini was no match for Matteoli, the wizard of wine. Why he even chose to challenge him was a point of issue brought up by the rest of the paesani, who had joined in the argument in support of Matteoli. The whole affair had ended up in humiliation for Contini. This didn't help his already grumpy disposition any. As was his habit, he was the first one up in the morning. Therefore, the coffee making was his duty on a regular basis. However, on this particular morning, it turned out somewhat unusual. No one bothered to switch the valves back the night before, so obviously, the system was still full of wine. Contini, pretending that he hadn't noticed, filled the big coffeemaker from the kitchen faucet and brewed up the usual pot of coffee.

The paesani were eager for a good cup of coffee. It was needed to flush out that stale, cotton-chewing residue taste left behind in their mouths from a night of drinking. However, this particular cup of coffee was, indeed, a bit unusual since it was made with wine. But rather than complain and play into Contini's hands, they chose to praise him for his new, ingenious discovery.

"Contini, we understand your highly technical knowledge of wine, but we had no idea that it extended to coffee as well. This is amazingly good." They were now on a roll and Contini would be the ball.

"You, mean, you didn't know that Mr. Contini has travelled throughout the world making a study of coffee?" another put in.

"What vintage would you say this is?" said yet another. "It has such good balance. Look how the cup balances on my knife. And the body is something to behold. Like the whore who lives down by the tracks; every time the train goes by, her body quivers

124

and wiggles in delight. Have you considered obtaining a patent for the process? Surely you wouldn't want to lose control of such a stupendous idea?"

Well, none of this was to help Contini's disposition one bit. So while all the others were preparing to do the bottling, and since the chore of laundering was also assigned to him, and since Sunday morning was the day to wash the previous week's work clothes, he immediately set out to do just that before the system was switched back to water.

As was customary and usual, he partially filled the double concrete trays from their designated faucets, threw a cup of White King soap in the side with the motor-driven agitator, and proceeded to wash all of the paesani's clothing and long johns in the usual manner. This went unnoticed by the others until the wash was hung up on the clothes line to dry.

The first comment came from Aldoino in his simple manner and high-pitched voice. He said:

"Do you suppose it would be a good idea to switch the valves back to water before Contini decides to paint the house? Look at the clothes line."

For those who preferred to wear red long johns, it made no difference. But for those who didn't, they were now going to have to change their preferences.

Contini continued about his chores nonchalantly humming his favorite tunes as if everything was normal while the others, knowing damned well that they had asked for it, said little.

Mike dropped the pipe wrench in disgust and made his way back across the celery patch as the chuckling and amusing comments faded from earshot.

CHAPTER 19

Monday morning, dressed in his usual manner, worn vest and all, Mike arrived at the bank on schedule. The thought of Mr. Battisoldi and his methods weighed heavily on his mind. The bank was already open for business as he pulled up to the curb in his Model-T farm truck. Pucci and his friend, Sven, had just stepped in the door. As Mike came around the front of the Model-T and stepped over the curb heading for the door of the bank, the banker, Mr. Battisoldi, rushed up to greet him, reaching out as if to shake his hand. He was sporting a big smile exposing a mouthful of gold-capped teeth. They flashed in the morning sun like gold nuggets that only a banker could afford. He was smiling for good reason, for today he would make a killing at the expense of a hard-working Norwegian tugboat Captain, or so he thought.

Mike was in no mood for nonsense. Ignoring the banker's extended hand, he instead made a gesture by holding out the clenched fist of his extended right hand as he slapped down on his right arm with the palm of his left hand causing the clenched fist to jerk upwards. Translated meant, "Up your ass!" He never broke stride as he walked past the startled banker toward Pucci and his friend Sven, the tugboat captain.

While all this was taking place, Sven, not having met Mike before, was dumbfounded at the gesture used to address the banker, Battisoldi.

Pucci gently poked Sven in the ribs as he whispered: "Mike is mad as hell. That's good. We're in business."

Sven was now even more stunned. "Is this the way Italians do business," he thought? To him, it all seemed strange.

126

Pucci stepped forward and introduced the two men while the banker (not being aware of the real reason for Mike's presence) was looking for the little sack of cash he normally brought with him for deposit. However, this time, the only thing Mike had that resembled a sack was the beat-up topcoat which he wore over his vest with worn out pockets. What he did have in his hand was the passbook to his savings account.

The introduction was brief. "How much money do you need?" Mike asked of Sven in his best English.

The Norwegian cleared his throat and answered, "Five thousand dollars is what I owe on the boat."

Mike turned to Pucci. "That means he needs $5,000, doesn't it?" he asked in his native tongue.

"Yes, Mike, that's what he needs to save his tugboat. The bank wants it all right now."

"That's what I thought," answered Mike. He now turned to the banker, addressing him in the same manner. "I want to draw out $5,000 from my account," he said, handing him the passbook. It was now apparent to him that Sven was being bailed out, which would cause him to lose out on the foreclosure.

"But Mike," pleaded the banker, "let's talk this over."

"I don't want to talk. You get me the money right now!"

The banker was rocked back on his heels and shocked at the sharp answer. He was about to lose that big tugboat for which he already had a buyer at several times what he was getting it for at foreclosure. No question about it, Mike meant business. The thought that he could also stand to lose his entire account made him nervous as hell. He pleaded:

"All right, Mike! All right! Please calm down. Come now, sit down and we will talk about this."

"I will stand. Hurry up! I'm in a hurry. What's the matter, don't you have the cash? Maybe I should take it all out?"

Pucci was amused with the whole affair, but Sven was astounded. He never experienced anything like this before. This immigrant Italian standing up to the banker who was attempting to put him out of business was indeed to be admired.

In short order the cash was brought forward, counted, and handed to Mike. In turn, he handed it to Sven.

"Now you pay the banker. Get the boat documents and give them to me," said Mike.

This was done immediately. Then before Sven could say much of anything, Mike said to him:

"All right, you pay me back the money when you can, then I'll give you back the documents to your boat. But first, you take care of your family. I can wait. Let me know sometime how things are going in the boat business." With this, Mike walked out the door and took off in his Model-T.

As Pucci and Sven stepped out of the bank, Pucci gently poked his friend again and said: "You have just done business with my good friend, Mike."

In his pronounced Norwegian accent, Sven said, "He will be my good friend, too. A very good friend. You can be sure of that, by golly!"

Pucci chuckled. He was satisfied that the matter went so well for he had a thought in the back of his mind which centered on the need for the big tugboat some day in the future, and to lose it to the banker was unthinkable.

"Sven," said Pucci, "I have a feeling that some day soon you'll be given the opportunity to not only pay Mike back with a like favor but, also, maybe even pay off your boat in the process."

"I do hope so," said Sven. "I like that man, and I like the way he does business. My wife will be happy to hear of this day's events. Thank you, Pucci, for bringing us together. You are a real true friend. I will not forget it."

The banker peered out the window, then asked himself the question: "Who is this man Puccinelli? He seems to be so cool, so confident; doesn't say much, but certainly has influence over people. No question, he has expertise in handling money. He would make a good banker. Maybe I should get to know him better." He walked over to his desk, picked up the bundle of bills, shuffled the edges with his big fat thumb as a disturbing thought crossed his mind: "All this money changed hands right before my eyes, and I didn't make a dime. How can that be? And Mike, what was his purpose for intervening? He's in the vegetable business, not the banking business." He then mumbled: "Puccinelli. That's it. He bested me."

He was walking toward the vault with the cash in hand, when another thought came to mind that caused him to hesitate before entering. Throwing his massive chest out, he grunted and said: "They're all a bunch of yokels compared to me. I am a success" (as if to say they were not). He was so wrapped up in his world of money that he didn't realize that true success was not in how many dollars you have, but how you put them to use.

CHAPTER 20

The four agents were going over the details of the now well-planned acquisition of the load of wine from Napa County. They, like the "Banker," recognized Pucci's traits.

"That man Puccinelli could be of help to us," said the senior agent. "Maybe we can con him into doing the dirty work for us. As you know, we can't trust our superiors any more than the 'Mob'." The thought of pocketing the extra cash rather than pay for the missing wine was heavy on his mind. "Yes, I do think we should use him, get him up front," he said thoughtfully. The others agreed. So the call was put through to the fire station. The call was taken by the same dispatcher as before.

"Is Mr. Puccinelli, the Fire Inspector, in?" asked the senior agent calmly. He remembered what happened the last time.

"No, he's not. But we do expect him in shortly. Is this an emergency?"

"No, this is a personal matter." He was taking no chances of a misunderstanding. "Can you relay a message to him?"

The answer was obvious; Pucci was relayed the message. He complied with the agents wishes by showing up at the warehouse a short time later.

"Please come in, Mr. Puccinelli. Have a seat. Do you care for a cigar?"

Pucci accepted the offer to sit, but declined the cigar. He watched the agent light up, then blow a billow of smoke towards the ceiling. "What's this son-of-a-bitch up to," thought Pucci. The agent was now ready to make his pitch.

"Mr. Puccinelli," he said, "there are times when the

130

Government has to call upon civilians to assist in its endeavor to serve the community. You know, appeal to a person's patriotism."

As the senior agent said that, his eyes shifted to the other agents, then back again to Pucci. The movement was quick, but not quick enough. Pucci spotted it. He had dealt with enough arsonists to know that this sort of behavior was a sure indication of guilt. In this case, "guilty of what?"

"Well — yes, of course, patriotism should always be put ahead of one's personal interest," said Pucci.

"I knew you'd understand; you're a true patriot."

"I don't understand, Sir. Is there something I can do for the Government?"

"As a matter of fact, there is." The agent was quick to answer; too damned quick to suit Pucci.

"Sir, if its within my power, I'd be glad to serve." So far, he didn't know what the agent was driving at.

"Now listen carefully. About this Napa affair. We wish to have you as liaison between us and the winery because, as you already know, there are people in Washington that can't be trusted. So we agents here must stay undercover."

He couldn't believe his ears as the senior agent proceeded to lay out the plan. The very thing that he had been wracking his brains over on how to approach, was now being dumped in his lap. He, Pucci, would not only see to it that the wine was procured, but to also act as the courier for the money.

"Well, what do you say, do we have a deal?"

"Why, yes, of course," answered Pucci. "In the interest of patriotism, I guess it's my duty. Should I take care of the matter of trucks as well?"

"Yes, of course. I'm glad you thought of that."

Pucci now had it all. What he thought would be difficult, turned out to be easy; too damned easy. He worried about having jumped into it too readily. The agents may give it a second thought as to why. Patriotism alone may not be a strong enough reason. So he threw in a "clincher."

"Sir, it's always been my desire to be a Federal agent. Something I've always dreamed of. If I thought for a minute there was a chance . . ."

The senior agent cut Pucci off short. He didn't give him a

chance to finish his pitch. "Why of course, you'd make a fine agent. If that's what you had in mind, you should have told me sooner. I'll make mention of it in my next Washington correspondence."

"You mean, you'd do that for me, Sir?"

"Absolutely!"

Pucci departed from the warehouse in the usual manner, with the exception of his comments and finger gesture. He wondered, "Are they using me?" The agents peeked out the small window to watch him depart before bursting out in boisterous laughter. They were indeed proud of themselves. They had conned a public servant to do their dirty work for them. They were pacing back and forth chuckling and laughing in low tones, interrupting each other to emphasize their individual contributions. They resembled a pack of hyenas drooling over the fresh kill of a newly-born wildebeest. Little did they know that by now the "local authorities" were well aware of their activities, Pucci's as well, and they were not laughing. This was a serious matter which could disrupt the tranquility of the city because of their inability to do much about it. They knew the difficulty of dealing with federal lawmen having gone sour.

The Mayor organized a meeting of his top public officials. Those present were himself; his well-informed and capable Police Chief; the Fire Chief; and the San Francisco County Sheriff. These four men realized the seriousness of the problem. The question was how could they cope with this situation? What could or what should they do in this matter involving Federal agents? So far, interference by their departments appeared to not be needed.

Besides, they could never, under the circumstances, convict the persons involved, especially those in the higher levels of government. And they are the very ones, above all others, who should be apprehended and convicted. It was apparent that the best way to get at these rascals was through their pocketbooks, which the paesani were doing. The decision was made to let it keep going as it was and, if anything, clear the path for the paesani and to encourage rather than discourage the other ethnic groups to apply their talents as best they could to help them.

The officials, as individuals and public servants, would use their offices and connections to assist in an undercover manner the best way they could as long as they could reasonably stay within the law. Obviously, at some time or another they would each, no doubt, be called upon for some help. Therefore, it was agreed that the Fire Chief would continue giving Pucci a free hand backed by equipment and men if necessary. They were aware that the paesani did not carry guns but that their opponents did. So the Police Chief was instructed to keep a protective eye on Pucci and Primo, especially in the event of violence.

The Sheriff, having already been apprised of the situation by his good friend the Sheriff of San Mateo County, was to continue covering the paesani, especially Mike, since he was traveling across the county line back and forth from the ranch to the produce market during early morning hours.

It was apparent that the law enforcement agencies felt that it was just a matter of time before some rough characters would appear on the scene and would be too much for a handful of unarmed immigrants to handle.

Last, but not least, since it was felt there would be an ocean-going vessel involved, the Mayor would contact the local Coast Guard Commander, apprise him of the situation, and ask for whatever assistance he could offer.

The theory behind all this was that because of the circumstances, the unofficial people involved might just be able to accomplish more with better end results than the local authorities could.

CHAPTER 21

To no one's surprise, not even Pucci's, a black limousine with a New Jersey license plate appeared at the warehouse well ahead of the ship's expected arrival. Pucci happened to be there as the limousine pulled up to the curb and parked in front of the small warehouse office.

Three tough, street hardened men stepped out onto the sidewalk and carefully looked around before coming up to the door of the little office. Without bothering to knock, they opened the door and followed each other in, then closed the door behind them. For a moment, no words were exchanged between the two groups of men. They were looking each other over with extreme care. Although never having met them before, the agents instantly knew who they were, "Gangsters," and they, in turn, knew who the agents were. There was no need for formal introductions.

Of course, Pucci was an unexpected stranger to them. The fact that he was dressed in his customary fireman's uniform required an introduction as well as an explanation as to why he was there. At this point, they listened to the senior agent's explanation with interest while carefully looking Pucci over with suspicion as he carried on. Finally, the one man who appeared to be in command (the Boss) of this unsmiling, unpleasant trio, had something to say to Pucci:

"So, Puccinelli, you're an Italian. How nice!" he said, with an icy expression.

"Yes, Sir," Pucci answered in his usual polite but firm manner.

"And you're a Fireman, a public servant. How interesting," the Boss added dryly.

"A Fire Inspector, Sir."

"Oh, yes, that's right —— that's right. I'm sorry to have degraded you, Puccinelli," he apologized in a half cocky manner.

Pucci was trying desperately not to show his disregard for this cocky son-of-a-bitch who was interrogating him. He knew he was leading up to something, but the way he was going about it made him nervous as hell. If he made a break for it, he'd be dead before he reached the door. So there was only one thing to do and that was to answer the man's questions as briefly as possible and hope for the best.

The Boss continued his questioning with the obvious intention of extracting from Pucci all he knew about the operation. The fact that he was a public servant, a Fire Inspector no less, left some questionable doubts in this gangster's mind.

"Tell me something, Puccinelli, just how do you figure to fit in on this . . .", he was about to say "deal" but instead said, "you know, this government matter?"

At this point, the senior agent interrupted him in an attempt to explain, but he might just as well have attempted to kiss a rattlesnake. The Boss whirled to face the interrupter, then hissed a firm reminder that the answer to the question was to come from the person being asked the question, and not from him. If there were any doubts in his mind as to who was in charge here, they were now resolved. The Boss's two bodyguards stepped apart as if getting ready for a shootout.

Pucci sensed the tension. He didn't move a muscle except to swallow his saliva to avoid choking. "It's my responsibility to protect government property, Sir," Pucci answered timidly. He continued, "There have been some recent problems — at least one attempt to gain entry was made by use of an explosive device. You may have noticed the boarded-up entrance to the warehouse, Sir."

"Yes, I was going to ask about that. I'm glad you explained it. Tell me more."

"I feel it is not only my duty to protect but also my duty to assist in any way I can to see this undercover government operation successfully reach its conclusion, Sir."

The Boss liked that answer. A thin smile reflected his satisfaction. "Take it easy. There's no need to be uptight. And what's with this 'Sir', thing?"

"Well, Sir, we in public service are trained to address our superiors in this manner and since you appear to be a high-ranking representative of the Federal Government, even more so than these other gentlemen here (referring to the agents), makes it imperative that I address you in this manner, Sir."

The Boss was now even more pleased with Pucci, a fellow Italian, a dumb one at that (so he thought). He could now see the reason that the agents were using him in their endeavor. Yes, he could be very useful, he thought.

Pucci was not so calm on the inside as he appeared to be on the outside. It was obvious that he had better continue to come up with answers that made sense without fumbling around. The agents were one thing, but these three gangsters were something else.

The senior agent again interrupted the interrogation, only this time with somewhat better luck. He realized the reason for this line of questioning, and if Pucci didn't come up with the right answers, it would be bad for them as well. The senior agent explained how Pucci, through loyalty and patriotism and for no other reason whatever, made it possible for them to conceal the operation. He also stated that Pucci was pushing for acceptance in the Agency and that he, as a senior agent, was helping him achieve that goal. Therefore they, too, could rely on him for cooperation.

Although the Boss felt this to be ridiculous, the explanation appeared to be acceptable. Tension eased as the discussion now shifted to the details of transferring and loading the wine aboard the incoming ship. Once the sequence of the operation was understood, it was agreed that there should be no deviation from the already scheduled plans. The senior agent now led the group out of the office for an inspection of the warehouse. They made their way along the neatly stacked rows of barrels. As a matter of habit (such as kicking the tires on an automobile), they walked along tapping an occasional barrel with their knuckles. During the hijack switch (Saturday night raid), the plan had been to replace one full barrel as the second one up on the stack to take care of just this sort of situation. Pucci was now praying that Mike had not forgotten that requirement. The procession continued along toward the rear of the warehouse. They reached the far wall, looked around, and to the relief of the agents started back. Had the gangsters studied the exterior of the building such as Pucci had, they would have found that the warehouse ran the full length of the block, whereas the interior did not.

As they walked back, the matter of the extra 120 barrels came up. The Mob had invested that extra cash so obviously they wanted to be assured of its delivery on time. For some reason, the Boss insisted that Pucci explain the sequence of that part of the operation as if the agents would have nothing to do with it. So he did. Pucci reported that he was able to hire an independent trucker with a big truck and trailer at a much cheaper cost. The truck was from the southern part of the state and was to arrive at the winery, make the load, and deliver it to the freighter as the first load of barrels to be taken on. The so-called "southern truck" would, however, be none other than Primo's Mack. The Boss also bought the idea that this same truck, in order to take advantage of the savings, would then make at least one more load from the warehouse to the ship. All activities from the warehouse to the ship would be done at night. The Boss was pleased with the fact that the matter of transporting the barrels from the warehouse to the freighter was already pre-contracted.

Now, then, the last matter to discuss was the incoming freighter. But again, the Boss explained the schedule more for Pucci's benefit than to the eagerly listening agents. The freighter, called "Amigo Negro", was scheduled to arrive in San Francisco, dock at pier 15, load the contents of the warehouse (plus the 120 extra barrels), and ship out again without delay.

All this time Pucci was carefully studying the three gangsters. He detected guns in shoulder holsters on the two bodyguards. There were other movements and matters of interest. The tall one, the driver of the limo, constantly kept reaching in his left pocket as if to check its contents. There was something in there that was causing his pocket to bulge somewhat. The group made its way back through the office and out onto the sidewalk. As they did so, the driver made it a point to be the last one out of the office. As he stepped out, the bulge in his left pocket was now gone.

The Boss turned to the agents and said: "By the way, we have something for you." He now motioned to the driver to open the trunk of the limo.

Pucci moved in closer and carefully looked in the car as he moved up to the open trunk. He viewed the trunk and its contents with extreme interest. So did the agents. There, resting comfortably in their specially-made support brackets, were two "Thompson" submachine guns. Sitting alongside of them were two full boxes and two empty boxes of ammunition to go with them. Apparently, they were fully loaded and ready for action. In addition, there was one full box and one partially full box of .45 caliber automatic pistol ammunition as well.

Pucci could see the uncomfortable expressions on the agents' faces. They said nothing and neither did he, for he was just as uncomfortable, and maybe more so. It was obvious that they were intentionally displaying their firepower for them to see.

The mobster reached into the trunk and removed a package which was neatly wrapped as a gift and about the size of a two-pound box of candy. He handed it to the senior agent as he said: "This is a gift for you four gentlemen, compliments of our 'Capo', Consiglio De Vita." With this, the agents managed to change their expressions from looks of horror to somewhat sheepish smiles of satisfaction and gratitude.

The driver locked the trunk as the three men stepped into the limo with stern, expressionless faces. They were cool and showed no signs of nervousness, with the exception of the shorter, chain-smoking, third man. His cigarette smoking habit was apparently catching up to him. The limo eased away from the curb like a hearse leaving the funeral parlor.

They watched the limo disappear around the corner before re-entering the office. Pucci was not about to leave just yet. His curiosity was centered on the "gift box" in the hands of the senior agent. He followed them back into the office. With the gangsters gone, the real threat for the day was now passed.

The agents were not at all happy. The sight of the submachine guns had raised concerns. Why would those gangsters want to go through the trouble of intentionally displaying them?

The senior agent walked around the other side of the desk and proceeded to open the gift box. Across the top were several neatly-wrapped, thin bundles of one hundred dollar bills which were visible to Pucci. The agent set the open box down. His eyes never left it for an instant. The smaller box which was shaped differently was sitting on the desk unnoticed, at least for the moment, left there by the driver. This explained the bulge in his left pocket.

The senior agent picked up each thin bundle of bills and shuffled them through his fingers as if counting them rapidly. For a few seconds, he said nothing, an expression of disappointment crossed his face.

Pucci broke the silence by saying: "Hardly enough to pay the cost of the loading and drayage, is it?" He knew very well that this money was not intended for that purpose. However, by so stating, it would give them an out as to the true reason for having received the cash.

"Yes, you're right — nowhere near enough."

Pucci asked another question: "They, no doubt, plan to provide the balance of the required amount when the job is complete, wouldn't you say, Sir?"

"Yes — yes, of course. I'm sure you're right about that as well." The senior agent had been given an out as far as an explanation was concerned, but this was not what was on his mind.

It was obvious to Pucci that the true purpose of the cash was to be their share of the take. They were being paid off but the amount was only a mere fraction of what they should be getting or, at least, what they expected to get.

One of the others commented in disgust: "They sure as hell don't think much of us if that's all there is. Maybe there's more underneath?"

The senior agent was now inserting the letter opener under the paper separator, lifting it gently as you would to get to the second layer of chocolates. He was obviously hoping to find much more cash in even larger bills. They were all staring in anticipation as he lifted off the separator. The lower section contained no money. Instead, it was packed tight with chocolate teardrops, all in rows neatly wrapped in foil with a little paper flag sticking up from each one with the word, "kisses" printed on it.

"What the hell is this!?" he swore. "Is this supposed to be some kind of joke with those bastards!?" He had now blown his stack. One of the others reached in and picked off the foil from one of the teardrops, then dropped it back into the box. It was chocolate all right.

Pucci interrupted the outbursts of profanity. "It appears they left something else for you, Sir," pointing to the smaller box still sitting unnoticed on one corner of the desk. It was about six inches long, two inches wide, and about two inches deep. The lid was hinged so that it would open back like a coffin, leaving approximately 1-1/2 inches of depth when opened.

The senior agent was still standing when he gently opened it without picking it up from the desk. The lid settled back resting on its hinges and exposing its contents. To his horrified surprise, there lay in this coffin-like box, a dead bird.

This colorful songbird was resting on its back, its stiff little legs and feet in a bent position lying back on its breast, its beak sticking straight up. It looked as if it were sleeping. The senior agent with his right hand trembling, gently closed the lid and dropped back into his chair. The expression on his face negated the need for words. This was no joke. If the others failed to interpret this message, he certainly did not.

Pucci was also very familiar with this gruesome message. Now everything seemed to fit. The submachine gun display coincided with these new findings. The Italian interpretation of a "kiss" in this case was meant to be the "Kiss of Death." A "dead bird" found on your doorstep was to be interpreted as "You are a Dead Bird"; if not today, tomorrow for sure.

Pucci apologized for his sudden departure and closed the door gently behind him. He hurriedly walked to his vehicle. Once seated, he took a deep breath and exhaled in relief. Apparently, none of this was meant for him. At least not yet.

"Those goddamned agents," growled Pucci. "They set me up. It all fits. Once paid, they pocket the extra cash, and beat it. Leave the gangsters to deal with the winery up north, and leave me here to deal with the gangsters. Those sons-of-bitches."

Apparently, the gangsters were satisfied that the agents were now dispensable. They were being told to get the hell out of town or else. For the present, Pucci still had a job to do. They still needed him. They could deal with him later.

It didn't take a genius to figure out the terms of settlement being offered to the agents. They had a choice. Either accept the cash and get out of town immediately, or take the risk of a shootout that could result in their being cut in half by those submachine guns they had seen in the trunk of the limo. There was no way they could match that kind of firepower. Even if they were to prevail in a confrontation, they would always be on the run and hunted down anyway.

Pucci's heart sank to rock bottom. Granted, the agents had their problems, but so did he. The events of the day had screwed up his plans but good. He, no doubt, would not have the agents to deal with any longer but he now had to deal with these three, tough gangsters from New Jersey who were armed to the teeth.

"Of all the damned luck," he cursed as he thought of the predicament he was faced with. They just might get away with hijacking the extra load from Napa since he already had the cash to pay for it. That load would be worth going after. Besides, these gangsters had no idea that a hijack might take place. However, the extra load to be picked up at the warehouse and diverted away from the freighter could be way too risky.

His first thought was Primo. In his mind he could picture his buddy riddled full of holes, blood splattered all over the cab of the Mack. His beloved truck could very well become his coffin.

CHAPTER 22

That night Pucci caught up to Primo to inform him of the latest developments.

"You could be right, Pucci. No question that the agents are on a collision course with disaster. Let's hope we don't get caught in the middle."

"Let's drive over to the warehouse and take a look around," suggested Pucci.

They drove past the front of the warehouse; everything seemed quiet.

"Take it around back. Let's take a look at the garage. I'm curious," said Pucci.

"I was thinking the same thing," answered Primo as he slowed down coming around the corner of the back street.

"Pull up in front of the doors. I want to check them out."

The car stopped short of the garage doors. The headlights illuminated the entire end of the warehouse.

"Hold it a minute; let me take a better look." With this, Pucci stepped out in front of the doors; he suspected they were not quite closed. They were unlocked. He pushed them open enough to allow the light to expose the now empty garage. He pulled them closed again and reported back to Primo.

"That takes care of the agents. Their car is gone," he announced. "They no doubt exercised their option to blow town. We'll never see them again."

"How about the panel?" asked Primo.

"It hasn't been disturbed. They must have come in from this end to get the car," answered Pucci. He then continued with a more

142

sincere expression and tone of voice: "They didn't leave town with just the few hundred dollars they were given. You can be sure they took the extra cash they conned their cohorts in sending them as well. If the Mob doesn't catch up to those assholes first, you can be sure that bunch of Italians up there at the winery will when they find out they're not going to get paid for the missing load."

The thought of who was screwing whom was more than Primo could handle. He burst out laughing uncontrollably.

"Hey, shut up, you jerk," Pucci commanded as he too joined in with a chuckle. As serious as the matter was, it appeared to be funny. "For Christ's sake, let's get the hell out of here before we attract too much attention." With this, Primo took off leaving behind a cloud of black exhaust smoke. The car rattled across the cobblestones as the two men struggled to regain their composure.

First thing next morning, Pucci was at the paper company garage waiting for Primo to show up for work.

"What the hell are you doing here at this hour?" asked Primo in a cheerful manner, starting to chuckle as he thought of the night before at the warehouse.

"Listen, buddy, cut the horsing around. We have to talk this thing over before it gets out of hand," said Pucci.

"I guess you're right. What do you have in mind?"

"It's my opinion that the smartest thing to do is go to the Police Chief and tell him about yesterday's incident at the warehouse. He should be told about those mobsters."

"The Police Chief!" exclaimed Primo. "Hey, buddy, are you losing your marbles? That guy is tough. Jesus Christ, can't you come up with a better idea than that?"

"Now wait a minute! We don't have to mention anything about our involvement. I'll just tell him about the gangsters, nothing else. Maybe he can help us deal with them. Stop and think about it a minute!"

Primo gave it some thought then offered his own opinion. "Here's what you should do: First, talk it over with your Fire Chief and have him accompany you to see the Police Chief. The way I understand it, they're close friends. He can put you in a better light with the Police Chief. You're going to need all the help you can get to keep him off your back if he was to get wise to you."

"Good idea, Primo. I'll do just that; I'm on my way. See

you tonight." Pucci wasted no time getting to the Fire Chief.

After listening to Pucci's comments about the events of the previous day, the Chief said: "You're on the right track. Let's get over to O'Shaunassey's right now. He'll be interested in hearing your story. But let me tell you something, don't be surprised if you find that he knows a hell of a lot more than you think."

As they were driving over to the Police Chief's office, a worrisome thought crossed Pucci's mind. This could be a mistake, he thought, as he mulled over his Chief's earlier comment. It's a cinch that he and the Police Chief knew something, or he would not have made the comment.

They walked into the Police Chief's office where his Chief introduced him in an informal manner. Pucci couldn't help but feel as if this lawman already knew him even too well. The thought of it made him a little uneasy.

The Police Chief listened intensely to the details of the encounter with the gangsters the day before. As Pucci outlined it, he gave no indication of the paesani's involvement nor did he say anything about the secret garage at the other end of the warehouse.

It was no surprise when the Police Chief informed Pucci that he already had a general knowledge of the agents' activities in reference to the warehouse, but he mentioned nothing about the paesani's activities although there was the feeling that the Chief did, in fact, know something. It was obvious his main concerns were centered on the gangsters who were now on the scene.

"Tell me, Pucci. These men you refer to, can you tell me more about them? Their individual descriptions, actions, or any other information you feel might be helpful."

"Well, the one that the other two refer to as 'Boss' seems to be unarmed. He has a medium build; about my size; tough and unyielding; noticeable scars on his face, like maybe having been the result of a beating or a knife fight."

"The fact that he's unarmed doesn't surprise me," said the Chief. "He's smart. Experience has taught him to let others take the risk of being caught with weapons."

Pucci continued: "He's well-dressed — expensive clothes — carries cigars, but I never saw him smoke one. His actions indicate that he's right-handed. There's no question that he's of Italian extraction. No doubt, Sicilian."

"As for the other two — I would say the driver, called 'Lungo,' probably a nickname because of his height and slender appearance, is left-handed. He wears his shoulder holster under his right arm, no doubt with a .45 automatic to match the boxes of shells I saw in the trunk. This guy has the coolness of a cobra; the appearance of a real killer. I'd say an expert with the submachine gun. Doesn't smoke. Steady nerves. May or may not be a full-blooded Italian. If so, he has some mixed blood from Northern Italy. I'd watch out for him."

"The third man's short, answered to the name of 'Morino,' a possible nickname for the 'little dark one' which fits him well. Slightly built; right-handed. He carries his shoulder holster under his left arm; also a bulky .45 automatic that seems too big for his stature. A habitual chain smoker; cigarette dangling from the left corner of his mouth continuously. Somewhat nervous with a light cough as if his lungs were constantly irritated. He too would be comfortable with a submachine gun. He is definitely of Italian extraction, possibly from Naples."

"How about the car, anything unusual about it?"

"Well, it's a black limousine with whitewall tires. This year's model 'Cadillac' with New Jersey license plates. As I walked past it, I noticed a briefcase that could serve for carrying cash. No other luggage. The trunk displayed its contents well." Pucci proceeded to describe the submachine guns and boxes of shells in detail.

"Aside from what I have just told you, there's little else to offer. I'm sure those guns are loaded with lead slugs and not blanks," he added as a final comment.

The Chief thought about that last remark before continuing the conversation. "Do you think they might show up at the warehouse tomorrow morning?" he asked.

"Yes Sir. I'm sure they will," answered Pucci.

"Okay, I'm going to give this some thought. Maybe I can get a look at them in the morning. Be at the firehouse at 10:00 a.m. sharp. I'll see you then."

The next morning the two men met at the firehouse as planned. The Police Chief made it clear to Pucci that with that much firepower in the hands of those gangsters, it put him in a very dangerous position. He made a strong point:

"I'm not telling you to stay away from that warehouse, but

I'm sure as hell telling you that any false move on your part could trigger a confrontation which could end in disastrous results. I hope you understand that," he warned. "With the agents out of the picture, they may feel they can use you for awhile, but after that you will become dispensable. Be extremely careful in dealing with them," he added.

Pucci hadn't mentioned anything to the Chief about the next load to be picked up at the Napa winery. There's no way the Chief could know about it.

"I have an idea," said the Chief. "It might work. At least it can't hurt to give it a try. We'll meet again here in the morning at the same time. By the way," he added, "there's someone I want you to meet down at the Coast Guard Base. Follow me down."

The last twenty-four hours had been full of surprises for Pucci. Now he was about to get still another. At the Base he was introduced to the District Coast Guard Commander, an Englishman. He was also introduced to Captain Terranova, a descendant from a long line of Italian Navy officers from Palermo, Italy. The Captain was quite impressive with black piercing eyes and jet black wavy hair, neatly trimmed mustache, young and alert. Although not too tall, he was well-proportioned and extremely good looking. He wore his officer's uniform in a meticulous manner. These qualities, plus his Italian charisma, no doubt stimulated scores of sexually adventurous San Francisco women.

Captain Terranova was in command of a new Coast Guard Cutter called the "Skipjack" — the largest and best in the fleet.

The Commander announced that a ship of suspicious nature was in the Los Angeles harbor unloading its westbound cargo. It was scheduled to take on a partial load of sugar, then proceed up the coast and dock at San Francisco, approximately one week from this day, to finish its load before returning to the East Coast.

"The ship in question is believed to be the 'El Vento Este' (The East Wind) a rumrunner of Panamanian registration traveling as the 'Amigo Negro.' However, it came through the Panama Canal under the name 'Caribbean Caravel', also a fictitious name. The ship seems to be just an average, common freighter, apparently not too well maintained, at least by what can be determined from the exterior. But, we have our doubts because it's apparently armed with a cannon on the bow and possibly a fifty-caliber machine gun mounted on the top deck just above and behind the pilot house. These guns are cleverly camouflaged by shed-type enclosures which can be quickly pushed aside. They're constructed to resemble the entrance to a possible stairwell leading below deck. We've seen this sort of arrangement before. Something you don't see on common freighters. In any event, if it proves to be the 'El Vento Este,' we'll be obligated to take it, along with her Captain, both wanted. We believe both to be connected in some way with the warehouse in question." The Coast Guard had done its homework.

The Police Chief asked an obvious question:

"Do you intend to seize the vessel and take the Captain into custody upon its arrival?"

"No," said the Commander.

"Why not?" came the next question.

"Because we're not absolutely sure it's the 'El Vento Este,' and neither can we be sure it will be under the same command when it gets here. We intend to stay clear of it hoping something will develop that'll give us cause to seize the vessel and arrest its Captain. If it comes to that, we'll be looking to your department for cooperation and assistance," said the Commander.

The explanation satisfied the Police Chief. He'd not interfere until needed.

Pucci was appalled at how much was known about the Federal agents and their unscrupulous activities. He wondered how much was known about their own activities. He had mixed feelings about the attention he was getting. Were they, the authorities, using him as a decoy? If so, how could he avoid getting caught in the middle? He left the meeting with the thought weighing heavily on his mind. Well, at least we're not alone in this dirty battle, he thought as he searched the city for Primo.

The two buddies combined their thoughts. Their minds were now geared to taking advantage of this situation. To some extent, they might have to revise their plans somewhat. But regardless of the inherent risks, they were not about to back out of the Napa winery deal. This they felt could be pulled off.

"There are only three of those bastards," snorted Pucci. "They sure as hell can't be everywhere at the same time. Besides, I doubt that they would split up or leave the warehouse totally unguarded."

"Exactly," answered Primo. "Let's stay with the Napa deal,

and let's approach this thing under the assumption that in some way the Police Chief might be able to blunt the stingers of those three scorpions."

"Boy, wouldn't it be something if in some way they were to be disarmed," answered Pucci. "The Chief's got something up his sleeve. I'm sure of that." Then added: "That settles it. Let's plan accordingly. Maybe we can get more than a couple of loads out of this, after all."

"What the hell are you thinking of doing? Hijacking the damned freighter for Christ's sake? That thing's supposed to be armed!" answered Primo.

"I hardly believe it. They weren't all that sure of it," said Pucci, then bid his buddy good day and hurried off. He had important errands to run.

Primo watched him disappear down the street in his Reo runabout, zigzagging through traffic, dodging streetcars as if he was going to a fire. "That guy's serious," he thought. "Jesus Christ! Are we ever going to get our ass in a sling!"

CHAPTER 23

Convinced that the local authorities were somewhat sympathetic to their cause, but to some extent setting him up, using him, so to speak, Pucci felt their involvement could be used to his advantage so, therefore, planned accordingly. His first step was to contact Sven, who proved to be eager to take part. In addition, they could also count on his fellow tugboat captain and close friend, Swede. Swede was a husky, blond brute of a man with a neck as big as his head, muscular arms and shoulders that tapered down to narrow hips, supported by legs that resembled pilings.

Sven, in introducing the two men, pointed out to Swede that Pucci, together with his friend Mike, was responsible for having saved his tugboat from the clutches of the banker, Battisoldi.

Pucci had no idea what strength really was until Swede reached out with his powerful right hand and pumped his arm in a handshake that all but dislocated his shoulder.

"I understand that you two have the contract to dock that Panamanian freighter coming up from Los Angeles. Is that correct?" asked Pucci.

"Yes, that's right," answered Sven. "Why do you ask?"

"Well, our friend Mike is involved in a business deal, and I'm afraid he'll need some help with it. I'm hoping you two fellows might give him a hand." Pucci was purposely injecting Mike into the request.

Sven hadn't forgotten Mike for an instant. "You tell us how," he said eagerly as Swede grinned in anticipation of joining in on something exciting.

"Well," said Pucci, "there will be a big truck and trailer pulling

149

up to the freighter after dark on the day it docks. The truck will be loaded with barrels that are to be taken aboard ship. There is the possibility of trouble. The driver may need some protection at least until he departs empty."

"Is this man a friend of yours?" asked Sven.

"Yes, he is. As a matter of fact, his name is Primo; he's Mike's nephew."

"What? Mike's nephew!" exclaimed Sven as he straightened up with raised bushy eyebrows. "By golly! Nobody better touch that boy of Mike's, eh Swede?" Swede responded as if hoping there would be a fight.

The two adventurous Vikings made it clear that they would be on hand with their tugs ready to use their fire hoses to give Primo cover if needed.

The matter settled, Pucci outlined a plan in detail wherein they could profit, assuming things went well. They were all for it. They didn't need coaxing.

"There is one more thing, Sven," said Pucci. "I need some work done by that Danish boat-builder friend of yours. Could you introduce me to him?"

"Right away," answered Sven eagerly. "Come with me and I'll take you to him."

As Pucci had hoped, the Dane was receptive. Pucci laid out in detail his needs, without divulging the intended purpose of the shipping container to be constructed. An explanation as to why there was an urgent need was not necessary. The Dane agreed to drop everything and get with the project immediately. Pucci bid his heavily-accented friends good day and headed back downtown feeling much more confident.

His thoughts turned back to the gangsters. If only the Police Chief could figure out a way to disarm them and keep them that way. They, incidently, were being careful not to break any laws. They were too smart for that.

The Chief was working on the problem. He contacted a man he knew in the jewelry business whose name was Stein. Some years back, while still a cop on the beat, the Chief had foiled an attempted robbery at his jewelry store. Had he not risked his life, surely the jeweler could very well have been shot; maybe fatally. Since then, Mr. Stein always reminded him that if ever he needed a favor from him, he should not hesitate to ask.

Well, the time had come. The Chief had brought along the equivalent amount of ammunition as described by Pucci at their earlier meeting. He proceeded to explain the importance of his request to the jeweler. There was an urgent need to accomplish the feat. Time was short.

"Well," said Mr. Stein. "It's an unusual request that you are asking of me. You must remember that I make jewelry, not ammunition for machine guns and pistols. But I will do my very best for you."

The Chief had asked him if he could remove the lead slugs from each one of the bullets, then make up exact duplicates with some form of compressed harmless material. They'd have to look like real bullets, and hold together when fired, but still avoid any possibility of fatal injury.

The jeweler agreed that it could be done. He'd have them ready in two days.

Pucci made it a point to appear at the warehouse while the gangsters were there. He inquired about the agents and their whereabouts as if he didn't know of their departure. The answer he got was quite dry:

"Why do you ask, Puccinelli? What's your problem?"

"Well, Sir, for one thing, I wanted to report to them that all is ready to go. The truck from Napa Valley will meet the ship on schedule as planned."

"Fine — that's just fine," the Boss said. "You're efficient in your work — I like that."

"To hear you say that makes me feel good, Sir. I do hope Washington will look favorably upon my request for acceptance in the Agency."

"Oh, yes, I almost forgot about that. I'm sure they will."

"Would you, Sir, also put in a good word for me when you get back to Washington?"

"Why, of course! Of course! No problem," he answered in his big-shot manner. "Would you also like to be assigned permanently to San Francisco?"

Pucci mustered up a big, boyish grin as he answered: "Yes, Sir. That would be great. Thank you, Sir."

Who was kidding whom would remain to be seen.

The Police Chief met with Pucci the following day. They discussed his strategy in detail. "Tomorrow we will put it to the test. In the meantime, I want you to stay away from those gangsters." By the tone of his voice, it was apparent he meant exactly what he said. "I will let you know later in the day how things turn out. Wish me luck for you and your friends' sake more than anything else. You'll need it."

The Chief visited the jeweler late the same day.

"Ah, you're early," said the little jeweler. "I didn't expect you until first thing in the morning, but then, this will be just fine. They're ready."

"Good," answered the Chief.

"I think maybe we have something for you, my friend. Come take a look. See what you think." With this he opened the boxes of reworked shells and displayed them to the Chief.

"Very good, indeed. They look just like the real thing all right," said the Chief with delight. "And they're heavy as well. How did you do that?"

"Ah! You noticed that. My friends and I devised a method to fill them with a liquid just to give them weight and more authenticity." His Jewish accent was now more pronounced than ever; his expression took on an air of genius.

"You have done a very good job. Thank you, Mr. Stein. How much do I owe you?"

"If my friends thought that I would take money for this, they would disown me. I'm proud to have been able to help you. Whatever the outcome is, I'm sure you will find it colorful," he added with a sly grin.

"All right, Mr. Stein. For the time being, I thank you kindly. Please express my feelings to your friends as well."

The Chief gathered up the boxes of shells and headed straight for his office. There were things to be done in preparation for the events of the next day.

Mid-morning the next day the limo appeared, cruising towards the warehouse following the same route from the hotel as on the previous mornings. They had several blocks yet to go when they swung into a cross-street only to find a police barricade waiting for them. Fully armed with shotguns and submachine guns, policemen appeared instantly from various positions. Coming up behind them were two more police cars, blocking the street behind them, so they were now "boxed in."

The two armed gunmen reacted by reaching for their guns.

"No!" shouted the Boss. "Hold it. They don't have a damned thing on us. For Christ's sake, put those guns away. Let's hear what they've got to say."

He knew better. They could ill-afford a gunfight at this point in time. His past experience in situations like this had taught him to keep cool–think, not shoot, especially when the odds are stacked against you.

The Chief stepped up to the limo and ordered the trio out:

"Gentlemen, please step out and move up to the front of the car," he said in a firm, polite manner.

The Boss inquired of the Chief as to what the problem might be, but received no explanation, just another order:

"The Sergeant will remove your guns for inspection. Extend your arms out straight." No nonsense here.

After that chore was done, the Chief now answered the Boss's question:

"We just had a holdup at a jewelry store on Market Street. There was a shooting involved as well. Do you know anything about that?"

The Boss smiled, somewhat relieved. "Of course not. Do we look like jewel thieves to you? Come now, Chief, please give us more credit than that."

"Not really," responded the Chief. "But there were three men, all armed, who fit your descriptions; and there was a description of your car as well. By the way, where's your gun?"

The Boss, expressing a sly grin, answered: "I don't carry a gun. My bodyguards are always on hand." His answer was no surprise to the Chief.

"I see that. So if you had nothing to do with the holdup, we can clear up this matter right here and now."

By this time the limo had been searched — which included the trunk. While the Chief was questioning the men up front, the Sergeant, along with two police inspectors (under the pretense of looking for stolen jewelry), switched the magazines of the submachine guns and the .45 automatics along with the boxes of ammunition sitting in the trunk. There was no indication of the switch. It was fast and efficient. The Sergeant stepped up holding the .45's and said:

"Sir, I have checked the guns. As far as I can tell, there appears to be no evidence of their having been fired recently." He pointed out that had they been fired, they would probably still have a live shell in the chamber and some missing from the magazine. Besides, the barrels would be dirty with burned gunpowder and would smell accordingly.

"Well, then," said the Chief, "these men apparently are not the ones we are looking for. Give them back their guns, Sergeant."

The Chief made a lengthy issue about the submachine guns. They were not to display the weapons in any way during their stay in San Francisco. He continued to point out that if their business matters were such that this kind of armament was necessary, that it would be best if they contacted him at Police Headquarters and let the police provide them with protection. Armed bodyguards were not recommended. He continued to engage them in trivial

conversation until he heard Primo's Doane give a blast from its exhaust horn as he drove by the cross-street. Pucci had asked him to delay the gangsters until he heard the signal in order to give him time to supposedly check out the warehouse. The true reason for the diversion was to give Primo and a half dozen paesani enough time to transfer and position the shipping container built by the Dane, along with its contents, in the secret garage at the rear of the warehouse.

The Chief apologized for the inconvenience and wished them well. The gangsters in turn drove off satisfied that, under the circumstances, their having been stopped was justified.

"That was a close call," said the Boss, somewhat relieved. "Let's take it easy from now on. We can't even afford a traffic citation at a time like this."

That afternoon the Chief met with Pucci. Pucci expressed satisfaction with the Chief's accomplishments, but lingered on the matter of the de-leaded bullets.

"Well," said the Chief, "you better hope to Christ that little jeweler knows what he's doing."

"What if the gangsters discover the switch? What then?" inquired Pucci.

"I thought of that too. What my men are doing is enforcing a ban on all sales of guns and ammunition. We have also asked all the dealers in town to immediately notify us if any attempt is made by anyone to purchase armament of whatever sort. We're also maintaining a twenty-four hour surveillance on the limo." He then finalized his comments with a stiff warning to Pucci: "Don't flaunt the law because if you get out of hand, I'll be obligated to focus my attention on you as well. Do you understand me, Mr. Puccinelli!?"

The firm and formal manner of this statement caused Pucci to gulp and clear his throat as he answered:

"Yes, Sir. I understand. We wouldn't think of flaunting the law. No, Sir. We'll be extremely careful."

Pucci rose from his chair, bid him good day and departed hurriedly for fear of his sweaty feeling being detected.

CHAPTER 24

The three partners met once more to go over the details of this grand-slam hijack which would divert two loads, one from Napa and one from the warehouse to San Bruno. Regardless of the risk involved, they were determined to try it.

As they were about to depart, Primo put the matter of the mechanic, Al, to his partners.

Mike was surprised to hear that his friend, Al, worked at the paper company garage.

"I knew he was a mechanic and a darned good one, but I didn't know he commuted to the city to work. Sure, he's a good man, that'll be fine with me," said Mike. "That is, of course, if it's all right with Pucci."

"Sure," said Pucci. "It's not a bad idea that we have a good mechanic along. Have him bring his toolbox with him just in case," he suggested.

Primo was delighted. It would be a comfort to have a relief driver on this long journey. He remembered the earlier lonely, grueling drive from Sonoma County during the night. It was a tough ordeal.

It was now early Sunday morning. Mike was about to leave the ranch to join Primo and Pucci in San Francisco for their journey to Napa. This would be an overnight affair. If their schedule could be maintained, it would bring them back to the ranch late the following night.

During the previous visit to the ranch, Primo had assured Livia that there was no risk involved in this trip to Napa, therefore easing her mind. She bid her husband farewell and, as always, worried about his well-being.

The paesani understood that they must be on their best behavior over the next couple of days for they would be called upon to unload, then reload the Mack the minute it arrived regardless of the time, day or night.

The weekend watchman at the paper company let Primo in the garage, pushed the doors open, and waited for him to pull out with the Mack. The phantom would strike again.

The three partners met at the Embarcadero. Mike threw his bedding in Pucci's Reo. The Mack pulled onto the ferry first, then Pucci and Mike, riding together, pulled up behind it.

As expected, Al was waiting for them at the ferry slip on the Oakland side. He threw his gear in the Reo but climbed aboard the Mack. The promise of adventure was exciting.

"Al, we better light up before we move out," advised Primo.

"Not a bad idea," responded Al as he, too, reached in his shirt pocket for a cigarette. Striking a match, he first lit Primo's, then his own. The truck moved out; destination, Napa County.

"These damned coffin nails are irritating my throat something fierce," complained Al, clearing his throat.

"Those Lucky Strikes will do that. Maybe you should switch to Camels."

"Switch to Camels," snorted Al. "Those damned cigarettes will burn right through your lungs. Besides, who wants to smoke camel dung? That's what those Turks put in their tobacco, or didn't you know?"

Primo took a long drag from his Camel cigarette, coughed and spit, pondering Al's comment.

"You didn't know that, did you? Well, think about it," added Al with a grin.

The scuttlebutt was that the Turkish tobacco's pronounced flavor did have something to do with its association with camels. Some said it was derived from the camels' spitting on the tobacco leaves as they lay across racks to cure. They despised it, so they spit on it.

American tobacco had a different, more pungent flavor to it. To some, it was desirable. While to others, it was irritating if not nauseating. It was thought, and there seemed to be some documented proof, that the many dogs running around loose in the South were contributing to this phenomenon. The dogs were observed lifting their legs and urinating on the tobacco leaves as they cured draped from racks. Since a dog's philosophy is, "If you can't eat it or screw it, then piss on it," — it would obviously substantiate this argument.

Bull Durhams, "roll your owns," were the favorite with the cowhands working the great cattle herds of the West. But they were impossible to make up in some of these open cab trucks like the Mack, so obviously truckers preferred ready made cigarettes. However, "roll your owns" were ideal for the lonely cowhands. Although they spilled and wasted the better part of the tobacco while making them up with one hand and scratching their saddle-sore ass with the other, they didn't seem to mind. The spilling didn't seem to create much of a problem as long as the little sacks held up, because refills were always readily available. All they had to do was gather up a fresh supply of "heifer dust," as they referred to it, from around the edges of the cow corrals as they went along doing their chores in their leisurely manner.

The Italians who smoked Toscanelli cigars had the best of both worlds. They were impossible to inhale since it took all the drawing power you could muster up just to get the smoke from one end of the cigar to the other. Besides, unlike a cigarette, you would have to keep puffing continuously in order to keep it lit. The idea of taking one nice deep drag and holding the smoke in your lungs in a relaxed manner, then letting it gradually drift out through your nose and mouth, was simply out of the question. To do so meant you would have to relight it with each draw. This fact, coupled with the fact that they, no doubt, used the cheaper, more contaminated leaves from the bales for rolling their cigars did, to some extent, discourage heavy smoking, therefore reducing the actual tobacco intake; a healthier situation.

Al commented about the roughly twisted Toscanelli cigars, which he referred to as "Tule Roots" and to Mike's smoking habit. "You notice your Uncle Mike when he smokes tule roots; he never coughs and seldom spits."

"Yeah, I've noticed that. But that's because they're too strong to inhale, and Aunt Livia won't let him spit, so he swallows the damn stuff." Primo's comment cracked them up.

And so it was throughout the journey; a little horsing around helped pass the time.

They arrived at the Napa winery late that afternoon; their arrival was expected. After parking the Mack off to one side to await the loading first thing next morning, they piled into the Reo and headed back to town (Napa) for dinner.

Upon their return to the winery from dinner, they noticed a black Essex Sedan parked along the road in view of the winery.

"What do you suppose that car with those two men is doing there?" asked Mike.

"I was wondering the same thing," answered Pucci curiously. "It looks out of the ordinary for this county. I'm not sure what to think of it."

Upon disembarking from the back end of the Reo, Al and Primo mentioned it as well.

"Hell, let's not concern ourselves," said Primo. "It probably has nothing to do with us. Let's hit the sack. It's been one hell of a long day." Primo's suggestion was welcomed by all. They bedded down on the ground under the bed of the trailer.

Mike's thoughts wandered back to when he first landed in this country and joined a railroad building crew. "Sleeping on the ground like this reminds me of when I worked on the railroad in Montana," he said as he snuffed out his cigar.

"Uncle Mike," asked Primo, "what was it like to hire out on the railroad building crew?"

The question caused Pucci to roll over and face the others. He, too, wanted to hear this story. Al was also now at attention.

"It wasn't good or easy being dumped off in a strange land at the age of seventeen," answered Mike. "No money. Couldn't speak a word of English. All I had was a bundle of extra clothing under my arm and the will to survive, wondering where do I go from here. But, no sooner had we cleared customs at Ellis Island, a bunch of us immigrant men from all kinds of European nations signed up to work through the summer on the Northwestern Railroad in Montana." Mike continued to describe some of the hardships of the ordeal.

"We were herded like cattle onto railroad cars and were fed just as bad. We were treated like so many animals. My father, back in the old country, took better care of his horses and oxen, even his pigs — than the way we were treated on that train. You can never forget things like that. It's branded in your mind like you brand a cow. It's forever." After a thoughtful pause, he continued his story.

"The working conditions weren't like our beloved Italy. No rest. No afternoon siesta. And no beds to sleep in. Only the hard ground or a rail car. One was just as bad as the other. We worked from daylight to dark everyday for very little pay. And if you complained, it meant answering to a big, tough Irishman boss. You know what he would do?", he asked, then answered his own question: "Every morning, the first thing this Irishman would do was fill his pockets with small rocks, like maybe the size of your smallest fingernail." Mike held up his little finger to demonstrate the size. "Then he'd walk along the railroad bed that we were building with picks and shovels. As we worked down in the ditches, he would throw the rocks hitting us on the back, neck, and head to remind us that he was up there. You didn't dare look up or open your mouth because if you did, this meant more rocks and an occasional kick in the ass. Rain or shine, hot or cold, it made no difference to him. He was a tough son-of-a-gun." The story continued with a hint of depression.

"For some, maybe it wasn't too bad because they, too, were tough, especially the big Swedes. He didn't throw rocks at them. You can be sure of that. Those guys could break a man's neck with one hand if they wanted to. When the big Swedes walked amongst us little Italians, we stepped aside and gladly gave them the right of way. We were no match for them."

Mike's sad, depressed tone of voice changed to a chuckle as he continued his story. The others were now paying closer attention because they knew there'd have to be a funny side to the story.

"One day the boss threw a rock by mistake, hitting a husky Swede on the back of the neck. His head jerked up, causing his hat to fall in the mud. The Swede didn't say a word; with one hand he sunk his pick into almost solid rock, breaking the pick handle in half. He picked up his hat, put it back on his head, mud and all, climbed up on the roadbed and, with clenched fists, started to walk towards the Irishman. Everybody stopped working to watch him take on the boss. The Irishman hit him once, then twice; it hardly fazed the Swede. Now the Swede was really mad. Coming in leaning forward like a bull, he threw a left, then a stiff right, hitting the boss right smack in the face. The Irishman's feet came up off the ground, causing him to land on his ass, then roll down the bank and into the ditch where he lay in mud and water, out cold. The Swede reached down in the ditch, dragged him back up on the railroad bed and emptied his pockets of rocks. His face smeared with blood and mud, the Irishman finally came to. "By God!" exclaimed Mike. "He almost killed him."

Mike's manner of telling the story with his usual hand gestures made it sound hilariously funny. Their laughter echoed among the winery buildings like thunder. They continued to laugh and chuckle until sleepiness got the best of them.

The shuffle of sandaled feet brought the men back from their heavenly sleep to face the new day.

"You are being asked to join us at the Rectory for breakfast," said a man's voice in a pleasantly peaceful manner. Mike opened his eyes. The man was dressed in a typical religious robe, standing a few feet from the truck. The sun rising over the ridge to the east was at his back, brightening up his outline, casting his shadow over Mike who was still lying there half asleep.

Heaven was the first thought that crossed Mike's mind. But under the circumstances, and considering his sometimes questionable conduct, that just might not be possible. At least, not until he was to change his ways somewhat.

"Well, boys, I guess we better not pass up the offer for breakfast," he said, as he crawled out from under the trailer to pull his shoes on.

While preparations were being made to start the loading, Pucci (with the worrisome thought of the black Essex still on his mind) walked out to the entrance of the winery. Sure enough, a short way down the road, the same car, with two male occupants, had just pulled off to one side and parked.

"Damned bastards!" Pucci mumbled. "Those sons of bitches are keeping their eyes on us sure as hell." As he walked back toward the truck, Primo couldn't help but notice the mad look on his buddy's face. It concerned him.

"What's the matter? You look disturbed about something."

"It's those bastards in that black Essex again. They're parked down the street, no doubt watching us."

"The hell you say! What do you suppose they're up to?"

"I don't know but you can be sure it's not good."

Mike walked up, followed by Al. "What's the matter?" asked

Mike as Al, too, wondered

"We've got company," answered Primo. "And it may not be too good," he added.

The four men talked it over for a few minutes. The main concern centered on who they were and their purpose for keeping a close watch on them.

Regardless, the truck had to be loaded so they must get with it. The loading procedure would be slow because of the lack of equipment and help. Besides, Mike insisted on carefully selecting the wine. He picked out a few barrels at random, drew a small sample, then hammered the bung back in place. He knew all about the trick of watering down wine. However, the people they were doing business with were too holy in their beliefs to do such a thing. The wine was of the very best quality, not watered down; but nevertheless, Mike was cautious — therefore slowing down the loading operation.

Finally the loading was completed and tied down. Heavy tarps tied down on all sides gave the load added stability. Some of the rough stretches of highway demanded it. The phantom Mack was now ready to roll out.

Primo walked over to an old Priest standing off to one side who had been watching the loading operation with interest. It was obvious that he had long since retired. He no longer had a Parish of his own. You might say he had been put out to pasture to live out the rest of his life in the quiet tranquil atmosphere of this wine-making institution so skillfully administered by his fellow holy Christian wine makers.

As he took off his hat in a gesture of respect, Primo addressed the old Priest:

"Father, would it be an imposition for me to ask you to bless my truck?"

The old Priest was momentarily caught off guard for he hadn't ever been asked to bless a truckload of wine before.

"I would be very grateful if you'd do this for me, Father." Primo was mischievous, but he was also a believer.

"Yes, of course, my son," answered the Priest. "I'll bless your truck, and you as well, for being so kind as to have seen something worthwhile in an old soul such as mine. But tell me, son, why have you chosen me and not one of the others?"

Primo still holding his hat in hand answered: "Because only a mature man of experience and wisdom could possibly understand what we are doing here today."

The old Priest slowly nodded his head. "Yes, my son, I do understand." With this, he walked toward the front of the big Mack and stopped short — facing this monstrous, bulldog-looking machine. He proceeded to chant the Latin words of blessings as he held up his hand, moving it back and forth so as to cover all portions of the machine and its cargo. He continued deeper and deeper in his sacred task. But he refused to follow the printed word. He was drifting into his best English as his thoughts dictated the context of the blessing. He talked to the truck as if it were a human being.

"God made man but man made you," he said. "Your destiny is to carry out the tasks for which you were created. You must obey the commands and carry out the wishes of your master; and, in turn, your master must obey the will of God!" He was now speaking louder, pointing to heaven with right arm raised.

"For it is God's will that this cargo of life-giving wine be delivered to his flock! We must not concern ourselves with those unjust laws imposed by man!" He was now waving his hands towards the east as if trying to get the attention of the lawmakers in Washington.

"What kind of men dare defy the will of God in an attempt to deprive humanity of its God-given right to drink wine derived from the grape? The grapes that were put on this earth in such abundance for just this purpose — to provide this nectar to maintain tranquility among God's children. The Ten Commandments do not forbid the drinking of wine! Since the birth of Christ, wine has been recognized as a symbol of blood!" He emphasized the next comment with an angry question:

"Would you deny man the right of his own blood? Would the saying of Mass be complete without wine? Of course not! The men who make such foolish laws, did they not read the Constitution of the United States of America? Did the forefathers of this great nation insert a paragraph in the great written document that says: 'Thou shalt not drink wine'? What kinds of fools are these men who pass such laws? Are they guided by the Devil himself? If so, God help them for they are surely destined to join him in hell where they must drink from the cesspools of Purgatory!" He then recited a few well-chosen passages of prayer before adding his final blessing:

"God bless this machine and its cargo of wine. And bless all these men who stand before me today as they endeavor to restore our God-given right to drink wine — God's gracious gift to mankind." He ended with an, "Amen."

His small congregation which had gathered around him could be heard repeating the "Amen" as they made the sign of the cross and bowed their heads. The old Priest had blessed just about everything in sight.

Primo had received much more than expected. He walked up to the old Priest and warmly shook his hand. "Thank you, Father," he said graciously.

The old Priest felt good, especially when he withdrew his hand along with a $10 bill which Primo had so skillfully transferred to his palm.

Mike, with hat in hand, stepped forward. A meeting of palms swept the cigars he was holding into the eager clutches of the old Priest. He was overwhelmed with such generosity. He thanked Mike in his native Italian tongue in a personal, man-to-man, manner.

Al had a big grin on his face as he, too, withdrew his hand clutching a now empty package of cigarettes. He had shaken the entire pack into the old Priest's pocket.

As the old Priest turned to walk away, he saw Pucci coming out of the office with the now empty cash-carrying briefcase. He stopped momentarily, raised his right hand, made the sign of the cross, and cast a short blessing towards Pucci. The contribution of cash was very much needed by this Christian society for they not only had the expenses of running the winery to deal with, but also the needs of those poor unfortunate souls who, for whatever reason, could not compete for the necessities of everyday life.

The old Priest walked away satisfied that God had not forsaken him in his old age, and that "God" would look after those that believed.

CHAPTER 25

The sun was about to settle down behind the ridge to the west as Primo climbed up into the cab of the Mack. However, this time he had the comforting blessings administered by the old Priest. In addition, he had Al sitting alongside.

The big Mack let out a roar and a puff of black exhaust as its engine responded to the demand of the starter motor. Primo let it warm up before selecting the lowest gear, then gave it a chance to pick up slack, like a team of draft horses putting their weight against the harness to get the load moving before applying their full muscle to the task. The Mack moved out slowly, making a wide circle through the yard, and then headed for the highway. It was a sight to behold — these two rather short Italians in their wool-lined leather jackets sitting in the partially open cab of this mighty machine.

The old Priest and several of the other members of this religious order were standing off to one side as the Mack gave out with a blast from its exhaust horn announcing its departure. They raised their hands in unison as the old Priest said:

"Be on your way my friends, and may the good Lord guide you throughout your journey." Little did he know how much these men would need his blessings this night.

They pulled onto the highway heading south. "There's that Essex again," announced Al as they passed by it.

"Al, I don't like the looks of it one damned bit. Keep an eye on them. See what they do."

The Reo pulled out behind the Mack. Pucci commented to Mike: "You can be sure those bastards are going to follow us." He was referring to the Essex. Sure enough, a short distance down the

166

road it could be seen following them.

As preplanned, they pulled in at the same restaurant they had visited the night before. The Mack was parked across the yard parallel with the highway taking just about all the parking space available. The Reo parked behind it.

The four men seated themselves at the window overlooking the parking area in full view of the Mack. No sooner were they seated, then the Essex pulled in, parking just ahead of the Mack as if it were a part of the caravan.

"There they are again, parked in front of us. Brazen as hell, aren't they?" said Primo.

Pucci responded as if the questions as to who they were and what they represented were asked. "Those bastards make me nervous. No question their presence has something to do with us, and that can't possibly be good. Did anyone by any chance notice their license plates?"

"I did," answered Al. "They're Pennsylvania plates."

No sooner were the words out of his mouth, the man on the passenger side of the Essex disembarked and walked back towards the Mack.

Al rose up from his chair, stretching his neck. He could see the top of the man's head at the far side of the cab as if he were looking into it. He took off in a fast walk towards the door mumbling profanity as he jerked it open and hurried across the parking area and around the nose of the Mack.

"Al must have seen something we missed," said Pucci as he, too, rose from his chair with the intention of getting a better look. As he did so, he saw him being pushed abruptly back and to one side by the inquisitive stranger. It was apparent that he wasn't pleased with Al's interference in whatever his endeavor might have been.

Pucci, still standing, said: "Hey, Al's in trouble."

"No," said Mike. "Take it easy. He's not in trouble. The man doing the pushing is in trouble."

At that instant, all hell broke loose. A staccato combination of lefts and rights smashed into the face of the intruder like a riveting gun pounding home a hot rivet. The man went down on one knee with blood oozing from his nose. He reached to retrieve his fallen gun, whether it fell accidentally from its shoulder holster or from his hand was not known. What was known for sure was that he had now set himself up for the "coup de grace."

Al's right-hand uppercut started from the area of his thigh. It came up and out as if ejected from a catapult. You could detect the muscles of Al's neck bulging with the strain of the tremendous force he was putting behind it. The fist, backed by the stocky, muscular arm behind it, and the experience of street fighting to guide it, caught the intruder in the face. His head snapped back with a loud crack; his hat tumbled to the ground. The blow sent the man falling backwards into the dust. His body was now piled up against the front wheel of the Mack.

The driver of the Essex came in on a dead run. It was apparent that his intention was to recover the fallen gun which lay close to Al's feet. As the man stooped reaching to recover the gun, Al took a step forward and came down hard on his hand with the heel of his shoe. The man's hand was pinned to the ground as he grabbed at Al's pants leg with his free hand. At that same instant, Al cut loose. The first blow to connect was similar to the one received by his buddy a moment before. Only this time, it was a left uppercut that smashed him in the face, and sent his hat doing cartwheels through the air. The punch was followed by a series of lefts and rights as he tried to straighten himself out, only to collapse at Al's feet whose shoes were by now smeared with blood. If a mistake was made, it was when these two taller men stooped in a manner that reduced their height, putting them in range of this stocky, husky Italian street fighter's fists.

Al gave the gun a kick and sent it skidding along the ground in the general direction of the Essex. He wanted no part of it. He knew better than to pick it up or touch it for any reason.

"Holy Christ! Did you see that?" said Pucci as he headed for the door to join Al.

Primo was dumbfounded. He had no idea that this mechanic he thought he knew so well was such a fighter. He was now looking at his uncle as he nervously asked: "Does he fight like that all the time?"

"Only when he gets mad. And he gets mad when he's pushed around," answered Mike. "Those two guys out there would have been better off if they, too, had taken lessons from those tough cannery workers from 23rd Avenue. Those kinds of fights are going on all the time between those East Oakland gangs."

Pucci met Al as he was strutting back across the yard. His fists were still clenched. He was muttering his disgust for the two (as he described them) "pricks" who were now picking themselves up from the dust.

"That guy has a gun, doesn't he?" asked Pucci.

"Yeah, he has a gun," answered Al. "And the next time, he damned well better use it, or I'll shove it up his ass," he added with determination.

As they walked up to the table to sit down, Mike addressing Al in a somewhat joking manner, commented:

"I was going to come out and help you, but my suspenders were caught in the chair."

Al was just as fast with his rebuttals as he was with his fists. He knew Mike was not a fighter. He answered promptly:

"That could have been bad if you couldn't get your pants down because you would have crapped in them when that gun showed up."

Primo, knowing that Al's comment was more truth than fiction, triggered a nervous laughter among them as they watched the Essex hurriedly pull out of the yard with the two somewhat battered occupants.

Mike called over to the proprietor and the still-startled waiter: "Bring us four good steaks and don't forget, Italians don't drink coffee with their steaks."

As they ate their dinners, the question of the Essex and its occupants was discussed. There was one thing they were all in agreement with: once back on the road, those two men would be right back on their tails. They, no doubt, had been commissioned to stay with the Mack at all costs.

Pucci insisted that these men were sent here by the agents in Washington. No doubt the continued hijackings caused them to distrust the previous agents who had been run out of town. And for that matter, maybe the mobsters back in the city didn't even know of their presence.

"Maybe and maybe not," said Primo. "Doesn't it seem odd that the mobsters never as much as gave you an argument about the money you were entrusted with? Maybe no one is trusting you either. We may have been set up, hoping they could locate the other missing load of wine."

"I'll have to admit that's the most logical explanation," said Pucci. "Regardless, they spell trouble."

Al listened attentively before offering his suggestion as to how they should be dealt with.

"Wait a minute, Al," said Pucci. "What do you mean — wipe them out? These guys could be Federal agents."

"I don't mean kill 'em," said Al. He proceeded to explain how two race cars would team up to wipe out a third competitor who didn't play the game by the rules. He added the fact that the highway between Vallejo and Benicia was perfect for the job, especially since they'd be on it after dark; a lonely stretch of road that he was familiar with.

"There are several grades with straight sections in between that surely can be used to our advantage," Al argued. "Instead of crossing at the Strait, we'll head for the Benicia-Martinez ferry instead. We'll cross the Sacramento River there."

"Alright," said Pucci. "If they follow us, we'll head for Benicia. But don't forget we could be dealing with Federal agents."

They were in agreement. Al's plan would be tried and since he knew the road better than Primo, Primo insisted that Al should take the wheel. Pucci and Mike would follow in the Reo and hope to antagonize the Essex and force them into the trap. Al warned Pucci to be careful because the Essex outweighed the Reo and, therefore, could get the best of them.

Since the plan would call for severe stress on the Mack, it could put the load in jeopardy. Al, with the help of the others, used the steel cables stored in the storage box of the Mack to further secure the load on both truck and trailer.

Al was taking no chances. The Mack's huge brakes would lock up the big wheels on demand. Depending on the speed at the time, the load could shift forward disrupting its stability with disastrous consequences.

It was dark as they pulled out of the restaurant parking lot. There would be no moonlight this night. The plan would have its hazards but, under the circumstances, the risk had to be taken. Whoever those men in the Essex were, they had to be put out of commission now before they had a chance to report to anyone.

As expected, the Essex picked them up again following at a reasonable distance. It was now apparent that these intruders, whoever they may be, were letting it be known that they intended to stay on their heels all the way.

"Of all the damned luck," growled Pucci. "Those bastards are screwing us up but good."

"You don't think Al's plan will work?" asked Mike.

"If it does, it will be bad. And if it doesn't, it will be even worse. We could be screwed either way," answered Pucci with a worried look before continuing: "Al knows what he's doing all right. And that's the thing that worries me. He's liable to kill those two men."

"I don't think he intends to do that," stated Mike.

"No, but what he intends to do, and what could happen with a plan like that, are two different things."

Both men were silent for a while. Their thoughts were troubled as they followed the Mack. The Essex was staying in close; its headlights were in sight. It was apparent they were not about to lose sight of the Mack.

The caravan had now reached Vallejo which was the crucial point. Instead of staying on course and heading for the Carquinez Strait, the Mack veered to the left and headed for Benicia instead — a dark, lonely stretch of road at this hour of the night. This was an unexpected route for the Essex. It followed along traveling an unfamiliar road.

"Well, Mike," said Pucci, "let's keep our fingers crossed. It's apparent Al hasn't changed his mind. He's going to go through with it — win, lose, or draw."

"I don't think those men back there have changed their minds either," said Mike. He was having some second thoughts. As he was snuffing out his cigar, he added in a concerned manner: "We're taking the long way home. Livia will be worried."

Pucci didn't answer. His mind was occupied with the thought of how he was going to carry out his part of the plan. The Essex, being a much heavier vehicle, could force them over an embankment.

The big Mack picked its way through the outskirts of Vallejo as it headed for the open road on its way to Benicia. Each man was mentally rehearsing his part. Unless properly executed with perfect timing, the plan could fail. If that were to happen, the four paesani would find themselves at the mercy of two armed and sinister characters of unknown reputation who were determined to carry out their mission without consideration for the well-being of anyone, especially Al.

"What you expect of this truck is beyond reason," said Primo somewhat worrisome.

"What are you worried about?"

"For one thing, stopping it. We're overloaded."

"Don't worry about it. These Searle air brakes work. They've been stopping trains for years." Al was trying to put Primo's mind at ease by reminding him that he was aware of the Saturday night raid on the warehouse. The pronounced flat spots on the huge tires were a dead giveaway.

Primo grinned as he thought back on the night of the raid. He hadn't told him the whole story, especially the fact that the Mack almost got away from him.

"I've never used the gear splitter with a full load like this, let alone shifting in and out of it at top speed like you're wanting to do. It could tear it up?"

"According to the manual, it can be done if you catch it at the right speed and motor rpm's. This special Brown-Lipe, high-low auxiliary transmission has been proven." Al's faith in the Mack was unshakable.

"What're your plans if we rip the gears out of it?" asked Primo in a serious, no-nonsense manner.

"Don't worry about the truck, it'll hold together. You better worry about what we're really faced with — those guys back there in the Essex have guns. They really mean business. If we're forced to stop, I want you to grab a tire iron and knock the headlights out of the Essex before they get a chance to use their guns. Without lights, we still have a chance. And don't pull your punches either; crack their skulls wide open. And don't lose your grip on the tire iron, whatever you do."

These sorts of defense tactics in the event of failure to disable the Essex, gave Primo the jitters. He wasn't the fighter that Al was. Failure was unthinkable.

The headlights of the Mack illuminated the narrow highway up ahead. Rumbling on through the night, it took up the better part of the pavement as it gently swayed from side to side. Working the steering wheel, Al was compensating for the drift.

"There it is up ahead," said Al. "When we top that grade,

there's a straight section of road down the other side and up over the next grade. That's where we'll take them, on the next grade."

The Mack growled its way up the grade. Not having a run at it made for slow going. The other two cars followed at a respectful distance. It was now up to the Reo to start slowing down and to not let the Essex get past, at least not yet. Al blinked the running lights on and off several times; that was Pucci's signal to put the plan in motion.

The instant the Mack topped the grade, Al started to pick off higher gears to get up as much speed as he could while going down the hill. The roar of the engine was just as pronounced coming down the hill as it was going up. The load sway was, by now, forcing the Mack to hug the center of this lonely stretch of highway. Fog drifting up from the Sacramento River brought forth a comment from Primo:

"We're none too early," he said with concern. "In another hour it will be pretty well fogged in."

"All we need is another few minutes," answered Al as he glanced in the rear view mirror. No one had topped the hill behind him as yet.

"Al, you're going pretty fast. Keep your eyes on the road. I'll give you the tachometer readings when you're ready."

"I'll also need the speedometer reading at the same time. I want to get the gear splitter into high range just as we hit the bottom of the grade–before we flatten out. You can start giving me the readings any time now."

"Holy Christ!" exclaimed Primo. "You're up over 35 miles an hour and still picking up speed. For God's sake, hang onto the wheel and don't take your eyes off the road."

Al was concentrating on his driving rather than Primo's concern. "At 38 miles an hour we should be at two thousand rpm's. The instant they come together, give it to me. We can't hold it there too long," he said while hanging onto the vibrating steering wheel with his left hand. His right hand was on the splitter lever protruding up through the floorboards.

"They're coming up. Get ready!" called out Primo. At the instant the two readings coincided, he called them out. Al let up on the throttle, then pushed the pedal disengaging the clutch. Primo continued the readings: "Speed still at 38, engine rpm's dropping fast. Get ready."

As the truck's engine wound down, Al waited for just the precise moment.

"Okay.! Fifteen hundred!" announced Primo excitedly.

With that, Al moved the lever forward gently but firmly as if feeling his way around the gearbox. The transition from low to high range was smooth enough. The clutch, now in its re-engage position, put the load back on the engine just as they flattened out now heading for the next grade several miles ahead.

Throttle to the floorboard, the Mack roared on picking up speed as the engine labored to bring up its rpms.

"For Christ's sake!" yelled out Primo in an alarmed manner. "You're going over 45! For God's sake, keep your eyes on the road. I'll watch for the others."

"It should hit at least 48, maybe 50 at two-thousand rpms. That'll be it!" shouted Al above the roar of the engine and the whistling of the wind through the open cab.

Primo had his eyes glued to the rear view mirror. He could make out the two sets of headlights coming down the grade behind them. "I can see the Reo swinging back and forth holding back the Essex," he announced. "No doubt about it, they're trying to pass it. They suspect we're trying to make a run for it all right."

"Good." said Al. "With a little luck, maybe they can be held off until we reach the grade up ahead." Then added: "Let's hope this fog doesn't get much thicker."

The big Mack was charging ahead like a runaway freight train. Overhanging tree branches swayed back and away from the gush of wind, only to snap back, plucked clean of their leaves. The leaves swirled and tumbled behind the Mack as it plunged through the fog-shrouded darkness at break-neck speed.

The roaring engine and high-pitched singing of gears, combined with the slapping of drive chains and grappling growl of rubber tires being pressed to pavement, were deafening to the ears. The two men were yelling at the tops of their voices in order to overcome the added scream of wind swirling through the open cockpit and rumble of barrels. The dim, upward glare of the instrument panel, outlining the shadowed facial features of these two determined men, gave them the appearance of Satan's own teamsters racing against time to snare the souls of sinners before being cleansed by the blessings of saints.

Pucci had his hands full in trying to keep the Reo from being run off the road by the heavier Essex. But, an outright collision was not in the Essex's best interest. Neither was a shootout with an officially marked vehicle. In either case, the Mack would make its getaway.

As planned, the Reo was succeeding in slowing down the Essex. The two vehicles were engaged in a risky game of tag, scattering gravel over the pavement as they rode the shoulder in their efforts to out-maneuver each other.

As the push and shove continued, the occupants of the Essex were bothered by the Reo's Fire Department markings. They had something to say:

"How the hell does the San Francisco Fire Department fit into this thing?" swore the driver. "What's their game, anyway?"

"I was wondering the same thing," came the answer. "Give the word and I'll blast 'em."

"No, put the gun away — can't take any chances — we want the truck first — save it for later."

The taillights of the Mack were disappearing in the distance. Needless to say, the Essex was desperate. The struggle to get past the Reo continued as they now headed out across the flat stretch.

Finally, as planned, Pucci allowed the Essex to gain a foothold. It raced past the Reo along the shoulder, kicking up dust and scattering gravel as it picked up speed. But by now, the Mack had gained a comfortable lead.

"God damn, look at them go!" said Pucci, relieved to have come out of that risky game without being shot at or run completely off the road.

Mike was being of little help. Every time he reached down to retrieve his hat, he'd be slammed to the floor. His contribution to the campaign was, simply — profanity.

"Go, you stupid imbeciles!" he cursed. "Wait until you catch up to Al. He'll take care of you," he said, waving them on with his hands as if they were waiting for his signal to move out fast. Mike's faith in Al was unshakable.

Plunging through patches of tule fog, the Mack raced across the flat. Regardless of chuck holes, Al held it in dead center of the pavement. Rumbling of barrels commingled with the rattling of iron.

The washboard effect of tires rolling over rough spots sent shuttering vibrations through the men's bodies. Fog-chilled wind numbed their faces. Eyes watering, they peered through and around the windshield, watching for anything that might loom up through the gathering dense fog.

"Damn the fog," cursed Al. "Get your hands on the air brake lever, just in case!"

Primo got the message. He didn't need an explanation as to its purpose. Anything in the way of stopping this hurtling mass was going to be O.K. with him. He had a firm grip on both the trailer and truck levers.

"This is sheer madness. We're going to get ourselves killed," pleaded Primo.

"Never mind. What's our speed?"

Primo was glad he asked. "The needle's against the peg," he answered.

No sooner had he said that, they could sense the Mack laboring and starting to slow down. Primo was relieved; they were now ascending the grade. The ear-splitting noise and biting wind was gradually subsiding.

"What's going on back there, can you tell?" asked Al.

Looking into the side mirror, Primo answered: "I'm sure the Essex got past Pucci. Other than that, it's too foggy to tell." He then commented about the grade:

"You're going to have to go through too many gears. It's going to slow you down too much each time you shift."

"We'll take it all in one shot through the splitter. At least we'll cut out most of them."

"Keeping up this kind of pressure on the engine is going to scatter it sure as hell. You better back off a little."

"No way. The truck will take it. It's a question of whether we can handle it," answered Al as he reached for the shift lever with his gloved right hand in preparation to drop the splitter into its low range. "Watch the tachometer. Give it to me at fifteen hundred — no less — then again at two thousand as I rev it up. We'll pick it up again there. At that point our speed should be in the neighborhood of 38, maybe 40. That's not too important, but give it to me anyway."

The speedometer read to a maximum of 50 miles per hour. Even though the Mack had some of these special features, it was not intended that it should ever reach that speed, loaded or unloaded. But the downhill run, plus the fact that they were able to get the gear splitter into the high range at the crucial moment, had been jamming the needle against the stop peg.

"Get ready!" yelled Primo. Although he would have liked to question these tactics, he didn't dare argue. Besides, this wasn't the time to do anything but follow instructions and hope for the best. It was at his insistence that Al was behind the wheel. But at the time, he had no idea it would result in this mad, hell-bent for destruction race through this fog-shrouded night. He called out again:"That's it! Fifteen hundred at 38!"

Al was set to shift anyway. The laboring engine and the feel of the truck told him it was time. His face showed the strain of the ordeal. Expressions coincided with each movement of feet, hands and body. His left foot released the clutch. His right foot let up on the accelerator. At that instant, his right hand pulled the lever to its neutral position.

The drive chains slapped at the sprockets every which way. The slack would normally be on the bottom during the pull, but now the slack immediately reversed itself since the drivers — being carried by the momentum — momentarily became the pullers. The men up front could detect this chain activity by the sound of its sorrowful, singing complaints and the tugging feelings that surged throughout the truck.

The massive combined transmission and differential case directly behind the auxiliary transmission "splitter" housed a conglomeration of huge gears that drove the first set of sprockets and chains connected to the first set of dual-wheels. A drive shaft came out the rear of this case and into a second, smaller differential case which housed another set of tough gears that drove the second set of sprockets and chains that were connected to the second set of dual-wheels. The various sounds emitted by all this machinery was a message that had to be interpreted correctly and instantly by the driver. In effect, the driver is part of the machine.

The man in command up front who was calling the shots had several important things to consider: ripping the gears out of the splitter, tearing up gears in the differential, twisting a drive shaft, or snapping a chain link, and if the engine were to quit, the air brakes would also fail. On a grade such as this, any one incident could spell disaster.

Al's feet were tap dancing to the beat of whirling chains and churning gears, double kicking the clutch while pumping the accelerator.

"She's coming up to two thousand!" Primo yelled as the engine wound up in a free-running, high-pitched roar.

At the instant Al got the word, his right hand gave the shift lever a good, hard tug. The stripping sound of gears was well pronounced as faster-coasting gears engaged the positive-turning slower gears. This was to be expected. The lever came back tight against the seat as his left foot allowed the clutch to re-engage putting the load back on the engine. His right foot put the accelerator to the floorboard.

"You got it! You done it!" yelled Primo joyfully.

The tug of chains let it be known that everything was still intact. The new surge of power challenged the uphill drag as the big Mack continued its forward thrust. The transition only took a fraction of a minute, but to the two buddies who were sweating out this unprecedented maneuver, it seemed like an eternity. As for Al, breathing had been ignored until the feat was performed. He was now concentrating on the various sounds emitting from the drivetrain. He finally said:

"It's a tough pull — keep your fingers crossed!"

The demand on the engine was severe. Five-inch pistons were pushing connecting rods down into the massive crankcase churning up a bath of oil so badly needed for maximum lubrication. Hot oil induced smoke being picked up by the huge blower fan directly behind the engine was being forced, along with cooling air, up through the two radiators mounted on either side of the cab. To see this monster coming at you through the night with its lit up huge blunt snout, smoke and heat vapors blowing out either side through gill-like radiators, gave the appearance of a prehistoric creature of sorts. It was a heart-stopping, fearsome sight.

The Mack's speed was now at 30 miles per hour and slowly dropping. The two men were now breathing easier. The threat of mechanical failure was past. Another minute or so would take them over the top. The fog thinned as they climbed.

The Essex's headlights could be seen piercing patches of tule fog as it raced across the flat. By the same token, its occupants were getting intermittent glimpses of the Mack's taillights as it ascended the grade.

"By the looks of it, they must be pulling up a grade," said the driver of the Essex.

"Yeah, I was thinking the same thing," growled his cohort. "That'll slow 'em down to a crawl. That cocky, son-of-a-bitch," he added, referring to Al.

"That bugger's in for a pistol whipping," snarled the driver in response. "Those Dago hijacking bastards; we'll put them out of business if it's the last thing we do."

Their anticipation of what they'd do to Al especially was overriding their common sense. Charging through this fog-shrouded night with the accelerator to the floorboard may very well be the last thing these two sinister characters ever do.

"You better drop it to a lower gear," suggested Primo. "Keep up the rpms," he added, somewhat commanding.

"Can you still see the Essex back there?" asked Al as he busied himself with the shifting procedure.

"Yeah, it's half way across the flat. They'll be on us in a couple of minutes."

"Let the bastards come," answered Al in a defiant and confident manner.

"They're coming up on the hill at a pretty fast clip. No sooner we top over, they'll be on us," said Primo.

"All right, from now on we're guessing. Grab the air-brake levers and stand by."

The Mack was now topping over the hill, holding its speed. The intention was to catch the Essex just over the top on the downhill side. Vision was still good enough despite the swirling fog that hung in the air. As the Mack topped over, the sky to the rear started to illuminate as the Essex neared the top of the grade.

"They're coming over the top!" yelled Primo.

"Yeah, I see them," said Al, glancing into the side mirror. While letting up on the accelerator and his left foot resting on the clutch, he shifted his right foot onto the brake pedal in readiness to apply pressure to the massive brake bands on the drive sprockets, as the Mack started to descend the grade.

"We'll give it a couple more seconds," he said as he reached for the light switch. Al was purposely holding the Mack in dead center of the road. The Essex would be forced to hit it or, in an attempt to avoid collision, leave the road and roll down the embankment.

The fog-shrouded sky behind the truck lit up indicating the Essex was topping the grade. Within seconds it would come barreling down the opposite side, it too hugging the center of the road. Its two occupants were anxious to pick up the Mack's taillights again for fear it might turn off the main highway and ditch them. They were not about to let this happen. The score they had to settle with Al was heavy on their minds.

"They can't be too far ahead. That grade had to slow them down," stated the driver.

"Even with this fog, we can't help but see their taillights. We'll pick 'em up again, stay with it." The cohort was confident. He encouraged the driver to keep up the pace.

At the precise instant, Al shouted: "Now!" At the same time, switching off the entire lighting system of both truck and trailer. The whole mass was hurtling along in complete darkness as Primo pulled hard on both air-brake levers, locking up the wheels on both truck and trailer instantly, while Al came down hard on both clutch and brake pedal, locking up the drive sprockets directly at the massive differential, thus avoiding snapping the drive chains. The instant deceleration and halting, forward motion, was felt by both men and machine. The huge tires, grappling with the pavement, sent off clouds of smoke in their attempt to overcome the tremendous forces of inertia exerted by some 35 tons of payload, plus the added tons of iron that made up this thunderous mass hurtling headlong through the darkness.

Arms outstretched, Al held the huge steering wheel steady with both hands, his feet pressing the clutch and brake pedals to the floorboard as much to support himself against the forward thrust as the need to keep the sprockets locked up in conjunction with the locked-up wheels.

Primo, having seen what had happened in the Saturday night raid with Vasco almost going through the windshield, was prepared. He still had a firm grip on the brake levers, but he also had one foot propped up against the dash.

Neither man had anything to say until the whole mass came to an ear-splitting, screeching, snarling halt amongst a cloud of burnt rubber-induced smoke.

"Okay, let go of the brakes!" commanded Al as he, too, abruptly let up on the brake pedal. Now the remaining stop lights faded out completely, leaving the truck and trailer engulfed in complete darkness amongst a cloud of smoke intermixed with fog. At the instant the air-brake levers were pushed forward, a hissing blast of air pierced the ghostly stillness of the night. Now there was deathly silence. From a dead stop, the Mack started to roll again, slowly, downhill. As the Essex leveled off, it, too, starting its descent, however with accelerator pressed to the floorboards. Its headlights illuminated the mixture of smoke and fog up ahead. Nothing could be seen beyond the seemingly wall that lingered across the road.

The glare from the Essex headlights flashed on the Mack's rear view mirror.

Primo in an excited exclamation yelled out: "Here they come, like bats out of hell!"

"Come and get it, suckers!" Al added in a similar fashion.

At that instant, the Essex burst into the lingering cloud, but never came out the other side.

The big Mack, as heavy as it was, lurched forward from the tremendous force of the impact caused when the sedan slammed headlong into the end of the trailer in a thunderous, glass-shattering, metal-compressing roar.

"We got 'em," said Al in a satisfied no-nonsense manner. "You can forget those bastards for awhile."

"Holy Christ!–they hit us dead center," said Primo. Then added in a softer almost sympathetic manner, "We might have killed them. Maybe we ought to take a look."

"No! Looking isn't going to help them any," answered Al firmly. "Stay in the cab! We're going to get our ass out of here. If they're believers, God will handle it. If not, the hell with 'em!" He then switched on the lights of the Mack as it rolled away from the devastating scene.

"Now, listen, for God's sake. We can't just drive off and leave them like that."

"The hell we can't!" With that Al picked off the proper gear to match the rolling speed of the truck, then added: "We're not about to hang around here to try to explain that mess back there. Pull yourself together. We may not be out of this thing yet. We've got the ferry to catch."

Primo felt chilled. He had a feeling all along what the end result might be, but he just wasn't prepared for the inevitable. All the years he had been driving as a teamster had taught him to be very cautious about letting an accident like this happen; and yet, here now, he was a party to a scheme which brought on an intentional accident and caused disaster for two unfortunate men who had the misfortune of underestimating the determination of four, seemingly simple paesano descendants of the fun-loving Etruscans of ancient times.

CHAPTER 26

The scene left behind by the Mack was, to say the least, not pretty. If, in fact, the old Priest's prayers were "indeed" being answered, it would seem that the good Lord could have used a little discretion as to the method of removing the threat of these men from the midst of the paesani. Apparently when the old Priest gave his blessing, it was intended for everyone in sight of the Mack. But the Essex (with its two occupants) was out of sight and out of range.

This, then, opened the door for the Devil himself to step in. One can imagine his satisfaction, riding in the back seat of the Essex, gleefully urging the driver on through this ghostly, foggy night of death and destruction. Surely, he meant to have them dead, so that their souls could be carted off to Hell in his fiery chariot of despair. He always had room for a couple of extra passengers.

The scene was horribly sickening. The hissing sound of steam emitting from the compressed radiator gave the impression of a huge snake having been stationed there by the Devil to guard his prize catch until their souls were firmly established in Hell.

Pucci and Mike saw the taillights of the Mack disappear over the hill. Then within seconds, the taillights of the speeding Essex also disappeared.

"Those poor bastards are sure asking for it," said Pucci with an icy calm.

"Oh, they're going to get it all right! One way or another, Al will stop them." answered Mike in an assuring manner.

They had no idea what to expect as they cautiously approached the crest of the hill.

The Reo pulled up short as its headlights flashed on the

carnage that lay in the middle of the road. For whatever reason, reality is hard to envision until it hits you smack between the eyes. This was a gruesome sight.

"Holy smokes! Look at that!" Mike blurted out as he leaned forward wide-eyed.

"God damn it! This is bad," cursed Pucci as he viewed the scene of twisted, compressed metal. The positions of the two former occupants of the Essex pretty well told them what had taken place. There was no doubt the plan had worked well. As a matter of fact, too well. It appeared obvious, the Essex had come up on the Mack much too fast to take evasive action. There was no indication that the brakes had ever been applied. The impact had sent both men crashing through the windshield like thunderbolts. The bloodied body of the driver lay forward and to the left of the crumpled sedan. Pieces of the wooden steering wheel lay by the palm of his now relaxed hand, indicating that the instant horrifying thought of collision had frozen his hand to the wheel in a death-like grip.

The passenger was apparently airborne at the instant of impact. No doubt, he was catapulted through the windshield, splattering headlong at some sixty miles per hour against the first row of barrels across the rear of the trailer. Bleeding profusely about the face, fatal head injuries were apparent. He was kicking and jerking as he lay just ahead of the compressed front end of the Essex. The throes of death triggered uncontrollable frenzy. His fractured arms flapped crazily splattering blood every which way. Bones protruded out through flesh, no doubt fractured in an attempt to protect his head with his arms from the impact of the windshield. Death is never pleasant, but to view it in this fashion was outright nauseating; a vomit-inducing experience at best.

Pucci was able to cope with death. As a fireman, he occasionally had to deal with it. He'd seen horrified, unblinking eyes, staring in disbelief. The sight of death was ever present of mind. He made a quick sign of the cross as he said: "I was afraid something like this might happen. Now what the hell do we do?"

With Mike it was different. He had difficulty dealing with death, gruesome or otherwise, and reacted accordingly.

"Let's get the hell out of here," he answered in a fearful and unsteady voice. "And we better hurry." He dared not make the sign of the cross, for he feared the devil as much as he did God. He preferred not to antagonize either by taking sides.

They drove along the shoulder of the road to get past the wreck. The scene they left behind was dark and gruesome. Neither man looked back. It was almost as if they were scared of coming face to face with Satan. They didn't particularly care for his kind of congratulations, nor to shake hands with him.

The paesani were God-fearing, fun-loving, nonviolent men like their Etruscan ancestors were two thousand years before. They didn't premeditate willful violence.

They reacted to violence only when forced upon them. This could be lived with. God forgave them for their reckless horseplay for it was intent that brought out his wrath, not the reaction to self-preservation.

The fog suddenly disappeared. Its absence was noticed by both the drivers of the Mack and the Reo. The thought crossed their minds: "Was this a coincidence?"

In their minds they were rehashing the events of a few moments before. Why was the stage so perfectly set? Two grades set apart, perfectly spaced with a straight running stretch between them? Fog swirling around, not enough to obscure vision until blended with rubber-induced smoke? The Mack, overloaded and stressed, pushed to unreasonable limits, never once faltering?

The remarkable performance of the Essex? Although not a powerful, fast car, yet careening over the top of the grade as if fueled by the fires of Hell? Is it reasonable to believe that both Heaven and Hell had a hand in this? Each one looking out for his own? How could a Christian, believe otherwise? The old Priest back at the winery could certainly explain that all this was not a coincidence. No, not at all. For the moment, the thought put their minds at ease.

Up ahead, the running lights of the Mack could be seen, winding toward the quaint little city of Benicia. Pucci was pushing the Reo along as well. His intention was to catch up to the Mack before it reached the ferry slip so that both vehicles could board together for the crossing.

"I suppose that's the Reo coming up behind us, don't you think?" asked Al hopefully.

"It's them all right. They'll be up to us by the time we hit town," answered Primo.

Once again Primo expressed his concern for the two intruders caught up in the demolition of the Essex. But Al put him down with a sharp response: "For Christ's sake, Primo, back off! Those guys aren't Sunday school teachers. We'd be better off if they're . . . " Al stopped short of saying, "dead". He viewed the affair as a duel between two pieces of machinery. So somebody got hurt; all part of the game.

"I think they hit us too hard to have survived. That's what's bothering me," confessed Primo.

Al sensed that Primo was fiddling with the gold crucifix dangling from around his neck. He realized that Primo was praying. He was touched by it. The old Priest came to mind; he wondered: "Did God have a hand in this? If so, was it the intent to impart the intruders' souls to Hell impaled on the tines of Satan's fork?"

Primo, realizing his actions were noticeable, let the crucifix slip from his fingers, then glanced at Al, who appeared to be in a trance, no longer reflecting a tough determined expression. To think that Al had remorseful feelings made him feel better. He renewed the fondling of the crucifix.

Al broke his fixed expression with a swallow of accumulated saliva. Without looking in Primo's direction, he addressed the situation at hand:

"We're coming into town. We better take it easy. This thing will attract enough attention as it is without our roaring in."

"Bring it down gradually or the backfire and rumbling of barrels will arouse the whole town," responded Primo.

The Mack rumbled slowly down through the quiet streets of Benicia towards the ferry slip. Since the ferry boat was still halfway across the river on its way back from the Martinez side, there would be a ten or fifteen-minute wait.

Al pulled the Mack up behind the single file row of waiting cars. Pucci pulled up directly behind him. The Reo's headlights illuminated the rear end of the trailer.

"Mike, look — the canvas tarp — the barrels — over to the right," instructed Pucci.

"Switch off the lights. Quick!" said Mike. He didn't like what he saw either. The tarp along the bottom portion of the fold was noticeably smeared with fresh blood, as was the bottom row of barrels.

Both men scrambled out of the Reo. Mike headed up the

right side of the trailer to meet Primo who was now walking back toward him.

Pucci started out first to untie the tarp, but he suddenly changed his mind as headlights could be seen coming down the street behind him. He quickly jumped back into the Reo, started up the engine and set the throttle at a fast idle, at the same time engaging the water pump. He scrambled back out and proceeded to unravel the fire hose as he jerked the lever of the water valve to its open position.

Al, walking back along the left side, saw the maneuver. He stepped up his pace. "What's the matter? Why the fire hose?", he asked as he glanced around the undercarriage looking for something to justify the need for Pucci's action.

"Get back there and stop that car coming down behind us! Don't let it come in too close. Tell 'em you've got hot brakes — there could be a fire — tell 'em anything — keep them away."

Al took a quick glance at the back of the trailer. He didn't see anything unusual because he wasn't looking high enough. Besides, the dim lighting shadowed the back end of the trailer. He started walking back up to carry out Pucci's instructions. As he did so, he heard Pucci utter in a low tone:

"Damn it, there's blood all over this goddamned trailer."

The thought of blood sent chills up and down Al's spine. He quickened his pace. Hands waving, he signaled the car to stop. However, instead of stopping in line with the rest of the cars, it pulled off to the right and parked off to one side. The only occupant, the driver, stepped out as Al walked towards him.

"Having a problem?" he called out.

"Hot brakes," Al answered. "No big deal."

By now Pucci had a high-pressure stream of water concentrated on the blood-spattered canvas and barrels. Fortunately the blood hadn't had a chance to set up.

The slip tender left his little shack and was walking up toward the Mack. He had never seen a truck and trailer like this before. As he approached the truck, Pucci intentionally directed the stream of water over the top of the trailer and in his direction, forcing him to take evasive action. He changed course to avoid getting wet and was now walking toward Al and the other man whom the slip tender apparently knew.

"Jim," he called out, "have you ever seen a truck and trailer like this before?"

"Not around these parts. As a matter of fact, now that you mention it, I've never seen one anywhere. That's why I came down, to take a look."

The slip tender chuckled as he added: "Neither have I. God damn, it's a brute."

The fellow called Jim directed a question to Al: "Where the hell did that little fire truck come from? It's certainly not from around here."

Thinking fast, Al answered: "I really don't know. He just happened to be here waiting to board the ferry, I guess."

"Lucky for you. I've seen hot brakes set trucks on fire. By the way, what're you hauling?" came the next question.

Again Al had to think fast. "Molasses," he answered. "Pretty heavy stuff."

"Oh, yeah! Molasses is heavy all right." Then he added: "That little ferry will have its work cut out for it tonight with that truck and trailer," the man called Jim stated, directing the comment to the slip tender.

"There's the ferry. I'll have to get back to my truck. Nice talking to you fellows."

As he walked up to Pucci and the others, Al said in a low tone: "Pretend we're strangers and don't know each other."

"Why?" asked Mike.

"I think that guy's the town constable," answered Al as he headed for the truck's cab. Primo didn't say a word. He, too, immediately turned and headed for the sanctuary of the truck's cab. Once in the cab, Primo commented:

"We better hope to Christ they let us on the ferry — it ain't very big."

They watched the slip tender walk down to meet the ferry. The first mate, having seen the big Mack up the line, stepped off to join the slip tender. Cars were coming off the ferry as the two men made their way up to the Mack. They stepped around the front to the driver's side. Only the tops of their heads could be seen as they came around the hood. Looking up at Al, the first mate asked: "What's your gross weight?"

This was to be a night of all nights for Al. His ability to

respond with quick reflexes and fast, sharp answers was being tested at every step of the way.

"Thirty tons," he answered briskly as if he had just weighed the truck.

"Appears to be a hell of a lot heavier than that," put in the mate. "I'm talking about both truck and trailer," he added as if Al had misunderstood the question.

"Yeah, I understood what you said. I've got the weight tag right here," Al said as he started fumbling around in his pockets in the dimly-lit cab.

"Did I give you the tag?" he asked of Primo.

"No, you didn't. The last time I saw it, it was sticking out of your shirt pocket," came the answer.

They were both lying like hell, but at least they were not contradicting each other.

"No doubt the darkness makes it loom up even bigger than it is," commented the tender.

"Yeah, you're probably right. We'll load most of the cars on the opposite side first," said the mate.

"Hell, you don't have that many cars. Why not put them all on the opposite side?" said the tender knowing damned well that the Mack's gross weight exceeded well over the stated amount.

"Well, okay," answered the mate. Then addressing Al, he said: "Stay where you're at until we get all the others on. When you see my signal, pull on. Hug the center as much as you can. We'll stop you dead center of the ferry." He then instructed the tender: "What the hell, charge him for 30 tons."

Pucci had his head hanging halfway out the window of the Reo, wondering what was going on up front, when the slip tender walked up and instructed him to pull around the Mack and follow the cars that were now loading on the left side of the ferry.

The Reo pulled around and passed the Mack. Mike turned his head and looked into the cab of the Mack as they went by. Both Primo and Al were looking straight at him with slight grins on their faces. The headlight glare was enough to light up Mike's face and disclose his ghostly look.

"Old Mike is scared to death," commented Al in a respectful manner.

"He probably thinks we're going to be left behind,"

commented Primo.

The Mack literally crawled onto the right side of the ferry boat. At first, it was tilted way up from the weight of the already loaded cars. But as the Mack made its way on the ferry, it tilted back down until the water lapped onto the edge of the deck. Once on board and in position, the ferry leveled off with the exception of a pronounced tilt to the right. Apparently, the truck outweighed the cars. The ferry settled down, then pulled away from the slip as the four men got together once again.

"What was going on back there?" asked Pucci. "For a while, I didn't think they were going to let you on."

"If Al had told them the truth, we wouldn't have got on," answered Primo. "For Christ's sake, the truck and trailer alone are heavy enough for this ferry while empty. Add another some 35-plus tons of cargo to that." He hesitated a moment before continuing. "Holy Christ! Wait till this thing hits the main current out there."

Once into the main current, the little ferry boat did indeed have its work cut out for it. The Captain was at the wheel keeping its bow angled upstream so as not to drift off course. The ferry took on the appearance of a fully loaded truck with its right side springs broken and a misaligned frame, moving somewhat sideways down the highway.

"I hope you Dagos know how to swim," said Al, looking straight at Mike. Mike's nervous reaction to Primo's comment was still apparent; he didn't respond.

"I'll breathe easier once we're across the county line. I'd rather see the whole damn thing sink rather than get caught after that mess you guys left behind," commented Pucci.

"Was it that bad?" asked Al.

"Worse than you could possibly imagine."

Al was looking right at Pucci. He could see the sickening expression on his face as he said it. Shaking his head slowly as if truly disappointed, Al said:

"Those poor saps. I never in God's world thought they would hit us dead center. The worst I expected was maybe a glancing blow or that they would lose control and roll over, but not killing the poor bastards."

"Yeah, I know," said Pucci in a slow, understandable manner. "But unfortunately that's the way it turned out. Let's agree on one thing for sure. Let's not talk about this ever again, not among ourselves, or mention a word to anyone, immediate family and friends included."

They had no trouble agreeing on this.

Al broke up the gruesome conversation with a humorous comment such as his witty mind was capable of: "What you Dagos are going through to get this stuff, even getting it for nothing, is paying too much."

The comment was meant to be funny although there was a great deal of truth to the statement. However, aside from the fatal disaster, they were well satisfied and content with their achievement. And such as it was with these Italian immigrants, they could find something to be pleased about even in the face of the end of the world. God intended them to be this way.

CHAPTER 27

Julio looked at his watch again. It was 3:00 a.m. He had been up for several hours wondering and waiting. "They should have been here by now," he stated.

His cousin, Matteoli, joined him. He, too, was concerned. "Mike said no later than midnight. Do you suppose they had trouble?" he asked seriously.

"Maybe, but that's a long trip. A couple hours more or less can be expected."

Julio was sounding reassuring, but deep in his mind he felt that, if anything, they should have been back even before midnight. He couldn't hide his concerns very well. He walked out the front door with a cup of coffee in his hand, made his way to the end of the porch and stood there, looking in the direction of Mike's ranch house. Matteoli followed him out as he also expressed the concern he was feeling.

"There's a light in the kitchen. Livia must be up with the baby," commented Julio.

"Yes" said Matteoli, then added: "He stays awake crying all night then sleeps all day." His next comment caused Julio to chuckle with laughter. "Mike made a mistake. He conceived him when the moon was wrong. I've always told him never to plant seeds until at least three days past the full moon — always on a declining moon."

After the comment was made, he too found it to be somewhat ridiculous and joined in on the laughter, for it was meant to be a joke in the first place. It would have ended there were it not for Contini overhearing the comment as he stood in the doorway in his longjohns and bare feet.

192

"You men are laughing about a very serious matter," announced Contini in a scholarly manner. He then continued: "Are you not aware of the tremendous pull the moon has on planet Earth: its tides; its inhabitants; the animals; you and I as well? Do you not know, that the Portuguese dairy men don't breed their cows unless the moon is in its right position?"

"You don't say?" interrupted Matteoli as he gave thought to a challenging argument. "And why is that?" he asked.

"Yes, I do say. And I will tell you why." Contini was now on a roll. It's not often he can out-best this man. "It's important to have the calf born at the right position of the moon — at its strongest point of pull — makes it easier on the cow. The calf practically comes out on its own — it literally hangs out of the womb," stated Contini.

Matteoli was impressed with Contini's remarkable knowledge of husbandry. He looked at Contini standing there in his longjohns with deep admiration, then walked to the very end of the porch, leaned out as far as he could, looked out across the vegetable fields at the late-rising waning moon that could be seen over the hills across the Bay to the east. He studied it for a few minutes before turning back to face Contini.

"Would you say that the moon at this hour of the morning could have enough pull to accomplish the fete you have just described?" he asked in all seriousness.

Julio was now leaning against the corner post of the porch. The ever-pleasant smile he was so much admired for was now forming across his face. He had a pretty good idea that his witty cousin, Matteoli, had come up with a good counterblow that would eliminate Contini as a contender for the world's championship of philosophers.

"Of course it could. The hour of day has nothing to do with it. Why do you ask such a foolish question?" answered Contini with a wise, old owlish look, complete with bushy eyebrows.

"Well! I . . . you see," stammered Matteoli with raised eyebrows, intentionally humble, faking defeat, "I notice your dong dangling out the fly of your underwear. No doubt the moon pulled it out as well." As he said this, his right hand was extended with its index finger wriggling in a curved downward, limp manner depicting Contini's appearance.

Contini's jaw dropped as he quickly glanced down in the direction of his crotch. A wide-eyed expression came over him like he had just been dowsed with a bucket of cold water. This, of course, explained the drafty feeling brought about by a missing button on his fly. The fact was, he got caught with his dong dangling. He hastily reinstated his penis back into the comfort of his longjohns and retreated back in the house, grumbling disgustedly as he stomped along. Others, that had been listening in, joined the two cousins in hilarious laughter. The joke was passed on from one bedroom to the other with each group having their own set of clowns reenacting the scene in the fashion they thought to be the funniest. The joke by now had been altered and magnified to incredible proportions. It reached its apex when someone injected the subject of wine, and its relation to the moon. Therefore, Matteoli was called upon to settle that issue as well.

"Yes," said Matteoli, "the position of the moon does have a definite relationship with wine. Wine should always be racked or bottled on the declining moon for maximum clarity and purity."

"Ha, you see," said Contini. "Even he admits it, and if it applies to wine, then it applies to other things as well."

The mere mention of wine united them once again for this was one subject they were in agreement on. Their great thirst for it, dictated it.

The old house seemed to rattle and roll in harmony with the paesani's laughter and horseplay. From the kitchen window, Livia, up with the baby, saw the lights come on over at the paesani's house. She could also hear the laughter and wa-hooping that broke the still of darkness. It was a welcome sound. It assured her that God was close by. She, as were the paesani, was concerned. Mike and the others should have been here by now.

It was late, but still dark, when the Mack, followed by the Reo, pulled in the driveway of Mike's ranch. Needless to say, the paesani were jubilant when they saw the Mack's headlights illuminate the buildings across the vegetable field. A contingency of them was immediately dispatched to Mike's ranch with lanterns. This time, extreme care was exercised so as to not cause damage such as the one previous trip when the Mack tore down the hen house. They were being extra careful. Men with lanterns guided the truck through Mike's yard around the right of the sheds and then to the backside of the big barn. Here the Mack parked in front of the barn doors.

Livia, guided by Julio, followed the truck around back through the semi-darkness. She was surprised to see Al step down from the Mack; but then, by now her life was full of surprises. She was happy to see him regardless of the reason for his being there. As Mike let himself out of the Reo, her first question was:

"Michele, have you had any breakfast?"

"No," he answered wearily. "We thought it best not to stop for breakfast. I'm sure the others are hungry, and so am I."

"Good," she said. "I'll prepare something for the four of you — don't be long." She then made her way back to the house.

Mike was making his way towards the Mack when Julio intercepted him. "Mike. Tell me, did something go wrong? You men appear to be worried as well as weary."

The lantern's glare held at Julio's side was enough to disclose Mike's solemn expression as he answered:

"This is one matter that would be best not discussed. Hopefully, you'll understand."

"I was afraid it might be something of an unpleasant nature; thank God you're here."

"Julio, I've already thanked him enough times. Hopefully, he'll understand as well." No more need be said, for Julio understood.

"Livia will need some help with breakfast," said Julio. And with that, he made his way towards the house stopping briefly to extinguish his lantern, his pleasant, mild features fading in the semi-darkness.

The men milled around the Mack. They listened attentively to each creak and crack as the metal cooled off. It would be unloaded at daylight without having to break their backs in the process. Preparations had been made. The one thing these men had in common was their admiration for Pucci's ability to mastermind these hijacking raids. However, unbeknownst to them, this time, Pucci had misjudged his adversaries. Neither did they know what part Al had played in making this one successful, or the methods used.

Daylight was breaking fast. Livia (with the help of Julio) was preparing breakfast. Mike and the three others were walking back out to the truck. Some of the other paesani were on their way over from the adjoining ranch walking along the dirt road connecting the two barnyards. The barn doors were swung open. Some discussion took place as to how the unloading ramp should be used and how and where the first row should be started. Those few paesani present thought they understood what should be done. The others about to join them would follow their instructions. Mike heard Livia's call to breakfast.

"Come on, let's go!" he said. "They can unload the truck without us. We'll have breakfast, then a few hours' rest. It's just what we need."

They turned and walked away leaving the few men to get things set up, satisfied that the unloading procedure was understood. Mike added a final comment: "At least, for once, they appear to be sober."

A few minutes later, the rest of the crew showed up to start the unloading. They were all still in a fairly joyful mood carried over from the earlier hilarious encounter between Matteoli and Contini.

Three men up on the truck were to position the barrels on the rail-type ramps. Others on either side of the ramp stood on raised platforms and at ground level. They would control the barrels as the top man would ease them down. The two men at the bottom end would roll them out of the way and place them in their final resting place. It so happens that neither of these two men or Vasco up on the top end of the ramp were present during the earlier instruction session.

The first barrel was let down. It reached the bottom just fine. As it was being rolled aside, Alberto yelled out to Vasco as he was about to ease the second barrel to the others below.

"Hey, Vasco! What end does Mike want us to start from?"

Well, Vasco had no idea but, nevertheless, the question must be answered.

Now, as one well knows, an Italian, in order to give an "I don't know answer," must gesture with both hands. The arms are held close to the body straight down the sides with elbows jammed against the rib cage, forearms straight out, both palms open to the sky as if checking for raindrops. At the instant words are spoken, both hands venture away from each other, left to left, and right to right, as the shoulders jerk upward at the same instant. With this gesture, the words "who knows" are spoken from pursed lips.

Well, this procedure was followed right to the letter. Vasco let go of the barrel. Both hands came up in position in order to get his tongue in gear for the spoken words. At that instant, the heavy barrel started down the steep ramp on its own. It picked up speed instantly. It careened down the ramp like a rumbling run-away freight train. With the exception of the clickety clack of wheels to rails, hissing of steam, and the dismal howling sound of a train whistle, it resembled old Engine #99 coming down the grade with wide open throttle. The rumble and creaking sound of stressed

timber rose above the yelling and scrambling among the paesani in their effort to get clear of the ramp. The barrel, hell bent for destruction, shot past the men on either side. They made no attempt to stop it. In a clowning gesture, several men saluted as it zoomed on by. It was now traveling at the maximum speed that gravity could dictate. It reached the bottom of the ramp where it leveled off for several yards before hitting the back wall of the barn. The momentum of the 600-pound barrel sent it across the floor in a flash. It hit the wall with a splintering crash, redwood boards shattered into kindling. Those that chose to resist the impact were popped from their supporting wood members and sent flying through the air. Their square nails were never intended to hold back such a missile launched from a catapult.

The barrel continued on its journey of destruction. The next target was the feed shed. Directly in its path, a plank of some sort was lying on the ground. Its position was such that it acted like a ski ramp sending the barrel in an upward direction, therefore causing it to hit the shed half way up the side. As the barrel emerged out the opposite side, the entire shed exploded as if hit by a huge cannonball. The shed was thoroughly pulverized with its contents scattered helter skelter. Fortunately, the barrel was now losing its momentum as it thumped back down onto the ground sending out earth-shaking vibrations as it rolled and bounced out across the yard churning up a cloud of dust. It came to rest up against the basement door with a sharp thump, sending vibrations throughout the house. It appeared as if it was purposely intended to be rolled into the basement. Needless to say, Livia and the others at breakfast were startled by the rapid succession of thundering crashes, vibrations, and commotion that shattered the peacefulness of the early morning. Each person had a different interpretation as to the cause of the disturbance and, therefore, reacted accordingly.

Mike leaped from his chair and headed for the back door grabbing a white dishtowel along the way for the purpose of waving a flag of surrender. He felt certain that the revenue agents had caught up to their operation and were lobbing mortar shells into the yard.

Pucci, reacting to his fireman's instinct, grabbed his fireman's cap and headed in the same direction. He assumed an explosion had occurred and a fire would follow.

Primo didn't bother picking up anything but speed. He raced

past Mike and Pucci, out the back door, down the steps, and into the dust-filled yard. He felt sure that one of those nuts tried to move the Mack and it got away from him, therefore churning its way through the buildings and yard like a war tank. He was peering through the dust, poised and ready to grab onto it as it came by, like hopping a moving freight train.

Al did the logical thing by following Primo, but was having second thoughts about the whole affair. What he first thought to be a joyride was turning out to be more of a military campaign.

Livia, encouraged by Julio — the earthquake of 1906 still fresh on his mind — gathered up her three children and headed out the front door and away from the house. Her children's safety was all that mattered to her.

A half-dozen men came trotting through the dust in hot pursuit of the barrel. With clenched fists, arms swinging in rhythm with their steps, all eyes were looking upward at Mike as if paying tribute to Caesar. They looked like a group of gladiators heading into the dusty arena of the Coliseum in Rome to retrieve a fallen comrade.

Seeing the barrel at the basement door and the men marching up to it, Mike thought they were rolling it into the basement with the intentions of tapping it. This thought caused him to fly into a rage. He cut loose with a barrage of cuss words not becoming to the great Caesar. He proceeded to berate not only the men present, but also their ancestors, both living and dead, and including the ships that brought them here in the first place. The old country that produced them was also well defined in his barrage of insults. In the meantime, the men wasted no time in rolling the barrel back to the barn where it belonged. For they knew that Mike was justified in his behavior even though his reason was wrong. His final and parting words were:

"No wonder they call you Dagos. Never a day goes by that you don't have wine on the mind of your crazy heads!"

Having regained their senses, Mike and the rest of the occupants of the house returned to the matter of breakfast. There was no sense getting more upset by assessing damages now. It could wait until after breakfast. As usual, Mike caught hell from Livia. In her mind, whatever happened for whatever reason was surely his fault. No matter what explanation he submitted, it was not sufficient cause to relieve him of total responsibility. As far as she was concerned, the paesani were like children. They should be guided, not condemned.

Back at the barn there was great relief in the fact that no one was injured. It was now a matter of engaging in argument as to who was at fault and why. An Italian never makes a mistake on his own. It may appear that way, but when all facts are in and all arguments heard, you will find yourself in complete confusion as to who or what caused the incident. The obvious one to speak first on the matter was Vasco who let go of the barrel in the first place:

"You see what you have done!" addressing Alberto. "If you didn't know where to start, why didn't you leave the job to someone who did know?"

"Me?" answered Alberto as if in great surprise. "My fault, you say?"

"Yes, you! That's exactly who I am referring to."

"Who else should I have asked?" pleaded Alberto. "You are up there like a king on a throne. When a person needs an answer to a question, he should ask the highest man, and you are the highest."

"And you, Gino!" said Vasco addressing the first man below him alongside the ramp. "Once I let go of the barrel, it is your obligation to take control, is it not?"

"Oh, yes. Of course. But was that a barrel that went by?" snorted Gino. "I thought it was a cable car that had lost its grip on the cable. If I had known it was a barrel, I would have grabbed at it gladly and passed it down to Santi so he could have broken his arm as well."

By now the accusations were pretty well distributed among the group when the great philosopher Contini, who was much better at philosophy than working, announced that he knew without a doubt where the fault should lie. Before proceeding further, he looked down at his crotch to be sure his fly was buttoned. This act in itself brought things to a standstill. All work stopped. No one wanted to miss anything this man had to say or the rebuttal that was sure to come from Matteoli.

"The fault lies with the fact that you were all born in Italy and therefore of Italian extraction: a mixture of untraceable nationalities that range from North Africa to the South, Asia to the East, Europe to the North, and the Rock of Gibraltar to the West, with the open sea beyond that."

The men were attentive and really paying attention so they could fully comprehend what Contini had uncovered in their genes. Matteoli relaxed. His rebuttal would not be needed for he sensed what was coming. Contini would even the score for their making sport at his expense earlier in the morning.

Contini continued: "Were it not for the ambitions of Julius Caesar that caused the Roman Empire to overflow across these aforementioned lands, this mixture would not have taken place in the first place. Therefore, because of the recruiting of all sorts of men and women that took place as armies marched from one ethnic society to another, the cross-breeding that took place produced a new breed of . . ." At this instant a new voice added the word "jackass" to the rest of Contini's sentence. He was delighted to see Mike standing in the newly made opening as he added: "Yes, that is the very word I was about to say," said Contini.

Mike stepped through the opening and interrupted him again. Then continued in a very formal manner:

"What Mr. Contini is trying to tell you is, Jesus Christ's donkey was breeding Julius Caesar's mare while the two men were discussing the question as to who or what created an Italian. God answered their question in part by producing a new kind of animal, a 'jackass'. The product of love instigated by his magic. But the magic that God sprinkled to perform this great feat spilled over on your ancestors as well, therefore producing more kinds of 'jackasses', only with shorter ears."

Contini interrupted at this point. "Exactly what I was going to say!" he announced. Then added: "So you see, none of you are at fault at all. It was the carelessness of the good Lord in the first place that caused the incident." He knew he had them this time, dead to rights.

"Bravo, Contini!" Matteoli announced. He concurred as if he had spoken the words himself. As for Mike, he couldn't help but join in on the boisterous laughter that followed. After all, what the hell would life be like without the good fellowship of his paesani. The barn is nothing but boards, but these men are God's creation put on this earth because they were needed to lift the spirit of their fellow man.

Al's comment helped prolong the laughter and gaiety as they worked:

201

"Who needs a circus when you have clowns like this around?" he said.

The unloading complete, the Mack was moved over to the paesani's barn. Now it would be reloaded with the same equivalent amount of barrels. However, filled with water instead of wine. By late afternoon, the job was complete. The Mack was now ready for the last leg of the journey: deliver the barrels, supposedly filled with wine, directly to the freighter for loading. Primo and Al would be there at the dock at 9:00 p.m. as scheduled.

"Al, be sure to give your wife my best wishes," said Livia as the men were about to leave. The empty pots and pans still sitting on the dining room table were testimony to a fine, old-fashioned Italian dinner.

Al turned to Livia and gave her a customary hug. "Not only will I do that, but I'll also tell her that you are the best cook in the world. The 'baccala' and 'polenta' were out of this world."

In her mind, Al was leaving to go home. She had some idea of the methods being used to acquire this continuous supply of wine; however, this was limited to what could be determined by the activities in and about the ranch. The ordeal that these men were being subjected to was certainly not within the grasp of an immigrant housewife and mother of three children. The paesani were careful not to say too much while in her presence. They understood the anguish this could cause.

Al, too, was careful not to divulge the extent of what had taken place the night before or the fact that they were about to embark on the second phase of this "double hijack" that could prove to be a real tough bugger to pull off. He mentioned nothing of the fact that if all went well, he would be there for breakfast next morning. The concerned glances exchanged with Primo went unnoticed as he bid her goodnight.

CHAPTER 28

With Al at the wheel and Primo seated alongside, the loaded Mack made its way slowly around the buildings, then out the driveway, turned right, and headed north to the predetermined rendezvous with the freighter.

Pucci's parting words to Mike were: "If all goes well, we'll have another load back here for you late tonight. However, if not, somehow, someone will get word back to you."

"Be careful. Watch your step," said Mike while puffing on his cigar.

The Reo then moved out the driveway to follow the Mack into the city. Pucci wondered as he followed along: Were the men in the Essex connected with the mob? They had to be, he thought, answering his own question. We'll damned soon find out how fast news travels when we get there with this load. He thought this out as best he could for there was no way of knowing what to expect upon their arrival at the dock.

The Mack rolled into San Francisco via Third Street, then onto the Embarcadero, the last leg of its journey. The docks were to its right.

"Okay," said Primo. "Pier 15 is up ahead past the Ferry Building."

"What's the freighter called?" asked Al.

"It's called — 'Amigo Negro' — or something like that," answered Primo.

"Amigo Negro!" exclaimed Al. Apparently to him the name had a sinister meaning. He let Primo know how he felt about it.

"That ain't nothing," said Primo. "We've got gangsters to

deal with up at the warehouse. According to Pucci, they're something else again."

Al was speechless. He figured to be into something adventurous, but this now was beyond his wildest dreams.

"There it is — up ahead," announced Primo. "Just as Pucci said it would be."

Al glanced in the direction Primo was pointing, then commented: "Sinister looking bugger, isn't it?"

"Yeah, it ain't pretty," concurred Primo.

The freighter was moored with its sharp bow facing the Embarcadero, the loading dock to its right, its starboard side. The Mack went past it then swung right onto the dock, came around in a tight right circle, pulled in close to the dock's edge, and stopped alongside facing the same direction as the freighter.

The maneuver was intentional. If their scheme was to be discovered, they wanted to get out of there fast. Hopefully, there would be no hang-up. The crew was ready for them. The Mack's cargo would be the first load taken on board. Then others with smaller trucks would follow, shuttling back and forth from the warehouse.

Primo noticed the two big tugs: one just ahead of the freighter, and one just behind it. He wondered why they were hanging around this late at night especially since the freighter was moored and needing no further assistance. He wasn't aware that Pucci had asked Sven and Swede to be there.

The Mack went first. As the trailer was being unloaded, tarps and ropes were folded and placed on the truck ready to roll out the minute the last barrel came off the trailer. Now, the first loaded truck from the warehouse came in close behind the Mack's trailer. But, before the Mack could pull out, another loaded truck pulled in directly in front of the Mack blocking its exit. There were two teamsters in each truck, both Fageols.

"Now, what the hell is this?" asked Al as he started up the engine. He then added: "These bastards are up to something other than just unloading their cargo."

Primo called out: "Hey, you've got us blocked off! Pull up!"

But instead of pulling up, two burly teamsters stepped out of the cab. It was obvious to Primo what they had in mind. This hauling job was paying a fat bonus, and the locals were not about to have an outsider come in from out of town with a truck twice their capacity, plus a trailer, and horn in on their deal.

Primo couldn't very well tell them that he was a driver for the paper company and not an independent from out of town (or in town for that matter). If, in fact, that was their problem, any attempt to explain it could backfire.

Through the rearview mirrors, Al could see the two men from the Fageol to the rear coming up on them. "We've got more company coming from out behind us," he said.

"I see them," answered Primo. "These guys are going to be more than we can handle." Then added: "No use trying to talk our way out of this. We better try to make a run for it."

"You mean literally run and leave the truck at their mercy? No way!" answered Al.

Sven, on the closest tug, saw the incident taking shape. He ordered the fire pumps activated immediately.

From his position on the rear tug, Swede couldn't see much of the drama unfolding up front; but he could see, and was watching, the two men from the rear Fageol that were now walking slowly on either side of the rear of the trailer as if waiting for a signal to come from up front. He concluded that they were up to no good. Since they were some distance from him, he decided to step out onto the dock and catch up to the driver that was moving slowly between the trailer and the edge of the dock. From what little he could see going on up front, he didn't like it any more than what he saw going on back there. He sped up his pace.

It was obvious that a fight was about to take place. The ship's crew had standing orders to avoid involvement of any sort in these waterfront disputes. They, therefore, retreated to the sanctuary of the freighter to wait it out. Swede's tug crew was standing by with fire hoses at full pressure. They well knew of their captain's love to fight. They would not interfere until needed.

Pucci was at the corner of the closest building ready to pull the fire alarm in the event Sven was not able to handle the situation with the fire hose. He couldn't see Swede or the other drivers out back, although he had a pretty good idea what was going on. The Mack was being trapped.

What no one was aware of yet was the unmarked police car parked across the Embarcadero. Its two occupants were also viewing the situation. Their orders were to keep an eye on the Mack and to not interfere in any way unless there was an actual threat to life. So far, this was not the case, so they merely watched and held their positions.

The gangster, "Lungo", parked in a side street, was also maintaining surveillance on the loading procedure. He noticed the unmarked police car with its two occupants, but assumed them to be the Federal agents sent out from Washington who, instead, got wiped out in Benicia by the Mack. The mobsters had been advised there'd be two replacements sent out, but had never as yet seen or met them. Lungo would erroneously report back to the Boss at the warehouse of their presence.

The two missing Federal agents were supposed to be undercover so to speak, and so they were. Only, by now, they were undercover lying on slabs at the Solano County Morgue, somewhere in the vicinity of Benicia.

As far as the four teamsters were concerned, they would have no interference in dealing with these two little Italians. They appeared to be even smaller while sitting in this big, Mack truck.

Primo had seen these teamsters in action before. He was not about to stick around regardless of what their beef was. As the two teamsters from the Fageol up front advanced towards the Mack, he turned to Al and said: "For Christ's sake, Al, hurry up and get us out of here!"

Al responded instantly. He picked off reverse gear and let out the clutch abruptly while the engine was revving up. The Mack lurched backwards with a slamming clatter as slack was being taken up in the trailer hitch. The rear end of the trailer smashed into the the Fageol behind it, all but demolishing its entire front end. The impact sent the Fageol rolling backward. Its driver turned and started for it with the intention of catching up to it, but didn't get very far. For standing in his way, legs spread apart, fists in fighting position, was the big Swede, and he wasn't smiling.

A left jab smashed into the driver's face, stopping his forward advance dead in his tracks. Blood and teeth splattered down onto the dock instantly as he rocked back, then forward again. The Swede's right fist was already on its way. It connected with the lower portion of the man's jaw with a sickening crunch as jawbones fractured. His head jerked back as the rest of his body was still in a forward motion. He was out cold before hitting the dock in a pool of blood.

While this short scuffle was taking place, the other teamster had caught up to the rolling Fageol stopping its backward roll just opposite Swede's tug. At that instant, a high-pressure surge of water came crashing through the open cab blasting the driver clean out the opposite side. The teamster picked himself up only to find the big Swede standing there ready to work him over as well. He turned to run, but the big left hand that took a hold of his collar jerked him back. He felt his belt buckle press against his bellybutton as the Swede's right hand took a firm grip on the back side of his wide belt. He was now looking up at the stars as he was being carried above the Swede's head like a sack full of trash about to be tossed into the Bay.

The teamster never saw the murky bay waters rushing up at him as he went sailing through the air head first, arms outstretched like he was doing a backward swan dive. The tug crew, using a pole hook, fished him out of the bay and tossed him back up on the dock in a half-drowned condition.

At the front end of the Mack, Sven was in perfect range for his high-pressure fire hose. The two teamsters came running towards the Mack, side by side. The hiss of air pushing its way out the nozzle ahead of the high-pressure water coming through resembled a huge snake.

The running men were met head-on with a surge of water that sent them reeling backwards. Their hats went sailing through the air as they stumbled and fell to the pavement. Sven kept concentrating the blast of water from one to the other as he rolled them back under their own truck. Whatever was on their minds this night was being washed down the drain and out to sea.

Pucci relaxed his grip on the fire alarm handles. No sense bringing those eager young firefighters out now. No telling what that crazy Indian with the ax might do to these bastards, he thought.

Al saw his opportunity. He cranked the wheel around tight to the right and gave 'er the gun. The big Mack gave out with a roar of approval. It charged forward and around to hard right, but it couldn't clear the right front end of the Fageol blocking its path. No matter, it continued its swing regardless of circumstances. The fact that the whole right front end of the Fageol was about to be demolished was of no concern to this monstrous machine. It showed no mercy. As the old Priest had said in his blessing: "You must obey the command of your master."

When the huge front bumper of the Mack finally cleared the wreckage, Al worked the big steering wheel to the left and now headed the Mack back down the Embarcadero.

Pucci came running up alongside, jumped up on the running board while yelling new instructions to Primo on the opposite side of the cab: "Forget the warehouse. Get your ass out of here! Head for the garage, I'll pick you up there."

"You got it, buddy!" Primo hollered back.

"Wait a minute, you guys!" growled Al. "Those guys aren't going to give us no more trouble tonight. They're all through." He was now slowing down to a practical standstill.

"Maybe so. But what about that car across the street? Do you see those two men over there taking all this in?" asked Pucci.

"Yeah, I noticed it," answered Primo. "But I'll bet you they're a couple of cops in an unmarked car. Bet you anything," he insisted.

"They sure as hell aren't the two jerks from the Essex, that's for sure," put in Al. "What the hell, let's go after that load too. If things look hostile, we can pull out empty," he reasoned.

"Okay, damn it!" said Pucci in a half-mad fashion. "It's against my better judgment, but let's do it."

"I'm all for it too. What the hell, we've come this far so let's go for it. Besides, it could be our last load ever," stated Primo in concurrence.

"Now, listen to me," requested Pucci. "Take the Mack up and around like you did on the Saturday night raid. Park short of the corner and wait for me. I'm going to the station and pick up a fire crew." His mind was working as fast as they were talking. "We're not going to take any chances of getting caught between union goon squads and New Jersey gangsters, by God!"

"Good idea," said Primo. "We'll be waiting for you."

"Al, you better let me take the wheel. I know exactly how to approach the warehouse," said Primo. Al jumped out of the driver's side and came around as Primo slid over behind the wheel.

No sooner had the Mack started down the Embarcadero, than the unmarked car pulled out following, its two occupants roaring with laughter. "Wait'll the Chief hears about this. I can hardly wait to turn in our report," said the driver. "That was one hell of a fight. We better tag along. I'm sure the Chief will want to know where the truck and trailer goes from here."

The two big tugs chugging along side by side, disappeared into the night heading for their berths. Their captains satisfied with the results of this night's activities.

"What the hell were those two tugs doing there?" asked Al as they made their way towards the warehouse.

"You can be sure Pucci had something to do with that too," answered Primo. "That guy thinks of everything."

"What about that car that's following us? You still think they're cops?"

"Yeah, but they don't worry me too much. If the Police Chief really wanted us, he could have nailed us long before this."

Al wasn't sure whether to be comfortable with that answer or not. The way these paesani were operating was something else again.

CHAPTER 29

Pucci pulled up behind the Mack with a fire engine and a full company of firemen.

"What the hell are you doing with all those firemen?" asked Primo.

"They'll come in handy," answered Pucci. "Now listen carefully. Wait until the last Fageol pulls out of the warehouse, then back the truck and trailer in all the way. We'll assume those four drivers that were worked over at the dock will come back with their buddies. We'll keep them away from the warehouse. Once you're loaded and tied down, pull out and don't stop for anything, just beat it out of here. I'll have the street cleared for you. As soon as you're out of sight, head south but stay off the Embarcadero. Pick up Third Street at about Townsend and give a blast from your exhaust horn before you cross the bridge at China Basin. Remember, stay off the Embarcadero."

"Okay, but what about the cop's car that followed us?"

"Where are they now?" asked Pucci as they walked up to the corner while keeping to the shadows.

"That's them down the street at the end of the block facing away from us."

"That's okay. If they don't follow the next truck out, we'll know they're waiting for us. I'll use that fire hydrant just in front of them. They'll have so damned many hoses strung out around them, they won't be able to move an inch."

As they were talking, the limousine pulled up to the warehouse. The Boss and his henchman "Morino" could be seen talking to the driver "Lungo" as he motioned in the direction of the unmarked car parked across the street.

"What do you suppose they're talking about?" asked Pucci inquisitively.

"Whatever it is, it does have something to do with the car and its occupants," answered Primo. "Maybe they're not cops after all. Who knows?"

"There goes another truck right past the parked car. They sure get them loaded fast," said Al. "There can't be more than one more left."

"They didn't move. That means they're waiting for us," said Pucci, then added: "Okay, let's go. Pull up past the entrance and line yourself up for backing in. This will force the last truck to pull out in the other direction. I'll get the fire crew down there and trap that damned car."

Primo was at the wheel of the Mack. He swung past the entrance and down the street then commenced backing up, lining himself up with the entrance.

As he did so, Pucci came cruising in from the opposite end of the street with the fire engine and crew, blocking the whole street.

The mobsters were not surprised to see the Mack although the size of it astounded them. But they were surprised to see a fire engine loaded with fire-fighters. Pucci walked over towards the three mobsters, while the crew busied themselves hooking up hoses to fire hydrants in a manner to trap the unmarked police car.

"What the hell's with that fire truck?" the Boss demanded angrily of Pucci.

"Precautions, Sir. Just precautions," answered Pucci.

"What do you mean precautions? You're going to screw up this whole goddamned loading procedure with this nonsense!" The Boss continued to berate Pucci's unorthodox maneuvers with an assortment of profanity.

About that time, the last truck pulled out only to find the Mack blocking his intended left turn. Al guiding Primo signaled the driver to go right instead of left. The Fageol's driver let out with a barrage of cuss words, plus calling Al a "Dago" in an insulting manner.

"Hold it a minute!" said Al to Primo. "Wait'll I have a talk with the asshole in the Fageol."

211

Al walked alongside the Mack towards the Fageol. The driver also stepped down from his truck and started towards Al. But, realizing that he was no match for Al, he suddenly changed his tone of voice.

"Hey, nice truck you have there fella. I thought I'd get a better look at it," he said, in a half-assed sheepish smile. In so doing he exposed a mouthful of rotten cigarette-stained teeth. Al kept coming straight at him with fists clenched ready for action.

"You better hope your eyesight's better than your teeth, mister, because you're about to start looking for them on your hands and knees," said Al sternly.

"Now wait a minute!" said the driver as he turned and retreated back towards his own truck.

"Only my friends call me a Dago, and they smile at that, you prick." With that Al took a fast step forward, came up hard with a right kick catching the driver square in the butt and sending him in an unbalanced, headlong crash up against the Fageol.

"Now get that damned truck out of here, and fast, before I get mad!" said Al with an added assortment of profanity. The driver got the message and hastily departed in a right turn.

As the Mack disappeared through the entrance, Pucci signaled to the fire engine driver to pull up opposite the entrance. He proceeded to shout instructions to his men regardless of the protesting boss mobster.

"This is official business. Please step aside," he politely but firmly told the Boss as if he were now in charge of the entire operation.

Inside, the Mack was being instantly loaded from both sides by hydraulic lift machinery. As truck and trailer were being loaded, ropes were following along securing the load. Then tarps were rolled out from the bulkhead ready to come down over the last stack as it was set in place. The faster they got out of there, the better.

While the truck and trailer were being loaded, four Fageols came in from the upper street such as Primo had done. They parked up at the corner as if waiting their turns to pull into the warehouse. The drivers piled out, along with the four teamsters from the wrecked trucks left back at the dock. They walked down the street as a group, skirting the fire engine, and onto the sidewalk just up from the warehouse entrance.

"Back off!" yelled Pucci. "You can't go in there while the truck is being loaded."

"Who the hell are you to tell us what to do?" said the cigarette-smoking leader of the gang sarcastically.

"It's against fire regulations to have smokers around gasoline-powered equipment while performing loading operations," came the answer.

Al heard the comment about smokers and quickly snuffed out his own cigarette as if it was meant for him as well.

These teamsters were determined to even the score for the defeat they had suffered at the hands of the tug captains and the devastating wreckage left behind by the Mack. A heated, to-the-point argument was taking place as firemen gathered around with hoses and nozzles at ready.

"Mr. Puccinelli is about to get the hell kicked out of him, and it'll serve him right," commented the Boss to his grinning henchmen.

The teamsters were grouped along the warehouse wall. Pucci was back on the street with several firemen on either side of him, holding their fire hose nozzles ready, as the exchange of profanity was about to give way to action.

Pucci knew where the ax throwing Indian would be, and without looking up and over to the fire engine behind him, he said to the ax thrower: "Let them know we mean business!"

With that the Indian let fly an ax in the direction of the group.

"I suggest you better duck unless you want your heads split open," Pucci calmly informed them at the same instant the ax was airborne.

The group of teamsters saw the flash of the ax as the light from the entrance reflected off the blade as it cartwheeled in their direction. It was purposely intended to clear their heads. The blade sunk itself into the wooden wall of the warehouse behind them with a thudding crunch of splintering wood.

The instant the first ax left his hand, the Indian immediately started a second one in motion. Only this time, he intentionally aimed lower. His ancestral hunting instincts dictated this maneuver. For when an arrow directed at an animal is high of its mark, the animal's instincts cause it to bend its knees in a somewhat crouched position as it springs to safety. Therefore, the second shaft is aimed to come in somewhat lower, and slightly ahead. And so it was with the second ax.

The second ax was now coming in just seconds behind the first one. As expected, the group ducked when the first one sailed over their heads. The Indian had purposely targeted the one teamster that was wearing a felt Stetson with a row of brightly flashing union buttons pinned to the wide band. The ax was on course. The instant the group had ducked, the sharp pick end of the second ax picked off the man's Stetson and pinned it firmly to the wall behind him. Pucci raised his hand so as to stop the third ax from being launched as he said:

"Now back off, or I'll turn these guys loose with the fire hoses!"

They broke ranks. The men that had joined them from the dock were the first to hightail it back up the street. They'd already had enough water for one night. This left only four men facing as many fire hose nozzles and an eager ax-throwing Indian.

Taking a step or two towards the remaining teamsters, Pucci added a to-the-point order:

"Get back to your trucks and get ready to start loading the minute that Mack truck pulls out!" His commands were not questioned. He then turned to address the astounded Boss standing off to one side with his henchmen close at hand.

"Pay those drivers in there! They're ready to pull out!" he commanded.

The Boss immediately turned and headed for the office, only to stop in his tracks and turn back towards Pucci. "What the hell am I taking orders from him for?" he mumbled while sizing up the situation. He hadn't intended to pay them off until the load was on the ship; if at all. This man, Puccinelli, he thought, he sure as hell isn't the same timid idiot we were dealing with before. What's his game? He was annoyed with him but did have to admit to himself that Pucci had stepped in at just the right time to avoid a jurisdictional dispute that would probably have stopped the loading procedure completely.

He glanced across and down the street towards the unmarked car. They'll see to it the load gets on board, he thought.

Satisfied, he went directly to the trailer and called up to Primo who was unfolding tarps:

"Here's your money, fella," he said as he extended his hand upwards.

"Oh, yeah," said Primo. "Give it to him down below." He wasn't about to waste time to take money or count it. As a matter of fact, he was content to just pull out, pay or no pay.

The Boss walked around the end of the trailer and handed Al several bills. Without saying a word, he turned and walked away, grumbling. He had intended to settle the account after the freighter was loaded.

Al looked up at Primo and with hand gestures asked the question: "What's this?"

Primo also answered in the proper hand-gesture technique so popular among Italians: "Stick it in your pocket and keep your mouth shut."

Primo let himself down off the trailer as Al was securing the last canvas tiedown. He came running up to him wide-eyed and jabbering nervously:

"Al, I don't like this. For Christ's sake, let's get out of here!"

"Yeah, I don't like it either. There's too damned much squabbling going on outside. Let's blow!"

"Al, you drive," said Primo as they trotted briskly towards the cab.

"No! You drive, and don't stop for nothing!"

Primo was in the cab in a flash. Not bothering to run around to the passenger side, Al jumped on the running board and hung on. He reached under the seat with his free hand and retrieved a sturdy tire iron. The maneuver caused Primo to raise a worrisome question:

"What're you going to do with that?" he asked as the Mack started up with a roar.

"Never mind . . . just go . . .!"

Out front the gangster, Lungo, was scrutinizing Pucci's activities. Having seen him down at the dock ready to pull the fire alarm, and now this nonsense, led him to believe they'd been double crossed. His left hand moved towards the .45 automatic tucked in the shoulder holster. But the Indian had spotted the movement. Lungo hesitated. He'd have to get him first. He was now studying the circular motion of the ax in the Indian's hand as it was rotating in a forward swing over his head, then back down past his ankles as if ready to give it one last whirl before letting it go. He had heard about the ax-throwing abilities of the high plains Indians, but always believed it to be only a myth, nothing else. His thoughts were now centered on timing. In order for the Indian to throw the ax, he would have to speed it up on the downward swing, bring it up fast behind him, and let go. That would be the time to nail him. He kept watching him, like a cat watching a mouse, waiting tensely for the right moment to pounce.

The Indian up on the fire engine, with eagle-sharp eyes and feet braced from one stack of hoses to the other, was watching the gunman. No question, these two men were squaring off, eager to try it. The challenge to take each other on was apparent. The draw of the gun versus the swing of the ax. The left-handed gangster had to consider the time it would take him to bring his left hand up, reach the shoulder holster under the right flap of his coat, pull the gun out, then slide the bolt with his right hand as he brought it up and around and lined it up to the target. The fact that he was left-handed might fool the Indian. Yes, it could be done, he thought. Except for the fact that the movement would cause the ax to be launched instantly, meaning it would be on course before the slug would reach him. The gangster would have to duck fast to avoid the ax, but then this could cause him to miss. Or, if he didn't take evasive action fast enough, the ax would indeed imbed itself in his chest for sure.

He glanced over to the two perfectly thrown axes still imbedded in the warehouse wall. They would have taken the lives of two men easily if so intended. No, he thought, not yet. The Indian has the advantage. I'll wait.

As the Boss stepped out the office, he called to Lungo. The instant Lungo's eyes shifted in that direction, the ax came sailing through the air. The gangster was partially turned when the blade buried itself in the wall directly alongside his head. An intentional miss. His instant reaction was to go for his gun, but as he turned back with the intention of going for it, another ax was already whirling in the hands of the Indian, ready to be released.

"Hold it, you damn fool! He'll split your skull wide open!"

screamed the Boss. "He's got the drop on ya! For Christ's sake, don't ya know anything about Indians?"

At that instant, the Mack came roaring out of the warehouse entrance, swung to the left past the startled Boss and bearing down on Lungo. "Run over the son-of-a-bitch," snarled Al, while hanging on standing on the running board. While yelling at the firemen to clear out of the way, he raised the tire iron with the intent of crushing Lungo's skull as the gangster jumped clear.

Firemen scrambled to safety as the Mack raced down the street, crushing high pressure fire hoses in the process. Several hoses whipped and flailed in a water-spraying frenzy sending surges of water in all directions. Responding to Pucci's hand signals, the water was shut off both at the fire hydrant and at the engine's booster pump. This stopped the life-threatening flailing action of the hoses. Pucci's intention was to "entrap" the unmarked police car all right, but certainly not by wrapping it up in fire hoses like a fly caught in a spider's web as it now was.

The gangster, Lungo, was now convinced that a hijack was in progress. His Boss, having stepped into the street screaming at Pucci, saw his henchman coming towards him in a swinging-swaying gait like a "cobra" about to strike. He'd seen him in this mood before, and it meant trouble.

217

"What the hell's with you?" the Boss demanded to know. "Haven't I got enough frigg'n trouble as it is?"

"It's a hijack!" hissed his henchman through tight lips.

"What? — A hijack! Why those frigg'n, sons-of-bitches!" swore the Boss.

He then made a bee-line for the unmarked police car. He yelled at the occupants through the now open window:

"Why the hell aren't you following that frigg'n truck!?" he demanded to know.

"Can't you see we're tangled up in fire hoses? Besides, what the hell business is it of yours what we do?" came the sharp answer.

"You better goddamned well believe its my business!" cursed the Boss. "I'm running this goddamned show and you'll do what I say, or else!"

This really irritated the two occupants. "Listen, Mister, we take our orders directly from the Chief of Police and no one else. Do you understand!?" came the retort.

"Chief of Police!" exclaimed the Boss as if he had just seen a ghost. "You mean you're not from Washington?"

"What the hell's Washington got to do with us? We're city cops on special assignment. Anything else you wanna know?"

"Oh, Jesus Christ!" exclaimed the Boss. He stumbled over fire hoses as he retreated back towards his henchman. He needed time to think this out.

As it was with Primo, Pucci also wanted out of there fast. He screamed orders to the fire crew: "Get back on the engine! Forget the frigg'n hoses! Come on, let's go! On the double!"

Diverting his attention to the Indian up on the fire engine, Pucci shouted: "And you, you damn crazy Indian, drop that frigg'n axe! Get down, hang on, we're getting our ass out of here!"

The Indian heard the command, but ignored it. He wasn't about to take his eyes off Lungo, he sensed the gangster to be an enemy. It was his vigilance that was keeping the gangster from drawing his gun.

The Boss was quick to get his act together. He addressed his henchman, whose eyes were following the Indian's rotating ax like a rope skipper, ready to jump in at the precise moment.

"Damn it, forget that frigg'n Indian! Get over to the limo and beat it down to the dock! If the truck's not there, then hightail it south on the Embarcadero!"

Lungo broke his fixed gaze. He'd follow orders. He ran to the limo in the same swinging-swaying gait. He was in a killing mood. He was also aware that the Embarcadero ended abruptly to the north at Fisherman's Wharf. It was logical that the hijackers would head south. Tires screamed as the limo took off with a killer at the wheel.

"That son-of-a-bitch — Puccinelli!" swore the Boss as he now ran to the entrance of the warehouse. Morino, his other henchman who was overseeing the loading, heard his boss's call: "Morino! Get your frigg'n ass out here — we've been hijacked!"

Morino came running with gun drawn, but it was too late; the fire engine with its crew had already rounded the corner.

The Mack, its lights extinguished, had turned south before reaching the Embarcadero. Primo was guiding it by dimly reflecting street lighting. It made its way through the various narrow city streets; crossed Market Street, picked up Second, then onto Townsend Street. Primo looked down Townsend to his left towards the Embarcadero as they made the right turn. The hook-and-ladder truck could be seen stretched across the street creating a roadblock. Its presence, along with the fire engine at hand, indicated there was something going on back up the street.

"What the hell do you suppose that's all about?" asked Al as he, too, was stretching his neck to get a better look.

"You can be sure it's some more of Pucci's doings. Whatever the hell it is," answered Primo.

The Mack rolled on up Townsend, made a left onto Third Street without being noticed. The Mack was now on its way out of town. "The phantom had struck again!" The loud echoing blasts from its exhaust horn caught the ear of the fire captain at the roadblock giving out the only indication of its presence.

As anticipated, the limo came heading down the Embarcadero looking for the Mack. It came upon the roadblock. The fire engine interfered with its attempt to get turned around.

For once the tillerman was in the middle of the action. His skill and experience at jumping curbs put the tiller directly up on the sidewalk while the tractor portion of this long ladder-transporting apparatus was on the opposite side of the street. Therefore, creating the perfect roadblock. Fortunately for him, he was wearing his rain gear when the action started with the fire hoses to stop the limo from running the roadblock. The eager firemen handling the hoses, so used to him hardly ever being close to the action, completely forgot that he was there sitting on the tiller. The blasts of high-pressure water directed at the limo directly alongside and below him all but knocked him clean off his perch. The profanity that followed the drenching he took was not fit for a foul-mouthed, knuckle-skinned plumber or a thumb-smashed carpenter for that matter.

The blast of high-pressure water through the open window of the limo was so great that it practically ripped the coat off the gangster as well as knocking his gun out of its holster and onto the seat next to him. Needless to say, he was thoroughly soaked. Water was running out the seams of the floorboards of the limo like a sieve when draining spaghetti.

The Captain, not mincing words, accused the gangster of being an arsonist. The gangster denied it with a foul-mouthed barrage of profanity.

"All right!" said the Captain to the limousine driver. "So you're not an arsonist. So why did you try to run the road block? And another thing, what are you doing with that gun over there? Don't tell me you were hunting rabbits! I won't buy it!"

"The gun is none of your business!" sputtered the soaked driver in a mad, furious manner.

"Maybe so, but arson is. Step out of the car!" commanded the Captain. The gangster hesitated.

The Captain jerked the door open, and as he did so, a gush of water cascaded out the door, down across the running board and onto the street.

To assure that the Mack would be well on its way south, the Fire Captain stalled the driver even more by making out an elaborate report. He had taken everything down he could think of in the way of information including the size hat he was wearing.

Finally, the Captain released him on condition that he'd return in the direction he had come. He would have done this anyway since the Mack had disappeared like a ghost in the night.

"Incredible . . . absolutely incredible!" said Al gleefully as he held the $100 bills in the light of the instrument panel. "We hijacked their wine from right under their noses, and got paid to boot.

Amazing . . . absolutely amazing. Jesus Christ, what a racket!"

"Hell, you don't know the half of it," said Primo in a chuckling, grinning manner. "The first 120 barrels the Fageols hauled out of the warehouse were half full of water."

"You mean, they were breaking their ass and wrecked two trucks . . . all for water?"

"Exactly!" answered Primo. "That was the switch that took place on the Saturday night raid."

For some mysterious reason, the big Mack hit a stretch of cobblestones that caused it to gently rumble and bounce as if it, too, was laughing along with its paesano masters who, by now, had lost complete control of their wits, roaring with laughter.

CHAPTER 30

First thing next morning, Pucci made an official visit to the Coast Guard cutter, "Skipjack," moored to its berth. Captain Terranova greeted him with the courtesy of a sharp salute.

"What brings you here this bright early morning, Sir?" he asked as he offered him a cup of hot coffee.

"Well," answered Pucci, "it may be of no great concern, but the freighter in question appears to be an outright fire trap."

"Oh, you don't say," answered the Captain. "How do you know? Did you inspect it?"

"By what I can see from standing on the dock, there are numerous fire code violations that could pose a hazard to the dock and crew as well. The Captain appears to be hostile. He could give me a bad time when I ask him for permission to come aboard for an inspection, you know — jurisdiction — that sort of thing."

"He damned well better not refuse your request!" snorted Captain Terranova. "If it's not within your jurisdiction, it's certainly within mine. Seagoing vessels are Coast Guard business. I'll be here standing by; let me know if you need my help."

"Good," answered Pucci. "It's a comfort to know you'll back me up." They parted company with a wave of hand signifying agreement.

Pucci now drove down the Embarcadero past the freighter. Since the transferring of wine was done only after dark, all was quiet. Without stopping, he continued on down to where the two big tugs were berthed. He was first greeted by Sven:

"Good morning my good friend. How are you this fine morning?"

222

Swede looked up from his chores and extended a similar greeting with a wave of his hand.

Sven continued in his heavy Norwegian dialect: "I saw you at the dock last night but there was no time to talk. By the way, did you see the fight on the other end of the dock last night?"

"No," said Pucci. "Not really."

"That was one helluva fight. Too bad you missed it," said Sven, amused. He then asked about their deal in reference to the freighter and its cargo.

Pucci had outlined a plan which they would participate in and benefit by. But he now had some second thoughts: "Well, there could be some problems that might require a slight change of plans. If such be the case, would you fellas still want to stay with it?" asked Pucci.

"Of course. Just tell us what you want us to do."

"Well, when you get ready to push the freighter out to the channel tomorrow morning, stall around until you see Primo go by the Embarcadero with his old Doane truck. If all goes well, he'll have the big container your friend, the Danish boat builder, made for me. In order to get your attention, he'll give out with a blast from his exhaust horn as he goes by."

"Very well. We'll do that," said Sven. "But suppose all doesn't go well? Then what?"

"Well, in that case, you'll see a limousine show up with three tough looking men. It's supposed to be loaded on the freighter along with the cargo of barrels. Now, if that happens, I don't know what to tell you except that once loaded, either way, the Captain will want to ship out without delay."

"All right," said Sven. "If the limo and the tough looking men show up, we will push the damn thing into the mud and the hell with it. But if Primo goes by and the Captain wants to get under way, we'll then follow the plan we originally agreed upon. Is that correct?"

"Yes," said Pucci. With that understanding the men parted with a good-luck farewell.

He then drove up to the warehouse to check the garage to the rear. Apparently the gangsters hadn't discovered the secret garage or the container left there by Primo. Pucci was pleased with his findings. Although things were quiet, he stayed away from the front

223

entrance altogether. It would be too risky to be seen or, especially, to confront those dangerous gangsters now, especially after last night, he thought. His next stop was to visit the Police Chief. The car he had entrapped with fire hoses was still on his mind — he wondered?

"I heard about last night," said the Chief. "You better damned well be careful! You're dealing with dangerous gangsters as well as one hell of a tough bunch of teamsters. They may be laying for you tonight."

No question now. The car was in fact an unmarked police car; for whatever reason, they were keeping an eye on things.

"I realize that," said Pucci. "We're going to stay away from them altogether. That could have turned out pretty nasty all right." There was nothing mentioned about the two loads they managed to hijack.

"As for the three jackals and their limo," continued the Chief, "there has been no attempt to acquire anything in the way of replacement ammunition or firearms. I'll be glad when those bastards leave town with or without their damned machine guns."

"I'm with you one-hundred percent," answered Pucci, not letting on what his next move might be.

That night, Pucci caught up to Primo. In a relaxed mood over a cup of coffee, Pucci asked: "How did the unloading go at the ranch?"

"Just fine. They were waiting up for us," answered Primo.

"Did you fellows manage to get some sleep?"

"Yeah, we did. But only after we got that bunch of paesani settled down, you should have heard them. Like a bunch of kids."

As the two buddies sat in the all-night diner, Primo proceeded to describe the events of the night before:

"We pulled in at the paesani's ranch with the intention of driving right out to the back of the barn, but decided it best to have a couple of paesani guide us with lanterns. The whole interior of the ranch house was lit up. There were loud voices coming from within. The shouting was so intense that they didn't hear the Mack come rumbling into the yard." Primo continued: "I sent Al up to let them know we had arrived, but he came running back to report that apparently they were engaged in some sort of brawl. The two of us went back up and cautiously made our way through the back porch, opened the door to the kitchen and peered in. It took a few seconds to make out what the ruckus was all about. We could see one group of men in the kitchen and another in the dining room. They had two card games going simultaneously. You know, the card game, Pedro," grinned Primo, before continuing: "The players were involved in heated arguments, as were the onlookers."

What Primo was describing was a typical Pedro card game amongst a group of Italians having formed partners with teamed up onlookers participating as backups (seconds). They seldom break up the partners once they have set up signals between themselves. They all cheat incredibly and, of course, they all know it. So, for the most part, the arguments are between the two partners who are constantly getting their signals crossed. If you watch one of these games being played, you'll note that all the players are wearing hats, including the seconds standing behind them. The idea is to tilt the hat into various positions such as the coach does in signaling the player in a baseball game. With the ball game, there are only two men sending signals back and forth; but with Pedro, there could easily be a half dozen or so men all tilting, touching, and shifting their hats at the same time. Obviously, the four players must watch not only for signals from their partners and their seconds, but they must also study the movements by others as well.

They must also concentrate on facial expression that indicates satisfaction or disgust with the signal received. During the play, there are very few words spoken. Mostly, the slamming of the fleshy part of the palms slapping the table are predominant sounds until the last hand is played. At this point, all hell breaks loose amongst the players, especially those that lost the hand. The accusations and insulting dialogue brought about because of crossed-up signals resembles an Arab dispute over the sale of a misrepresented camel.

"To make matters even worse, both games were embroiled in heated arguments at the same time with the onlookers or seconds running back and forth to report to each other the stupid mistakes made by the players in their respective games. The whole affair was really nutty," said Primo, chuckling.

"What did Mike have to say about their conduct?" asked Pucci in a humorous manner.

"Hell, he was right in the middle of it — one of the participants. When they get in these Pedro games, my uncle's authority is meaningless. They don't treat or talk to him any different than the rest," said Primo with emphasis. "By Al working on one bunch and I on the other, we managed to finally get the games broken up. But, they continued to argue all the way out to the yard. When the glare from the lanterns illuminated the Mack's monstrous features, they quieted down. Now they wanted to know how we were able to return with another load of wine in such a short time. They demanded to know, so I let Al tell the story. Once they heard how it was done, and the fight that ensued between Swede and the teamsters, they went from an argumentative mood to a laughing, festive, clowning mood with some trying to imitate the fight between Swede and the teamsters. They even tried to pick each other up by the scruff of the neck and seat of the pants. No question that the nipping at the wine jug was a contributing factor to their behavior, but they were not totally drunk, just happy-go-lucky, as usual."

Pucci was grinning and laughing all the time Primo described the reaction of the paesani when they were told of the previous night's events. To those that participated at the time, it was serious business. But to those that were now hearing how and what events took place, they had to admit that it was hilariously funny. Once the two buddies calmed down, Pucci put a serious question to Primo:

"Do they understand what they're up against tomorrow? Will they be ready?" he asked.

"Yes, they do," answered Primo. "We went over it again in detail. They'll be ready to the last man. There's one thing about them; they love to clown around, but when the chips are down, you can depend on them. They'll be there."

They were to all meet the next morning at daybreak one block from the warehouse, Primo with the old Doane, and Mike with the Model-T Ford loaded with paesani eager to take on the supposedly armed gangsters and run them out of town. They had good cause to do so. The gangsters also being Italian was a bad reflection on themselves, the paesani. They knew the risk involved, but the cause outweighed the risk.

While the two buddies at the diner were going over the details of the next day's event, Mike, back at the ranch, was briefing the paesani. Livia listened in. She didn't like the looks on their faces. They were no longer happy-go-lucky and carefree men. They now looked serious, somewhat solemn. Like soldiers going to war — not really wanting to go, but knowing they must. She expressed her concern to Mike.

Please tell me!" she pleaded. "What are you asking our paesani to do that makes them look and feel so determined?"

"They are about to do what their hearts dictate them to do," he answered in a solemn tone of voice. "The paesani, including myself, must do what authorities cannot do to rid the city of undesirable Italians. We understand their ways and therefore know best how to deal with them."

"You mean you are going to fight with fellow Italians?" she inquired.

"Unfortunately, yes!" he answered.

"Michele," she said in a soft, concerned manner, "the paesani are not fighters; their ancestors were not fighters, and neither are you. Please reconsider."

In an assuring, respective manner, he asked of her: "Concern yourself with having a good supper ready for us. We will be hungry upon our return."

"Well, maybe it's what the good Lord wants," she responded with a sigh.

Mike thought for a second, then said: "Aldoino will stay here with you." He was a good, but simple man. The last place he should be is in a fight of any sort. In no way would he be able to defend himself, let alone be an aggressor. Livia was pleased with his decision.

CHAPTER 31

Early next morning the Model-T pulled out of the ranch yard loaded with a dozen paesani heading for the rendezvous in the city. They were to meet Pucci on the street above the warehouse, opposite the direction the truckers were hauling. Pucci was already there waiting. He informed Mike and the others that Primo was already parked in the back street of the warehouse with the old Doane.

"A few more loads and the warehouse will be cleaned out," he said. "Let's get down to the corner and take a look."

They took turns peeking around the corner. Nervous excitement was building up within them as they waited. By now the sun was trying to break through the light overcast cover. The city itself was coming to life as people scurried to their jobs and businesses, unaware of what was going on in this separate little world of the paesani. The last truck to be loaded finally pulled out. They would now wait for the transport trucks to move in, load, and haul out the hydraulic-lift machines before moving in on the three gangsters who would then be alone.

The paesani were engaged in a conversation. They insisted that it would serve no purpose for Mike to go in with them. After all, they reasoned, if things go badly, why lose a man like him with a family? Besides, if there are serious injuries, at least we have one sound person to help us, they argued. The issue was resolved. Mike would not go in.

The transport pulled out of the warehouse followed by the owner of the drayage company. Apparently, he had been paid off in full. There was no one else left in there except the three New Jersey gangsters with their limousine.

"All right," said Pucci. "Put on your safety glasses and button up your coats. Let's go!"

They hurried across the street and passed through the entrance as a group. The lights were still on. The limo was parked towards the rear and to the right. The three gangsters were walking back towards the limo. The sound of the men's footsteps echoing throughout the vacant warehouse caused them to stop and look around.

Primo, down at the end of the block to the rear of the warehouse, saw the men head out across the street. He hurried over to the secret garage, quietly opened the doors, entered, and waited.

Mike, having remained behind, was peeking around the corner watching the men disappear through the entrance. Being left alone made him nervous and jumpy. As he peered around the corner, hat pulled low shading his eyes, he heard footsteps coming up behind him. He whirled around in a state of fright, let out a gasp as he threw himself back against the wall in a defensive manner.

"Jesus Christ, you're jumpy!" said Al. "What's going on?"

"Oh, my God, am I glad it's you!" said Mike after catching his breath. "They told me to stay here while they went inside the warehouse. But I'm scared to stay here alone."

"I can see that. Is Primo with them?"

"You didn't come with him?" answered Mike with a question of his own.

"No. He left early before I got to work. He didn't say what was going on, but I had a hunch you guys would be here."

"He's down there around the corner in back of the warehouse. Something about a secret garage back there."

"I'll take a walk down there and join him."

"No, Primo doesn't need you. Stay here with me," pleaded Mike in desperation.

"Okay, if it makes you feel better. But what's Pucci with that bunch of nuts doing in there?"

"They're going to beat up the gangsters!" answered Mike, wide eyed.

"What the hell . . . ! Has Pucci lost his mind?"

The three gangsters were surprised to see Pucci leading this group of ragtag-dressed men wearing loose, heavy coats. They realized instantly that this meant trouble. The freighter would be ready to pull out shortly. They couldn't afford to miss it. The paesani were well spread out, walking steadily towards the trio who were now standing there sizing up the situation. They could see the paesani were not armed. "A mistake on their part," thought the Boss. With a nod of his head and a quick hand gesture, he indicated to his henchmen to get to the limo. As they did so, he addressed Pucci in a rather polite, but sneering, manner:

"How nice of you to come, Mr. Puccinelli. Where have you been since your friends with the big truck hijacked a load of our wine?"

Pucci would have liked to answer: "A truck load? Guess again!" But he chose to remain silent. He could only think of how nice it would be to get those strong hands of his on this bastard's throat. It was just about the size of a fire hose while under pressure, struggling to escape his grasp.

The intent of this strung-out, slow-marching group of men was no mystery to this jackal. The Boss had found himself in similar situations before. His scarred-up face disclosed his past well enough. His intent now was to stall the men a few seconds to give his henchmen time to get back with the submachine guns. "The sight of those guns alone should scatter Pucci's rag-tag backers," thought the Boss.

The Boss spoke again: "Mr. Puccinelli, we had been waiting for you. We want to settle with you for your services. In a business-like manner — of course."

"Fat chance," thought Pucci. "Who you trying to kid with that bullshit?"

The Boss grew more impatient as he continued: "I would like to stay and meet your friends, but we're in a hurry. You see, we must leave with the freighter. Surely, you can understand that?" he hissed through clenched teeth, like a snake hissing through deadly, venomous fangs.

Pucci remained silent. He was watching the two bastards with the submachine guns walking hurriedly towards their Boss. The little dark one, Morino, got there first. He took a position close to him — covering his Boss's left flank, with the submachine gun held in a right-hand shooting position. The ever-present cigarette dangling from his lips caused him to keep tilting his head back and to the right so the smoke could clear his hat rim, pulled down just above his eyebrows.

The tall one, Lungo, moving like a cobra, slithered behind his two companions, being sure not to get in the line of fire. He took a position to cover his Boss's right flank with his submachine gun held in a left-hand shooting position.

They were now ready. If a settlement couldn't be reached, they could cut Pucci and his men down in seconds. The gangsters were puzzled by how this unarmed, rag-tag group expected to stand up to them. They were now stepping backwards as the line of men drew closer. Experience had taught them, the shorter the distance between them, the better the chance of their being overrun. They wouldn't let that happen. The line was now forming into a pincer movement with the two ends starting to close in.

Pucci now had something to say: "You bastards!" was his first outburst in a tight-lipped cursing manner. "There'll be a settlement all right, but not the kind you've got in mind!" he growled. "You may get past us, but you still have a long way to go before you reach New Jersey. Our San Francisco authorities know all about you and your crooked associates in Washington!"

The trio were astounded to hear Pucci talk this way. They had misjudged him for sure. It was now clear they'd be forced to gun down the whole lot of them regardless of consequences, or have those submachine guns shoved up their ass if they didn't. The Boss was no longer cool. His sweaty hands rested gently on the two submachine guns on either side of him. To lift them off would start them chattering in the hands of the two eager gunmen.

Morino was having trouble. His hands were unsteady. His nerves were shot. He didn't dare release his grip on the gun to remove the cigarette from his lips. Besides, he didn't really want to. The cigarette was now bouncing to the nervous reaction of his lips. The smoke was drifting constantly into his eyes. They were watering, bloodshot, and irritated. He was having trouble focusing. Things were getting blurry. He appeared to be about to panic.

Lungo, however, was cool. No smoke in his eyes. They were clear, shifting back and forth from under the rim of his hat studying the situation carefully. Which end of the line to start from would be an important decision. As he glanced to his left, he couldn't help but notice the unstable condition of his so-called fellow gunman. This caused him to curse in a hissing, snarling manner:

"You little son-of-a-bitch, you get in my way and I'll kill you too!" He now directed his next comment to the Boss in a hissing whisper: "That little screwed-up idiot is falling apart! Take that gun away from him and get him out of the way!"

The Boss made a quick decision. He would take the submachine gun as suggested, but Morino's sweaty hands were frozen to it. The maneuver started the machine gun rattling, splattering projectiles in every which way. The little rattlesnake was striking blind. His finger was frozen to the trigger.

This now brought the left-handed gunman, Lungo, into action. He swung to the far right. The man at the end of the line coming in along the wall took the first burst of machine gun fire. Without letting up, he swung along from one to the other working his way around in an accurate, concentrated manner. Once around and past center, he planned to keep right on going, cutting down his two cohorts, along with the rest, if need be. The thought of killing them both in a crossfire didn't bother him one bit.

The gunman, Lungo, leaned into the bucking machine gun, twisting and swaying like a cobra with a fixed, cold gaze locked on his victims. The blood-red blotches oozing through the paesani's heavy clothing verified the effectiveness of the machine gun's fire power. He wouldn't concern himself with how many were dropping dead or dying until he reached the end of the line.

As the belching gun barrel came around, the Boss, in a fit of fear induced by rage, screamed at Morino:

"Step back! He's coming around!" The Boss made a desperate grab at the gun as he cursed: "You goddamned little frigg'n son-of-a-bitch! Give me that gun!" But Morino's hands were still frozen to it. With both hands now on the gun, the Boss jerked him out of the line of fire as he, too, stepped back out of the way.

The line was no longer orderly. The paesani raised their arms to protect their faces and ward off the stinging effect of the oncoming projectiles. They turned sideways to take the brunt of the bursts of machine gun fire against their arms and heavy coats rather than against their face and chest. They staggered and winced noticeably as the fake bullets filled with blood-red dye splattered against their bodies with concentrated accuracy.

The rattle of machine gun fire emitting from the warehouse entrance drove Mike and Al to near panic.

Al knew nothing about Pucci's assurance that the deadliness of the submachine guns had been neutralized. "Jesus Christ! Let's get in there!" he yelled out to Mike. "Those guys need help!"

"But Pucci said the guns wouldn't be shooting real bullets," responded Mike.

"How the hell can he be sure?"

Al's question raised some doubt in Mike's mind as well. He

responded to Al's urging with courage.

They jumped in the Model-T Ford and headed for the warehouse entrance at full throttle. Mike at the wheel, and Al hanging on standing on the running board. Neither one knowing for sure what they would do once in the warehouse. Instinct had caused them to ignore all precautions as the Ford came bouncing into the warehouse. Through the drifting gunsmoke, they could see the group of men at the far end of the warehouse. The "chit . . . chit" sound of the Ford echoing throughout the warehouse comingled with the staccato rattle of machine gun fire. The Ford was overtaking the group of men at a fast clip. Mike could see that unless he took immediate evasive action, he would run into his own men. He swung the wheel hard right as he let up on the throttle. The braking procedure (for what it was worth) came about simultaneously. However, oil concentrated on the concrete floor from the previous trucks and equipment caused the Ford truck to go into a spin, end for end, until the rear end of the truck smashed into the side of the limo in an ear splitting, echoing crash of twisted metal and breaking glass.

Al saw the collision coming. Instead of riding it out, he chose to jump off. In so doing, he went skidding on his butt across the oily floor. He came to rest in puddles and smears of red substance that appeared to be blood. "Holy Christ!" he exclaimed as he picked himself up off the floor in horror.

Primo, waiting in the secret garage, upon hearing the machine gun fire quietly pushed the sliding panel at the rear wall of the warehouse to a partially open position, thus exposing the shadowed, corridor-like opening to the shipping container. The opening was directly in back of the retreating trio, therefore offering them an escape route. The shadowed darkness of the corridor and container disguised its true intent. The trio were about to be overrun from all directions. They were mystified that the seemingly blood splattered men weren't collapsing to the floor.

The little gunman, Morino, was the first to break and make a run for it. As he did so, the Boss made another attempt to wrestle the submachine gun away from him. In so doing, he saw the corridor-like opening directly behind them. Giving no thought as to why it wasn't noticed before, he yelled out new instructions to the two hastily retreating gunmen:

"Come on, this way! Follow me!" He was running towards the corridor as he shouted further orders: "Use your automatics! We can finish them off as they come through!"

The machine guns, being out of ammunition, were discarded. The two gunmen followed their Boss, reaching for their automatics as they ran with the paesani bearing down on them.

The gangsters, reaching the corridor, dashed into it, unsure as to where it might lead. The paesani grabbed at them as they rushed headlong into the adjoining dark chamber of the shipping container.

Pucci quickly reached for the container's vault-like door recessed in the wall of the corridor, and with both hands slammed it shut. Sticking out from the outside of the door was a hardwood wedge intended to firmly secure it once driven into place. He picked up a discarded submachine gun, and holding the hot barrel in his hands, proceeded to pound the wedge into place with the stock of the gun until the wedge was flush with the rest of the exterior. There was no provision provided to open the door from either the inside or the outside once the wedge went into place. The vault-like chamber secured, the paesani backed off into the full light of the warehouse. They would now take time to assess the casualties.

Primo now pushed the panel open the rest of the way, stepped in, and looked at the men in disbelief. They were splattered with a blood-red sticky dye and complaining of the stinging effect of the fake bullets. Some had penetrated their heavy clothing and were actually drawing blood. But, at least, they were all alive. That was all that mattered now.

Mike was walking hurriedly in their direction when he overhead Pucci's comments: "Thank Christ we're alive, or maybe we should thank the Police Chief and his friend, the jeweler."

Mike added his comment as he walked up to them: "By God! The Chief and his friend better like wine because they're going to get a lot of it."

The mention of wine brought relief to the stressful ordeal.

CHAPTER 32

The pain was giving way to the joys of victory as the men prepared themselves for the next task. They must now load the heavy container and its contents back onto Primo's low-bed truck. The container was built to support life. Air circulating ducts were built into the thick, sound-proof walls in a manner to suppress sound. Slit-like openings provided oxygen for the occupants. It was soundproof in all respects. The container was stocked with water, bread, and several cases of chili beans. There was enough provisions to sustain life for at least a month, about the time it would take to make the journey to the East Coast.

As the loading progressed, the question was asked: "Why provide chili beans? Why not just bread and water?"

Pucci took his time in answering the question: "We want to be damned sure that in the event these slimy bastards survive — sane or insane . . . ," he paused for a moment, then went on, ". . . that they will never, ever, want to come near each other again for the rest of their lives. And, if in fact they are Mafiosi, their so-called family may refuse to lay claim to the no good sons-of-bitches." He paused again before continuing: "There is a good chance that their New Jersey associates might smell the container's contents before completely cutting it open and, therefore, bury it without opening it."

No one, but no one, laughed or even cracked a smile. They just went about the task of getting the container on the truck for they could sense that Pucci was not trying to be funny.

Meanwhile, down at the docks, the delayed limo's arrival was irritating the freighter's captain. The trio had better show up damned soon or he'd leave without them. The captain finally gave the signal to ship out. A long blast from the steam whistle could be heard throughout the waterfront. He wanted the tugs to move in and push him out into the channel.

However, Sven and Swede kept horsing around with their tugs, fumbling with lines, pretending to be having problems getting into position to move the freighter away from the dock. They were intent on stalling until Primo or the limo showed up.

"Okay, good enough," said Primo. "Move out of the way. There's no need to tie it down. I have to get going. See you guys down at the Embarcadero." Hesitating for a moment, he called out: "Hey, Al, how about taking a ride with me?"

The call broke up Al's thoughts. He was thinking about this man, Pucci, that he just met less than a week before. His determination, acting as if carrying out a vendetta, determined to destroy, if need be, anyone that had anything to do with this government warehouse affair. The very thought of it caused Al's skin to crawl. He wondered as he hopped on the truck and sat alongside Primo.

The Doane swung out of the driveway and down the street heading for the Embarcadero.

Once at the Embarcadero, Primo turned right heading south. As he passed the tugs and freighter, he let go with a loud "quok-ah, quok-ah, quok-ah," from his exhaust horn. Sven and Swede both let out a couple of long toots from their stack whistles in response. They were relieved to see him go by with the big container. They were now free to move the freighter out and away from the dock.

The freighter's captain, with bullhorn in hand, was bellowing profane obscenities at the tug boats; he wanted out of port right now. Obviously something had gone wrong; the limo hadn't shown up as planned. As far as he was concerned, the three gangsters may have been picked up by the police. He was not about to stick around to find out.

Primo kept right on going down the Embarcadero with Al asking questions: "What the hell was that all about? And where are we going with this container?" Al listened as the plan was explained to him.

"This container will be loaded on that other ship you see up ahead. It's scheduled to leave port later tonight. The container is assigned to the same fictitious-named company as the load of wine barrels. As for the two tugs, if everything goes as planned, you will see for yourself how they fit in."

"Is this more of Pucci's strategy?" he asked, as if he didn't already know it.

"Yeah, it sure as hell is," answered Primo as he pulled onto the dock ready to unload the container.

The ship, also a freighter, was scheduled to arrive on the East Coast in about a month after its San Francisco departure. There was no return address on the bill of lading. The container would have to sit back there on the dock until someone claimed it. Once they had seen to it that the container was taken aboard-ship, they returned and joined Pucci and the others where the Panamanian-registered "Amigo Negro" freighter had been moored. It was now being pushed out into the channel by the two big tugs.

The freighter certainly had the appearance of a rusty, messy-looking vessel. It was surprising that it had been allowed in port in the first place. The heavy load of wine barrels and sugar caused it to ride low in the water. You could now see the unkept and disorderly condition on deck with the crew looking just as bad as the freighter. It left the feeling that it was in no condition to put out to sea with such a heavy cargo. Surely it would flounder and sink before reaching its destination, thought the paesani who were standing around speculating as to what might come next.

Mike was puffing on his cigar as he sat in the Model-T Ford with Julio at his side. Julio's pleasant features were showing the strain of battle. But although he wasn't the fighting type either, he'd follow Mike no matter where he led him. In his pleasant manner, he asked the question: "What happens to the rest of the wine now, Mike?"

The answer was brief: "Who knows for sure? But as long as Pucci is here, we'll also stay."

"Maybe we should have cleaned out the warehouse while we had the chance," said Julio.

"Easier said than done. Pucci weighed the risks both ways and decided to let them load it." He took a couple of hard-pulling puffs on his cigar before adding: "The fight's not over yet. You'll see soon enough."

They sat there watching the two big tugs working the loaded

rusty hulk out and away from the dock. "I'm glad I was able to save that tugboat for that man, Sven," Mike mumbled. "He's a good man, and he keeps his boat looking real good. He knows what he's doing and so does his friend, the big Swede."

Mike grinned. Every time he saw a big Swede, his mind wandered back to some of the fights he'd witnessed between them and the Irishmen. They couldn't say hello to each other without getting into a fight. Their idea of a handshake was a right chop to the jaw.

Al was still sitting in the open cab of the Doane taking in the conversation between Pucci and Primo, who were off to one side leaning on the vehicle. They were admiring the performance of the two big tugs as they maneuvered the freighter out towards the channel. The sea gulls were following it out, hovering constantly looking for its cargo of garbage, and rightfully so, because it sure as hell smelled like a garbage scow. They would, no doubt, stay with it until they found out otherwise.

"I hope Sven understands that even though the freighter's captain may be a wanted man, there are some things that can't be done. There are laws," said Pucci. "Christ! Look at the amount of men on those two tugs, will ya? What the hell do they think they're going to do? Pirate the damned thing? That's not the plan for Christ's sake!"

This comment struck Primo somewhat funny. He answered in a laughing manner: "That would be something if they did and got away with it."

"I suppose no one would give a damn," said Pucci dryly. "They'd probably get a reward for bringing in that greasy-looking captain. I could smell that dirty bastard from down on the dock the other night. He's the one Swede should have dunked in the Bay instead of the teamster, or maybe both of them, for that matter."

The paesani were watching the big tugs push the freighter out closer and closer to the deep channel. It was belching puffs of black smoke from its tall, single stack, building up a head of steam in preparation for a full-speed-ahead run out through the Golden Gate, once the tugs backed off. They were jabbering amongst themselves:

"Too bad all that fine wine has to fall into the hands of a bunch of villains," commented one of the men. "No doubt the

Captain and his crew will drink more than their fair share. They may even take it slow so they'll have more time to drink more wine," he added in a sad down-in-the-mouth manner.

"No," said another. "Those kinds of people don't drink wine. They're like monkeys, they drink coconut milk."

"Coconut milk!" exclaimed yet another. "I don't believe you. Besides, how do you milk a coconut? What do you take me for, a complete fool?" he asked.

This now was the cue for Contini, the great Etruscan philosopher, to explain the nomenclature of the coconut and its contribution to mankind. Sensing a lively discussion about to commence, all ears were now tuned to the scholarly voice of the "Learned One," Mr. Contini.

He started out by explaining the shape and height of the coconut tree and how the coconuts hang in hairy-like clusters below the skirt-shaped palm fronds.

"Wait a minute," called out one of the men. "I think I saw them one time in a Scottish bagpipe parade, but I didn't know that you could milk them."

It took some time to quiet the paesani down after that comment but, nevertheless, Contini was encouraged to continue:

"Once the coconut is harvested, the outer husk is peeled off, therefore leaving a hairy, hard surface with what appears to be little eyes grouped together on one end much like the head of a hairy monkey," he explained.

"Contini, you are amazing," interrupted Vasco. "You have just described little Pietro here. I can hardly wait to milk his coconut head. But, tell me, where does the milk come from? His nose or his ears?"

Well, there was no point in Contini trying to explain such a technical matter as deriving milk from a coconut to this bunch of nuts. They were laughing and commenting disrepectfully like self-interest-oriented congressmen shouting down a sensible political opponent that was trying to promote good legislation.

Matteoli was not about to spar with him on this one. He knew better. To try to describe the matter of coconuts that look like so many hairy elephant balls with little eyes to an immigrant Italian was completely out of the question.

Contini walked away from his laughing colleagues in

complete disgust. As he passed the cab of the Model-T Ford, he stopped long enough to look in at Mike and Julio. They, too, were laughing along with the rest of the others.

"You, too, Mike," said Contini, as Caesar had said to Brutus. He then turned away in disappointment, but stopping short, turned back and once again faced his two laughing friends and said: "God makes them, and Christ pairs them."

To the delight of the others, Contini, the proven master of wit, had cleverly made reference to a pair of fools.

Back away from the Embarcadero, there were others watching this event as well. The Police Chief and the Mayor were standing alongside the unmarked police car listening to what the two plainclothes policemen had to report. The one doing the talking was pointing to the cargo container now being strapped down on the deck of the cargo ship moored several piers down the Embarcadero. The ship bore the name of its owners in large letters, "Atlantic Coast Shipping Corp."

"We just can't make out the connection, Chief," he said. "We saw the men from the Model-T Ford enter the warehouse. We heard the rattle of machine gun fire like you couldn't believe. As ordered, we didn't intervene. The Ford then charged into the warehouse, hell-bent for destruction. A short time later, it came back out loaded with all those men you see over there standing around it, smeared with blood-red paint or whatever. About the same time, that low-bed truck you see over there came out from around the back side with that huge container taking up the whole bed, and headed for the Embarcadero. We took a quick look through the entrance of the warehouse. All we could see through the still-lingering gunsmoke was the limo with one side of it smashed in. The three gangsters were nowhere in sight."

The Chief was pondering the report when the Mayor asked the question: "Do you suppose those men down there got the best of them (referring to the gangsters), and their bodies are in that container?"

"I hardly believe that, your Honor," answered the Chief. "Those men over there are unarmed. They're not really even fighters, let alone killers. No way. If the gangsters are in the container, they're alive; unfortunately." The Chief thought for a moment, before adding: "There's nothing we can do here now. The ship is on its way out, so let's go up and take a look at the warehouse."

"Good idea; maybe it will reveal something useful," answered the Mayor.

The smell of gunpowder was still strong to the nostrils as the four men entered and looked around the all but vacant warehouse. The limo was smashed up on one side all right, like being kicked in by a couple of irate mules. The two submachine guns were laying on the floor amongst empty shell casings. Blood-red dye was splashed and smeared just about everywhere.

"So this is what the little Jewish jeweler meant when he said, 'I'm sure it will be a colorful event,'" thought the Chief. Turning to the Mayor, the Chief asked: "Do you see any evidence that the missing gangsters may have been killed, your Honor?"

The Mayor answered the question promptly: "All it looks like to me is a bunch of Italians having been horsing around in their customary manner, Chief. I see no blood, no bodies, no signs of foul play whatever. The guns were obviously harmless."

"Well, then," stated the Chief, "since we're all in agreement that there has been no crime committed, the case is closed."

CHAPTER 33

The freighter was now in the channel headed in the direction of the Golden Gate and the open Pacific. The tugs were backed away from it but not yet leaving. They were sort of hanging around, standing by.

Pucci was keeping a close watch as a churning wake developed at the stern of the freighter; obviously the full-speed-ahead order had been given as the bow commenced plowing into the swells. She was heading out to sea in the face of the afternoon winds and a developing fog bank that could be seen out towards the Farallon Islands. Without saying a word to the others, he jumped into his little Reo run-about fire truck and took off in the direction of the Coast Guard cutter, Skipjack, moored at its berth a short way up the Embarcadero.

Through binoculars, Captain Terranova was eying the freighter suspiciously. It was moving out at too high a rate of speed for an old dilapidated vessel. There was something fishy about it, he thought.

"You look upset," commented the captain as Pucci hurried up to him. "What's the matter?" he asked.

"That damned captain refused to let me inspect the freighter before pulling out," lied Pucci.

"He did what!?" exclaimed the captain.

"Just as I said, Captain. And what's worst of all, those seamen's lives could be at stake. That thing's a firetrap if I ever saw one, Sir." What Pucci had said was not entirely a lie because had he asked for permission to board the vessel, he would have been flatly refused anyway. As for the seamen's lives being at stake,

243

that too had merit. What with the freighter's cargo worth a king's ransom, who knows what they may be confronted with before reaching their destination.

Captain Terranova flew into action. This was just the excuse he needed to go after it. He was convinced that its old dilapidated appearance was merely a disguise for a powerful, modern, high-speed vessel, something that hadn't occurred to Pucci. Besides, according to reports, it was possibly armed. Another feature that stuck in his craw. He barked commands:

"Prepare to cast off! All hands to their posts, on the double! Come on now, let's go!" he yelled out to his men. "I'll bring her back, don't you worry about that one bit! Step off, we're pulling out, pronto!" he said to Pucci.

Pucci stepped off onto the dock as the cutter cleared its moorings. As it pulled out, the captain shouted to the commander of the slower, smaller cutter berthed just ahead of the Skipjack: "Follow me out, we may need help!"

Once clear of the docks, the Skipjack's sharp bow rose above the waters in response to the thrust of its powerful engines, its flag snapping in the breeze while its radio crackled messages to Coast Guard headquarters.

Out in the Bay, the two big tugs' skippers were eagerly watching and searching the waterfront for something to happen. "If that cutter doesn't come out pretty soon, it will be too late," commented Sven as he glanced towards the other tug.

Swede was walking back and forth from one end of his tug to the other like a pit bull itching for a fight. He had commented to Sven sometime earlier that he had never had so much fun since they had teamed up with these Italians. They, like Pucci, had no idea what kind of vessel they were dealing with. As for its name, God only knows how often its been changed to thwart positive identification.

The two tugs were chugging along, side by side, riding the freighter's wake like a pair of huge porpoises when Sven hollered out over the radio excitedly:

"Here she comes, Swede! Man, look at her go! By golly, the cutter is skipping across the water like nothing I've ever seen before."

"Look at the flag, will ya! It's snapping like a bull whip!" yelled Swede in delight. "We may get a fight out of this yet, Sven."

"My God, man, don't you ever think of anything else besides fighting?" commented Sven, then said: "Okay. We better get going. But remember, let the cutter stay well ahead of us."

"How would you do otherwise?" commented Swede. "We surely can't catch it."

The freighter, under a full head of steam, was picking up speed surprisingly fast. Like a battered-up looking hot rod, the exterior doesn't necessarily reveal what it has under the hood. But, Captain Terranova knew what he was doing. He was heading out ahead of the freighter in order to intercept it where it will be, rather than where it is now, similar to the lead a duck hunter gives a fast-moving target.

Pucci was now back with his friends. Without taking time to explain, he called out to them: "Come on, let's get up on the other side of Fort Point. Primo, leave your truck here. You and Al ride with me. Mike, you follow us. I'll clear the way with my siren."

His cool, all-business-like manner had now given way to excitement; the very thing the paesani needed to lift their spirits. For surely, it was depressing to think that all that wine was being lost forever.

Al, sitting up front with Pucci and Primo, was satisfied that he hadn't misjudged Pucci. His actions were indicative of his determination to continue the campaign. But, was there a plan?

Primo put a question to Pucci:

"What do you think, can Captain Terranova bring the freighter back to port?"

"He has the authority, but we need more than that," answered Pucci. "Unless the freighter's captain is taken into custody, there's no way we can get at its cargo."

So that's the strategy, thought Al: A freighter, loaded with contraband cargo moored to a dock without its captain; the watch dogs locked up in a shipping crate; a crew of questionable loyalty, and authorities sympathetic to the cause. "Jesus Christ, what a deal," mumbled Al.

Primo, overhearing Al's mumbled comment, asked: "What'd you say, Al?"

"Nothing, nothing really, just thinking out loud, I guess."

The Ford, despite its load of wah-hooping paesani, was keeping pace with the siren-wailing Reo. Julio, riding up front with

245

Mike, posed a question:

"Mike," said Julio, "what do you think, is the wine lost for good?"

"You know Pucci!" answered Mike. "He's always got something up his sleeve, but he can't win them all." There was a plan of some sort, but knowing nothing about the sea or ships, he wasn't really banking on it.

"What you're saying is that Pucci does have something going, but you're not sold on the idea."

"You could say that."

"Well, in that case, my friend, I'll make you a wager," offered Julio in all seriousness. "My share of tonight's dinner wine, against a whole Toscanello cigar, that Pucci will have a measure of success."

Mike thought about the offer while dodging traffic along Lombard Street, at the same time glancing up to see his sister, Rosina, pull back the window curtain as they were going by her flat. She was attracted to the window by the Reo's wailing siren. She recognized Pucci's fire truck, but was surprised to see her son, Primo and Al riding with him, and Mike's Model-T loaded with hand-waving paesani following close behind. She waved back all right — but with a clenched fist. She was condemning their actions and presence, without knowing anything about reasons. Woman's instinct told her that they were up to something mischievous, for sure. Her fist was still clenched tight as she watched them go by, except that she was now biting down hard on the knuckles — an Italian expression of frustrated anger.

Her husband, Teodoro, a heavyset man with a pumpkin-like head, having just stepped out of the toilet down the hall and seeing his wife sinking her teeth into her knuckles, realized that something was wrong. He thought she was irritated because he had smoked a cigarette while sitting on the throne — a practice she strongly detested. He moved fast in the opposite direction, down the hall through the kitchen and back porch, grabbing his hat as he moved along hurriedly, then out the back door in a flash for he was not about to have her catch up to him with a clenched fist. The 1906 Earthquake had taught him to head for the open fields when disaster was about to strike.

Mike fumbled around in his coat pockets and came up with a fresh, whole Toscanello cigar and handed it to Julio. "Here. Take it," he said. "I might forget to pay you on our bet."

Julio grinned with satisfaction. His bet was a sure thing. He would not only enjoy his share of wine but the cigar as well.

It was, indeed, a strange sight to see. This little fire truck, siren blowing, being followed by a Model-T Ford truck full of paesani hanging onto the side racks while urging the driver on for fear of losing sight of the leader. By the time they had left Lombard Street and were winding their way up and around through the Presidio, the Model-T was spurting steam vapors like an overworked ox on a cold, frosty morning.

When they finally pulled up and stopped on the west side of Fort Point facing the ocean, the freighter had just passed through the Gate with the cutter gaining on her.

The paesani had a commanding view of the drama that was about to take place, but what made it even more exciting to them was the announcement by Pucci that the cutter was commanded by Captain Terranova, their countryman, no less.

The cutter was closing the gap while signaling the freighter to heave to. But, the freighter was ignoring customary signals to stop. Tailing behind and closer to shore was the smaller cutter doing all it could to hold its own against the windswept swells. The freighter would have easily outrun it if that was all she had to deal with, but the faster, new Skipjack was another matter.

The two tugs were crashing through the swells at a steady pace. They didn't intend to get in too close, even if they could have. This was a Coast Guard matter. They weren't about to interfere; but, nevertheless, they tagged along.

From up on the Point, the cutter could be seen coming in on the starboard (right) side of the freighter. It had now caught up to it and was running alongside at a safe distance. Captain Terranova once again signaled the ship to heave to, but the freighter's captain chose to ignore his request. The cutter moved in closer. With bull horn in hand, Captain Terranova demanded of its captain that he bring the vessel to a stop immediately.

The freighter's captain, also with bull horn in hand, stepped out the starboard side of the wheelhouse and onto the bridge, to face the cutter: "I demand an explanation for this interference. Your presence puts my vessel at risk!"

Captain Terranova responded in no uncertain terms: "You

were not to leave port until your vessel was cleared by the City of San Francisco's Fire Inspector. Not having done so, you must, therefore, return to port at once!"

The freighter's captain responded by saying: "Since this cargo is made up of sugar and molasses, (lying of course) and is therefore not considered a fire hazard, I'm not about to do that!" With this, he turned to re-enter the wheelhouse. As he did so, he gestured with his right arm outstretched and middle finger pointed upwards as if to say, "Screw you!"

This infuriated Captain Terranova. This was an outright insult. The pride that had been bred into him would not permit such conduct to be passed off just like that. No, sir, the freighter's captain would be dealt with in Naval-Officer tradition.

"Helmsman, pull away and up ahead!" ordered Captain Terranova. "Gunner, to your station at the cannon! Let me know when you're ready." At the bow of the cutter, the gunner, with assistance of other guardsmen, quickly removed the gun coverings exposing the bright, shiny new cannon.

"Ready, Sir!" came the word from the gunner.

"All right! Fire a round across her bow, now!"

The gunner was meticulous about such matters. He just didn't press the trigger at random. He waited for the cutter to rise up on the next swell, level off, hesitate for a split second — and at that instant, fired the cannon.

From up on the Point a puff of smoke could be seen emitting from the cannon, then the roar of the cannon followed, music to the ears of the paesani. The shell careened across the bow of the freighter and splashed into the ocean some distance beyond. The action could be seen by all. The freighter spewed out a puff of black smoke out the stack as more fuel was being injected into the furnaces. It was obvious that she was picking up more speed rather than heaving to.

"They're going to make a run for it!" said Pucci excitedly.

Any further conversation was drowned out by the yelling and shouting of the paesani. They were calling out encouragement to the cutter's captain. They'd rather see the freighter sunk, than to escape with all that wine. The wine barrels would, no doubt, float and wash ashore. One by one they would eventually get them all — they were acting like a bunch of kids just having discovered a horde of marbles.

The cutter's radioman dispatched an urgent message back to Coast Guard Headquarters. It said:

"The vessel appears to be something other than a common freighter. Her captain refuses to acknowledge my authority. Request permission to use force to bring the vessel about."

Back at Coast Guard Headquarters, having just received confirmation of the captain's and vessel's true identity, the District Commander along with the Police Chief and the Mayor, were discussing a possible course of action when they were relayed the cutter's urgent message.

"It looks like they're going to disobey the cutter's request and make a run for it," the Commander announced. Then added: "It's the 'El Vento Este' all right. We've got to stop it!"

The Mayor asked, "What can be done about it, and how can you stop it?"

"I'd rather not speculate, your Honor. Under the circumstances, it's more or less up to the captain of the cutter as to how he stops it, unless I order him to do otherwise."

"I see. Well, what're your thoughts then?"

"My preference is to let Captain Terranova make the decisions. He's the one closest to the problem. If he has to use force, so be it."

His Honor, the Mayor, looked directly at the Police Chief as he asked for his opinion.

"I go along with the Commander. Besides, it's not in my jurisdiction," answered the Chief.

"Well, then . . . since I have no authority or jurisdiction either, I'll obviously also agree."

The Commander immediately instructed the radioman to relay the answer back to the cutter. The radio crackled:

"The vessel must be brought about! Use your discretion as to the method."

Captain Terranova had his "orders."

As for the freighter's captain, he didn't really think the cutter would take drastic measures to stop him. In his mind, he hadn't given it reason to do so. But, he wasn't aware that his and the freighter's identity had been uncovered.

Back on the cutter's bridge, Captain Terranova, bull horn in hand, was barking orders to the battle-ready crew. He wasn't told what he was dealing with, only that he must take the vessel.

"Helmsman, drop 'er back a little and hold 'er steady!" he ordered. "Gunner, stand by to fire cannon!" The gunner announced he was ready. "Okay, take that shed off the bow! Let's see what's under there — Fire!"

The gunner again waited a few seconds for the upcoming swell. The cutter rose up, leveled off, hesitated. With that, he let fly the second round. In a split second, the shell crashed into the shed-like structure, sending chunks of debris into the ocean, and exposing the freighter's cannon. Amongst the chunks of debris that splashed into the ocean was the remnants of a life preserver. The pieces were big enough to make out the stenciled letters of the vessel's true name, "S.S. El Vento Este."

For an instant Captain Terranova shuddered. He was out there alone taking on the notorious "rumrunner," El Vento Este, that in its plying of the nation's coastline transporting contraband from port to port, had eluded or destroyed every authoritative vessel that ever tried to take it. He knew what he was up against; for an instant his coolness faded, but not his wits. When the shot hit its mark, men aboard the rumrunner had ducked out of sight only to reappear again heading for the cannon.

Captain Terranova had already seen the gunner take his position at the fifty-caliber machine gun at the stern of the cutter. While pointing at the men, he barked an order:

"Gunner on the fifty! Keep those men away from the cannon! Avoid casualties if possible!" His intent was to take the vessel — not kill men.

No sooner said than done. Each time the cutter settled down for a few seconds, the gunner would let go a burst of machine gun fire ahead and around the crew forcing them to take cover. The whining, ricocheting slugs from the fifty sent men tumbling into recesses that they themselves never knew existed.

"Hold it fifty!" snapped the captain. "Gunner on the cannon! Take that cannon off the deck of that bugger!" he ordered with regained coolness.

The first of the next two rounds hit the vessel's railing closest to the cutter sending metal shrapnel flying in all directions further suppressing movements of the crew as they scrambled for cover.

In the meantime, Captain Terranova could see men working

their way up the ladders of the superstructure heading towards the shed on top of the wheelhouse directly in front of the smokestack. He yelled out:

"Gunner on the fifty!" Keep those men away from that shed up there!"

The machine gun instantly chattered as bullets poked holes in the superstructure in even lines back and forth above the crew's heads. It was beginning to look like the trunk of an apple tree being worked over by a meticulous woodpecker.

Meantime, the cannon roared again. Only this time, the shell found its mark. It exploded against the cannon mount sending pieces of metal skyward. The gun barrel spun around in a crazy-like pattern before coming to rest pointing in a lopsided angle towards the sky. It was clearly disabled.

Sven and Swede were close enough to see the action. Their only regrets were that they had not joined the military services.

"There's where the action is, by golly!" Swede was telling Sven over his radio.

"Maybe they can't sink her, but they sure as hell are getting the best of her!" answered Sven in delight. But the battle had just begun.

"Gunner on the fifty! Work on the shed up there! Men are coming up from the other side!" announced the Captain again. "Helmsman, drop 'er back a little more! Give the cannon a better shot at that shed!"

The cutter having dropped further back, put itself in position to be rammed. Taking quick advantage of the blunder, the rumrunner veered sharply to starboard, leaning heavily to port side and putting herself on a collision course with the cutter. You would think barnacles the size of baseballs would expose themselves on the lower extremes of the hull, but such was not the case. She was extremely clean below normal waterline, and slick as a whistle, typical of a high-speed rumrunner.

"You damned son-of-a-bitch!" swore Captain Terranova, as he saw the sharp bow slicing through the swells intent on splitting the cutter in half. The helmsman also saw the horrifying predicament they were in and was about to act accordingly when he heard the captain's frantic shout:

"Hard to starboard! Hard to starboard!"

The cutter, such as the rumrunner, leaned heavily to port side as she swung to starboard. The captain was drenched with sea water as the maneuver sent wind-swept ocean spray high and across the breadth of the cutter. Having dropped his bull horn, he was hanging on with both hands in order to keep from being catapulted over the dipping bridge's railing. Through the confusion, the machine gunner heard the captain's urgent, screaming order:

"Fifty! Blast her wheelhouse! Blast her wheelhouse!"

The machine gun bucked, sending lead slugs the size of acorns into the rumrunner's wheelhouse, splattering glass throughout its interior as well as on the decks below. Rather than sending off bursts of fire, the hot steaming gunbarrel was spurting a steady stream of bullets. The gunner was taking advantage of the cooling effect of the ocean spray sweeping across the cutter's stern. Instruments were being chewed off the walls as the concentrated machine-gun fire worked its way back and forth through the interior, devastating everything in its path. No doubt there were small arms aboard ship, but who had the guts to expose one of them in a threatening manner in the face of that deadly machine gun. Besides, there were crack-shot guardsmen with rifles standing by eager to put their training to the test.

The rumrunner's helmsman was forced to let go of the wheel and take cover. In so doing, the wheel spun back like a wheel of fortune. The vessel was answering to the will of resistance and the demands of memory. It now veered to port side while leaning heavily to starboard as it was reinstating its original course. Had the rumrunner's captain been standing on the starboard bridge, he could have shaken hands with Captain Terranova.

"Gunner on the cannon, you've got it now! Take out the shed!" yelled the captain urgently. He wanted that shot off before the vessel rolled back up to its normal upright position.

The gunner could have hit it with his eyes closed. It was like shooting at a garage door from across the street. The cannon shell entered the shed in an almost downward direction. The vessel's roll had put the railing at water level. The swell the gunner had waited for was timed perfectly. It put the cutter high up, causing the shell to barely clear its railing as it departed from the muzzle of the cannon. The debris from the explosion was dropping back onto the cutter in sizeable chunks. It had blasted the machine-gun mount, and parts of decking clear off the rumrunner. That was, indeed, the end of its heavy armament. Again, the two vessels were running side by side.

Captain Terranova was not about to ask the rumrunner's captain to "heave to" again. He was indeed mad, but hadn't lost his sense of caution. The near collision taught him to be wary of his opponent, and to give no quarter. He issued his next command with confidence, sharp and to the point:

"Gunner on the cannon! Take the stack off that son-of-a-bitch! Gunner on the fifty! Put another burst high on the inside of the wheelhouse! Run those bastards out of there! Riflemen, pepper that frigg'n crew! Try to run me down, will you, you banana-weaned bastards!" he growled. "I'll burn you to waterline!" He was now addressing the vessel, captain, and crew alike.

Whether he really meant what he said or not was certainly not disputable since the next shell from the cannon hit the stack and exploded a few feet above the top of the wheelhouse roof deck. The stack teetered back, and then forward again. The explosion blew a gaping hole in the front portion of the stack, therefore leaving no support to carry its weight. It continued to lean forward; and finally came crashing down over the wheelhouse, spewing black smoke and soot as if the vessel was actually afire. And so it reflected below in the engine room as well. The chief engineer was to get no response from his inquiries to the wheelhouse, so he ordered a halt to the engines before scrambling up to the main deck. The men handling the boilers followed suit without bothering to shut the furnaces down. The instant backfire of soot and smoke had forced them away from the boilers.

As her engines came to an abrupt halt, the bow of the vessel nosedived into the sea, sending ocean spray high into the face of the wind, then settled back as seawater cascaded off the forward deck and down the sides, thus putting an end to the vessel's ability to continue the fight. The "S.S. El Vento Este", the notorious rumrunner, was now just a plain ship, dead in the water.

"Now, that's better," grumbled Captain Terranova as he viewed the situation searching for the ship's captain. He would now address him, if he could find him. But he was not in his line of sight.

Sven and Swede were following the wake of the rumrunner like a pair of bloodhounds following the trail of a wanted criminal. Sven yelled out:

"Did you see that? She'll go no further now, by golly."

Swede gave him a "thumbs up" sign. They had both backed off even farther when the shooting started. The smaller cutter was jabbering over its radio keeping home base informed of the action as it was coming up to the rear and port side of the rumrunner, well out of the line of fire.

"Sir, the Skipjack has succeeded in stopping her," reported the radioman rather excitedly to the District Commander back at headquarters.

"Well, gentlemen, you heard the report. I suppose we should further instruct the Skipjack to carry out our wishes, whatever they may be. What are your thoughts, gentlemen?"

"What is the normal procedure under the circumstances?" asked the Mayor.

"Again, that'll depend on the conduct or response of the vessel's captain. Since he's a wanted criminal, maybe you'd be interested in taking him in, Chief?" suggested the Commander.

"I doubt that it's in my jurisdiction to do so. I'd rather the Skipjack sink the vessel, along with the captain, Sir. It would be less trouble for all of us," answered the Police Chief sternly.

"Unless the vessel's captain refuses to surrender, I'm afraid that would be inappropriate. Besides, the cutter hasn't the ability to do that on its own, and since it's solely up to me to make the decision," said the Commander, "I'll instruct Captain Terranova to board the vessel, take its captain into custody, and bring the vessel back to port."

The radioman interrupted to report the vessel being afire. There were now few options left. So, the message went out leaving the final decisions to be made solely by Captain Terranova. The three officials then strolled out for a breath of fresh air.

"Commander, is there a military terminology for such a decision and situation such as this?" inquired the Mayor.

"Yes, there is, your Honor. It's called 'passing the buck.' We use it quite often when we're not sure of the consequences."

The comment drew chuckles and grins for it was not only a military practice, it applied at all sorts of authoritative levels.

Up on the Point, a sizable crowd had gathered to watch the battle at sea taking place a short distance outside the Golden Gate. News travels fast throughout a community when this sort of action takes place. Without having the slightest idea of what the issue was all about, the crowd naturally hooted and hollered their approval of the Skipjack's conduct, for it displayed the American flag in all its glory. This was to their liking.

The paesani up on the hill were dancing around in a circle to the imaginary beat of the song, "Tarantella." They were elated about the whole affair. Since they couldn't shake hands with their fellow Italian, the Skipjack's captain, they engaged in a backslapping, handshaking spree amongst themselves. Each one was expressing his version of the strategy employed by the cutter to subdue the armed vessel; all talking at the same time, no one listening to the other. In the interest of fairness to each other, it was decided that Contini be called upon to apply his expertise in his prudent manner so as to settle this issue of naval procedures.

He felt, indeed, honored to think that these men, his true friends, looked upon him to analyze and decipher the highly technical

255

military action that had taken place in this battle of vessels and, therefore, submit his findings to them in understandable layman's terms. The truth of the matter was he didn't know any more about such matters than they did. This time he was, indeed, in trouble; but he had to come up with something or lose his standing amongst them. So, he started out by asking them to search their memories:

"Do you remember the ship that carried you to these lands? You will recall, it too was a steamer with a smokestack. The purpose of the smokestack is to exhaust smoke and gasses from the boilers below."

He was now searching for something to add to this statement that could apply to the strategy when Julio, in his pleasant, soft-spoken manner interrupted him. The timing couldn't have been better.

"Contini," he said, "you're trying to explain a highly technical naval maneuver to a group of men that don't understand a coconut. Don't you think you're taxing your highly complex brain for nothing?"

This was perfect. An out for the great Etruscan philosopher without the discomfort of embarrassment. Julio had unknowingly come to his rescue. Contini was quick to answer:

"Yes, you're right, Julio. Therefore let's just say that the decision and actions of an Italian naval officer speak for themselves. There's no need to explain his strategy."

The men were dumbfounded. Not that they were satisfied with the answer to their technical question, but with the strategy exercised by Contini to work his way out of what could have been a highly embarrassing situation. This man is, indeed, a genius, so they thought. And a fellow paesano, at that!

CHAPTER 34

The ship's smokestack having collapsed across its shot-out base was impairing the normal draft required to maintain the boiler's fireboxes burning efficiently. The choking action was causing smoke from oxygen-starved fuel combustion to back up into the boiler room which, in turn, was being sucked up to the upper deck, especially the superstructure. Black oily smoke was pouring out of vents and openings as if the boiler room was ablaze.

On the port side of the ship, preparations were under way to launch the ship's motorized tender. The captain was not about to be taken in by the Coast Guard. And since it appeared the ship, or at least its cargo, would be lost anyway, he was therefore intent on making a run for it. Crew members also sized up the situation. There was no question the ship was being abandoned by the captain, first mate, and anyone else close enough to jump onto the tender as it descended down the port side of the ship. The rest of the crew proceeded to lower a lifeboat down the starboard side with the same intention.

The Skipjack was standing by. Captain Terranova was sizing up the situation. The normal procedure would be to put his men on board. But remembering Pucci's comments about it being a firetrap, and since it already appeared to be afire, caused him to have second thoughts. No, he thought, why risk his men's lives for a ship the captain himself was abandoning.

The small cutter, coming up on the ship's port side, moved in to take the tender. However, this was easier said than done for the tender took off at full throttle heading for the fog bank. This wasn't an ordinary tender. It was equipped with powerful twin engines and a sleek hull typical of coastal rumrunners. The chase was on; a real challenge for the small cutter. It wasn't about to overtake the tender that easily.

The Skipjack moved in and took the lifeboat in tow. The captain asked if there was anyone else left on board. The answer was no. Therefore, the ship was completely abandoned.

"All right, Helmsman," said the captain. "Move away from the vessel. Radioman, inform Headquarters that we can't risk boarding the ship; therefore, it being completely abandoned and on fire, it's being left for salvage."

The two tugboats were tuned in on the same radio frequency as the cutter's. When Sven and Swede heard the message announced over the radio, they let out a howl of joy. The tugs' propellers instantly churned up sea foam as they thrust the tugs forward. They were now bearing down on the crippled vessel giving it all they had. There was no time to lose. Every second was precious.

The tugboat captains had already assessed the situation. With quick, decisive action, they may just be able to save it. If so, it would surely be a valuable prize. The two tugs split.

Sven was coming up to the starboard side while Swede plowed through the blinding smoke to come up around to the port side. One of Sven's men shimmied up one of the same ropes left dangling over the side by the lifeboat. Once on deck, he threw the ship's rope ladder over the side, then ran around to the port side and did the same thing for Swede and his men. By the time he made it back again to the starboard side, Sven was already on deck struggling with a steel cable being fed off the tug's winch alongside while others were lending a hand along the way.

While this was going on, Swede and his men were crawling up the rope ladder on the opposite side of the ship, pulling dry fire hoses up from their tug as they worked their way up to the deck. Once on deck, two of Swede's men were swinging fire axes, smashing portholes in the general area of where the stack came up through the superstructure, while he scrambled up to the stack to lend Sven a hand. Men would disappear through the clouds of smoke pouring out of openings, only to reappear again above or below its source.

Fire pumps on both tugs were building up pressure, standing by to send high-pressure water through fire hoses when called upon.

Sea water was gushing out of relief valves since the men struggling with the hoses were not ready for it yet. They were not ready because the stack must be swung aside first.

The two skippers had reached the top roof deck where the stack lay horizontally with the open end towards the bow. The ship was being kept into the wind by the two tugs in order to keep it as free as possible of smoke that was boiling out around the base of the stack. The two skippers worked their way along towards its open end.

"Okay!" yelled Swede. "Throw me the hook!" With this, Sven threw the hook with sufficient slack in the cable over the top as he yelled back:

"Watch it! Here it comes!"

Grabbing both hook and cable, Swede called for more slack as he prepared to feed it back under. "Watch your feet, Sven, it's coming back to you!"

The big hook came sliding back under. Sven grabbed at it, hooked it over the cable making a slip loop that would tighten on the stack once slack was taken up. Both men scrambled down ladders shouting orders to their men to move up towards the bow on the double.

"Are your men in the clear?" called out Sven.

"Okay, take it," came the answer.

From the railing of the ship, Sven was signalling the tug's helmsman to start moving away from the ship. The cable was now picking itself off the rigging as it tightened up. To be at the stern of the ship would mean to suffocate with the amount of concentrated windswept smoke pouring out of the general area of the superstructure's vents and openings. The tug was now putting sideward pressure on the stack. It was coming around. The groaning and screeching of metal scraping against metal signified the stack was heavy. Railings and other protrusions were being scraped off the top deck as it continued coming around. Supported by the still-attached metal at its base and portions of the top deck, the angle of pull was forcing the stack around and down. It was about to break loose. In a sharp, crunching, swinging motion, the open end swung around and downward as resistance gave way to constant pressure. It hung there in a downward direction. There was still enough metal attached at the shot-out base to keep it from falling off, and tumbling into the sea.

"Hold it! Hold it!" yelled Sven while motioning frantically. "That's good enough. Back off! Back off!"

With a couple of long hook poles, the two skippers where able to work the cable off the end of the stack, sending the cable splashing down into the sea.

"Okay. Pick it up and get back over here with those fire hoses. Tie on to her and keep her into the wind," shouted Sven.

The obstruction was now cleared. The stubbed flue was belching up big clouds of billowing black smoke. However, there was nothing to rejoice about at this point because the men knew the worst was yet to come. As expected, orange flames were licking up through the flue mingling with the billowing black smoke. With the flue now cleared, the upward draft was increasing as hot gasses were allowed to escape, therefore drawing more oxygen into the furnaces below that were overloaded with heavy, unburned fuel oil.

Swede could be heard shouting orders to his men: "Get the water in those portholes and openings! Keep her cool! Stay away from the top; we don't want water down the stack!"

They were concentrating streams of water in areas closest to where the flue worked its way up through the superstructure. The other tug's fire hoses were now doing the same thing on the opposite side of the ship at Sven's direction. No way could they pour water down the hot flue and into the now roaring furnaces. A mistake like that could cause an explosion spewing hot, burning fuel oil throughout the entire boiler and engine room. The intention was to burn up the excess fuel without setting fire to the ship or causing an explosion. The more it burned, the hotter the gases; the increased flue temperatures created more upward draft pulling more oxygen into the furnaces, increasing combustion intensely. The more combustion, the more steam generated with no place to go except out the safety valves. The trick now was to get things in balance or blow up the ship in trying.

From up on the Point, it appeared that all was lost. What were cheers of joy were now sobs of sorrow. All was silent as the crowd watched a handful of brave men battle what appeared to be a hopeless beast of a fire. However, the men battling the beast knew it to be somewhat different. The fire was still confined to the furnaces. What they saw from up there was intense black smoke commingled with orange flames confined to the stub of the stack. Smoke that was drifting out of the other openings was merely what had backed up below from overloaded fire boxes. There was still a chance to save the ship providing, however, they could manage to regain stability before the intense heat set other parts of the ship on fire or a boiler was to let go. By now, the upward draft was so intense that smoke from below was actually being sucked back into the furnaces and out the flue along with the hot gases.

Swede and one of his men were now working their way down metal ladders towards the engine room. They were being followed down by a crew member dragging along a fire hose keeping them constantly saturated with a fine spray of cool water as they descended.

Sven was running around on deck opening whatever steam valves he could find. The intent being to use up as much excess steam as possible until Swede could reach the engine room. Once there, he could open up the main control valves putting the vessel's engines in full reverse. Thus, the resistance of the blunt stern would use up more steam without much directional movement. The smoke was clearing out, but the heat was unbearable. They reached the fire-box level as exhausting steam from relief valves added to the furnace heat.

Swede made a dash for the main fuel supply valve, spun it closed, then retreated back to take shelter under the spray of cool water. The two men would take turns. The next dash opened the valves to the fire pumps.

Sven was up on deck hoping for just that. They had more men up there than fire hoses. Now the ship's fire hoses, in addition to the tugs', were in action as water cascaded out of openings and down the side of the superstructure like waterfalls. The stubbed off stack was still belching hot flames and smoke into the sky. Paint was blistering off the steel plates around it.

Sven's voice could barely be heard above the roar of the emitting hot gases: "Use a fine spray when you can! Just keep it cool! And for God's sake, keep it out of the stack!" There was a lot more at stake now than the ship itself. Swede was down there with a couple of men. Their lives were at extreme risk.

From the Point above, the sizeable crowd that had gathered gasped in despair as they saw steam vapors in sizeable clouds shoot upwards from in and around the ship. They were shouting down instructions as if they could be heard: "Get those tugs out of there. Can't you see she's going to blow? It's hopeless."

Pucci, with one foot propped up on the front bumper of his little Reo fire truck, could hear the crowd's comments. However, as anxious and concerned as he was, he was not about to go along with them. He kept mumbling to himself: "Hang in there, Sven. You're going about it right. You'll succeed." Then in an audible voice, added: "God help you if you don't!"

Both Al and Primo looked at Pucci wondering what he meant by that remark. There was some conversation in low tones amongst the paesani, but they were not rejoicing or clowning around now. They realized the seriousness of conditions on the crippled vessel below. Suddenly the ship shuddered noticeably, creaked and groaned as she started her reverse movement bucking the outgoing tide.

"By golly, ol' Swede got her going!" Sven yelled out excitedly, then shouted out further instructions to the men manning the tugs: "Tie on! Use a little power! Let her drag you along! I'm going below with Swede."

As he descended the metal ladders, he could feel the intense heat from the engine room. There was no cool ocean breeze down here to keep you cool. The spray of cool water drifting down over him felt good; as a matter of fact, life saving.

"What's it look like?" he shouted above the roar of furnaces and pounding of the ship's engines.

"She's pretty damn hot!" answered Swede. "We managed to get all the dampers closed, but she's still sucking in air through the cracks and openings."

"You can expect that until all the oil is burned out, don't you think?" answered Sven.

"Yes, but the pressure keeps rising even though the relief valves are blowing off at full capacity. What the hell are we going to do with all that extra steam?"

"Say, did you get the bilge pumps going?" asked Sven.

"No, by God, I overlooked that. They will help some."

Swede didn't have to move a muscle. His man standing alongside of him covered with soot, sweat, and black oil, made a dash through the maze of pipes and machinery as if it were a matter of life or death, and it could very well be.

Pucci, from up on the Point grinned as he saw water, accompanied by hot vapors, come gushing out the discharge holes of the bilge pumps. He was assessing the various functions that he could see taking place down on the ship when Mike asked the question:

"What do you think? Can they save it?"

"By what I can see from here, they sure as hell are doing all the right things, all right," he answered. But he was still noncommittal. He had fought fires himself that finally appeared to be under control only to have a wind shift, or a wall collapse between buildings at the very last minute, and start the inferno all over again. On a ship fire, especially, there are many things that can go wrong at the last minute. Fighting a fire and/or struggling with overloaded boilers, overheated fire boxes, and excess steam pressures with a full load of fuel under your feet can make an old man out of you in a hurry. No, Pucci was not about to make any rash commitments, not just yet.

"You know something, Sven. This ship has bigger boilers than I've ever seen in a ship this size. Look at them, will you? And that goes for the engines and the rest of the equipment as well. What surprises me even more is how everything is in such real good shape down here. Good equipment and well-maintained. I don't think she's very old," said Swede.

"Yes, I see that," answered Sven. "And if it wasn't in such good shape, the boilers would have blown up by now. It's a good thing for the new cutter or they would never have caught her even with the full load she's carrying. I bet you this ship was built purposely to be a rumrunner, don't you think, Swede?"

"I believe that, all right," answered Swede as he glanced from one instrument to the other. He was also watching the water gauges on the boilers as they fluctuated up and down reacting to the surges of steam emitting from the boilers and the response to replenishing the diminishing water supply by the feed pumps. "My big concern now is to keep an eye on the feed pumps and condensers. We can't afford to have them fail now, by golly," he added.

Pressure gauges were indicating that steam pressure was starting to back down as the boiler relief valves were now starting to change their tone from a "roar" to a more sensible "hiss" as they were shutting down. The engines were still pounding away in full reverse which did bring a comment from Sven.

"I better get back up on top. I wouldn't want to run it aground now, by golly."

Things were beginning to come into balance. The heat was now bearable and the air breathable. Nevertheless, Swede stayed with the boilers even though several other men had joined him below. With the excess fuel oil completely burned off, it was now a matter of gradually bringing the engines back down to a complete stop. In order to avoid damage to the furnaces, they would have to be cooled down very gradually, even to the extent of firing them up occasionally over the next couple of days.

The flue area up through the superstructure was still sending off considerable harmless vapors due to cold water spray coming in contact with hot metal. There was no longer black smoke or flames coming out of the stubbed-off stack. They had it under control and stabilized. It was a grueling fight that took the better part of the afternoon. Young men that had first scrambled on board as mildly experienced seamen were now seasoned mariners, at least to the extent of handling an extreme emergency. What they learned from their skippers this day was not yet printed in the book.

CHAPTER 35

Gathered up on the Point, the crowd expressed delight in seeing the now obvious victory. They had no idea whatsoever as to how it all started or what or who was involved. They had heard reports that the ship had violated fire safety codes, thus the resulting fire aboard ship. They had also heard that the cargo supposedly contained molasses and sugar, and was in danger of being destroyed, with the crew's lives also in jeopardy. The question as to why the ship's crew had not joined the tugboat crews in battling the fire was going unanswered. The ship's tender having been lowered, then departing with the smaller cutter in hot pursuit, added mystery to the whole affair.

Pucci, the only official-looking person present, was being hounded by reporters seeking information about the violations. His only comments were: "Look out there, you can see for yourself." Every time a camera was positioned to take pictures, a couple of paesani would jump out in front of it, hats in hand, big smiles on their faces. They loved to have their pictures taken.

The smaller cutter had long since disappeared out through the fog bank in pursuit of the ship's tender. Indications were that the tender was too fast and had too much of a head start to be overtaken.

The two tugboat skippers were now up on deck directing their men with the chore of towing their prize back into port. Men were cleaning things up, restoring fire fighting equipment and hoses back to their respective places. The dangling stack was strapped to the side so as not to lose it. One tug had the ship in tow while the other assisted nudging it along.

As they moved back through the Gate, other tugs and boats intercepted them but kept their distance. The two skippers standing on the bow waved them away signaling them to stay clear. As they passed through the Gate, they could distinguish their Italian friends up on the Point waving their hats at them. They, in turn, waved their soiled caps as Sven yelled out as loud as he could in their direction. If it were not for the distance between them, they would have heard him say:

"We have your cargo for you, by golly, and we thank you for the ship."

Sven had no way of knowing that the gun battle was not of Pucci's doing. Pucci had asked him to stay with the ship just in case the Coast Guard was to need them to bring it back to port. And if such be the case, they would moor the ship at a predetermined pier so the paesani could hijack its cargo. The tug captains would then share in the bounty. As it turned out, they had it all, lock, stock, and barrel.

What a prize! An almost new vessel specially built for speed and maneuverability. With the exception of it being somewhat shot up, it was in excellent condition, besides having a hold full of hundreds of barrels of quality wine and thousands of sacks of sugar all intact, undamaged. Yes, indeed, quite a prize!

Al was the first to put a question to Pucci: "How the hell did you manage to get the Coast Guard to shoot up the ship?" he asked curiously.

"What makes you think I had anything to do with that?" answered Pucci with his own, to the point, question.

"Huh?" uttered Al in surprise. "You mean you didn't . . .?"

"Hell, no," interrupted Pucci. "I'm just as puzzled as you are. I don't know what got into Captain Terranova. All I said was . . ." Pucci briefly apprized Al and the others of his conversation with the Skipjack's captain, and how he'd hoped to somehow raid the ship's cargo if brought back to port. He readily admitted that his plan had backfired.

Mike fired the next question at Pucci: "How about the wine? We're going to get that, aren't we?"

"I think we will, and half a ship-load of sugar too, I guess, if we want it," answered Pucci.

"Jesus Christ!" said Primo excitedly. "Do you really think

266

they'll let us have the cargo?" he asked, hoping for a positive answer.

"Hell, yes," said Pucci with confidence. "Those guys are sea dogs. All they want is the ship, and they've got it. You don't think they'd risk their lives for sugar and wine, do you? Besides, it being contraband, they wouldn't know what to do with it. And don't forget, we had a deal; they'll honor it."

The answer was logical, especially since Swede was eager to throw in with the paesani. He liked their style; no question, they'd get the cargo.

Pucci, in a serious, concerned manner, turned to Mike and asked the question: "The disposition of the wine (so-called molasses) I can understand; but tell me, what are we going to do with all that sugar?"

Mike was purposely slow in getting his cigar out of his mouth to answer the question. He was thinking the answer over very carefully when Primo interrupted with the statement: "Are you kidding? Can't you see the grin on his face?"

Mike need not answer the question. The three partners walked off in the direction of their vehicles chuckling, snorting, and grinning as they walked along. They were like three young bulls just having been turned out into a green meadow amongst a herd of mature heifers.

It was now late afternoon. His men were eager to get back to the ranch. "Come on, you bunch of paesani," Mike called out in a proud, respectful manner. "Let's get back and open up a fresh barrel of uncut wine. Supper will be ready by the time we get there." Then added: "Al, you and Julio ride up front with me."

The surge of men converging on the bed of the Model-T almost tipped it over on its side. They were waving their hats as it took off down the road, seeking the shortest way home. The "chit, chit, chit" cricket-like sound of the Ford was the last thing heard at the Point as the Reo pulled out ahead to clear the road. It would take them a while to drive from the Point to the ranch at San Bruno. This would give Pucci a chance to discuss an important matter with Primo.

"I guess you know I was sort of pulling Mike's leg back there about the sugar, don't you?" said Pucci.

"Yeah, I knew that," answered Primo. "But I thought it was a good idea to say what I did at the time because he wasn't quite ready to give you an answer just yet. Knowing my uncle as I do, you can be sure the sugar isn't for sale. I'm afraid he has other plans for it."

"That's the very thing that bothers me," said Pucci. "It's not all that wine that worries me, but the sugar is another matter altogether."

"Meaning what?" asked Primo as if he didn't already have a pretty good idea.

"You know damned well that before your uncle unloads it off that ship, he will already be working on getting a still of some sort made up and set up somewhere around here, if not at the ranch itself. And that worries me no end."

"What's the problem? Don't you think my uncle can handle a moonshine operation?"

"Only too damned well." With this, Pucci expressed his concerns. "You know, buddy, the local authorities knew a hell of a lot more than we thought about that warehouse. And for that matter, to some extent, of our own activities in connection with it as well."

"So what? Of course they had to suspect something, for Christ's sake! I've been keeping them supplied with a river of wine. Besides, if they knew so much, how come they let us get as far as we have? Or for that matter, why don't they take the wine away from us right now?"

"My answer to your question is simple — because they needed us. They couldn't do what we could, and have, done. We rid the city of a nest of rats. That's what they wanted most of all. Besides, they're happy to see the wine distributed throughout the community. Wine is okay with them." Pucci continued, "Keep in mind, if they were to confiscate the wine, either the Federal Government will take it over or it'll be dumped. Either way is not acceptable. That would be an outright blunder on their part to put it right back in the hands of the crooked bastards we just took it away from."

"Yeah, I can see your point. You're right. If anything, they helped us. We lucked out on this one."

There was silence for a few minutes as Pucci worked his way through the city with Mike following not far behind. He opened the conversation again. "The way I see it, if we had been dealing in alcohol, we'd be on our way to San Quentin in handcuffs instead of going back to San Bruno."

268

"Hey, don't talk like that. It makes me nervous to even think about it," snapped Primo.

"We're not going to get away with dealing in alcohol without finding ourselves confronted with serious problems," stated Pucci. "We might as well face up to it right now. The authorities know we have the sugar, the main ingredient necessary for making good moonshine. They'll be watching us closely, you can be sure of that. The equipment to set up the still is really a secondary matter. It can be made up in no time."

Primo was listening to every word for he knew his buddy was one to think things out well in advance.

Pucci continued: "You have a good job and I have a good job. They're ours for as long as we want them providing, of course, we don't get caught doing something real stupid and bad. And alcohol is bad. Look at it this way, this Prohibition thing could be short lived. In the meantime, we may get caught. So now we have a criminal record. We, no doubt, would lose our jobs. Then what? You're not going to find it easy to get another one like it with a criminal record."

"I guess you're right, Pucci. Bootlegging is not a very stable business. I'll have to admit that. Do you think we might have some problems develop when the news reaches the Federal agents in Washington?"

"Good question. But my guess is, if anything, they'll disclaim any knowledge of the whole affair, if it were to come to light, that is. Besides, they're going to have their hands full dealing with the Mob. They lost it all: ship, money, wine, sugar, the works; and all legal-like."

The two men thought about that last comment for a few seconds, then started snickering, then chuckling, and finally bursting out in outright laughter.

". . . And a limousine plus two machine guns. But look what they'll get back in return," snorted Pucci. "Three of their prize henchmen neatly packaged and delivered right to their doors. Prepaid at that. And they have no idea who sent them, I hope," he added in a more solemn tone.

"Thank Christ we didn't put a return address on that container," blurted Primo nervously.

As they were driving back to the ranch, there were two other men talking about the sugar along similar lines, only for different objectives.

"Julio," asked Mike, "why don't you say what you're thinking? You have something on your mind. I can see it written all over your face."

Julio responded with a pleasant grin: "Yes," he said, "I do have something on my mind."

"Sugar?" questioned Mike.

"Yes, sugar. Do you know how much alcohol you can make with all that sugar?" he asked as if he didn't already know.

"I know what you're thinking, my friend. Your mind works different than some of the others. There is a fortune to be made in the alcohol business, but one can't do it alone. You must have loyal, dedicated men you can trust because it's a much riskier business than what we're doing now," stated Mike in a manner to excite Al as well.

As long as Mike wanted to talk, Julio let him do so for he remembered what he had been told by his father in the old country some years before: "When a thinking man begins to talk, listen carefully and keep your mouth shut, for you learn through your ears and not your mouth."

Mike continued to carry the conversation: "Julio, you have certain qualities that the others don't have. If I could be sure that you, especially, along with Al here, and a few of the others, would stay with me, I think we could all do well. So, since it is already on your mind, you must tell me how you feel about this moonshine business? Do you want to be involved?"

Now would come Julio's comments and conditional answer: "If I understand you correctly, there'd be some sort of incentive system set up for at least the key men, is that correct?"

"Yes," answered Mike.

"In that case, my answer would be 'yes', I do want to be involved, but only under certain conditions. You must understand, this life here in America is not for me. For you, yes; but for me, no. My ambition is to go back to Italy and join my family there, not bring them here as many others have done. I want to live there and raise my children there; but since I'm here now, it would be desirable to make some money first. And working with you, Mike, it could come about. It would be worth the risk."

Julio continued: "However," he emphasized, "you must promise me one thing. If things go bad and we get caught, don't leave me in jail. Get me out as soon as you can, and give me enough money to get me back to my family and my beloved Italy."

"I am happy to hear you put it in that manner," answered Mike. "My thoughts are to give shares to my closest and most trusted men. In this manner, we all make money to justify the risk. Al, for a talkative man, you have said nothing," inquired Mike with a smile, knowing damn well that up until now he was never given much of a chance to comment.

"Now that I can get a word in edgewise," answered Al, "count me in." He had no conditions to offer. The whole affair had the earmarkings of excitement. That was good enough for him. The money would be welcomed, but secondary.

"You better not discuss this matter in the presence of Livia," warned Al. "Unless you don't mind being hit on the head with a cast iron skillet."

"This matter should not be discussed at all, not even with the others, at least not yet," put in Mike. "Pucci and Primo know nothing about my thoughts. I would want to discuss this matter with them first. After all, they are my partners. They have a say in the disposition of the sugar."

Little did he know that his partners could read his mind like an open book; and little did he know that his thought, although not yet expressed, worried the hell out of them.

And to add to Pucci's concerns was the thought of two trustworthy tugboat skippers, especially Swede who now had a taste of good fortune thanks to their association with some enterprising paesani. They, too, or at least Swede, were contemplating throwing their hats in the ring even though they had not yet been asked. Swede had a couple of good ideas to offer that might catch their paesano friends by surprise; ideas that would never be expected from a couple of honest, hard-working sea dogs.

CHAPTER 36

The two tugs pulled, pushed, and shoved until they had the ship positioned where they wanted it, just off the main channel and opposite their own berths down at "Central Basin" where they finally dropped her anchor.

Swede, with a couple of his men, would spend the night on board ship keeping watch. Sven would relieve him the next day.

The following morning Sven came back out to the ship and tied up alongside. He was greeted by Swede with a cup of hot coffee in his hand. "They have some fine coffee on board, would you like a cup?" asked Swede.

"Sure, why not? What else did you find of interest?"

"Did you know that all those sacks contain brown sugar?" responded Swede.

"Brown sugar! No, I didn't know that," answered Sven somewhat surprised. They were well aware of the load of wine that had been taken on board and, of course, the paesani's anxiety to retrieve it. But all that brown sugar — at first thought, it appeared to be cargo that would be useless other than selling it at sacrifice prices.

"Maybe our Italian friends plan to get into the baking business?" commented Swede jokingly as he eyed his friend now in deep thought, brushing back his big mustache, then lifting off his cap and readjusting it on his head.

"Or maybe, the bootlegging business?" came Sven's answer as he looked directly at his friend with a cocked eye.

Swede was taken by surprise with that comment. "Do you really think so?" he asked.

"By golly, I sure do! That fellow Pucci is a smart one. You can be sure he knew what the cargo was all along."

Now their thoughts changed. From a cargo of brown sugar that they first thought would have to be disposed of at sacrifice prices, they now saw a cargo worth a king's ransom. They walked up to the bow of the ship, looked out across the Bay waters towards the city; there it lay, San Francisco, bustling with activity, abound with opportunity.

"By God, Sven, we should join up with those Italians; that is, if they'll have us."

"Yes Swede, I was thinking the same thing. We do have something to offer, by golly. But we better think it over carefully. They say bootlegging is a pretty risky business."

"Well, of course, any business venture has its risks, but if one doesn't venture, one doesn't gain. Don't you like the idea, Sven?"

"Oh, I like the idea all right; but tell me, Swede, do you think you could fight your way out of there with your fists?"

Sven was referring to Alcatraz looming up in the morning sun as the now dissipating fog swirled around it. It almost looked like it was purposely inviting them in.

"Well, I wouldn't like that too much," answered Swede. Nevertheless, they agreed to keep the door open.

Sven took his turn on watch. Keeping up enough steam to run the small generator for lighting purposes was about all there was to do. The rest of the afternoon was spent looking over the damage done to the wheelhouse. Those 50-caliber machine guns are sure devastating, he thought as he assessed the damage done by the cutter's machine gun. The holes could be plugged up easily enough, but much of the wiring and tubing was chewed up, to say nothing of the instruments and gauges. This, along with reinstating the stack back in its original position, will cost money. Money that we don't have, he thought to himself.

"That banker, Mr. Battisoldi, would like nothing better than to have me come to him looking for money," he said, talking to himself. "Those Italians," he muttered, "they know how to do business. And Mike, he helped me before; maybe he has more cash he can spare."

He grinned, exposing a mouthful of teeth from under his

mustache as his thoughts wandered back to the day he witnessed the confrontation between Mike and the banker. "Yes, it won't hurt to talk to our Italian friends."

Swede was pleased with Sven's idea on how to raise cash. However, his beaming smile betrayed his true thoughts. But, Sven was to remind him:

"Now remember," said Sven, "this has nothing to do with your idea of joining up with them."

"I understand. When do you plan to talk to them?"

"Well, tomorrow will be Monday. Mike will be at the vegetable market. Maybe I can catch him there."

"Good," said Swede, with a broad smile, for he felt the matter of their joining up with the paesani would enter into the conversation somewhere along the line if, in fact, bootlegging was on their minds. As far as he was concerned, risk be damned! This was exciting.

Swede wasn't surprised to see Sven's tug chugging its way across the channel this Monday morning. Neither was he surprised to see Mike and Pucci standing on the tug as it tied up alongside the ship, for there was no question that there would be much to discuss and plan in reference to the cargo. Once on board, and after the handshaking and backslapping, congratulations were finalized. The four men then made their way down into the ship's hold. They were impressed with what they saw:

"My God! Look at that!" said Mike as he viewed the stacks of wine barrels and neatly stacked sacks of sugar.

Pucci was grinning like a fox that had just captured a rabbit and was about to have it for supper. "Does anybody know for sure how much stuff we have here?" he asked.

Sven answered the question: "No, but there sure as hell is a lot of it, don't you think?"

"That's for sure!" answered Pucci as he stretched his neck trying to see the ends of the rows of cargo. "I would like to see the rest of the ship," he then announced inquisitively.

With this, Swede led them directly to the engine and boiler rooms. He explained the function of the engines and their relation to the boilers, making it a point to emphasize their size in relation to the ship.

"Most ships this size that I know of don't have twin screws or this much horsepower," he pointed out proudly.

274

At this point, Pucci interrupted him to ask the question: "What I want to know is how did you fellows manage to keep it from blowing up once the stack was shot off?"

Sven jumped in with an answer immediately by saying: "That's easy when you have a bull-headed Swede handy," along with other comments in a joking manner. The answer brought on a round of laughter.

Swede, however, was eager to explain the steps that were taken. Having worked their way through a maze of pipes and equipment, they were now standing before two condensers, piped in a manner so they could be used separately or together depending on demand. Valves and pressure gauges of various sorts and sizes were observed in amongst the piping and on the units themselves. To the two skippers, the conglomeration of equipment was well understood; and to some extent, by Pucci as well. But as for Mike, he didn't know what the hell he was looking at. For that matter, once they had left the ship's hold, the rest of this was just a mishmash of valves, pipes, gauges, and machinery that had something to do with making the ship go. Swede now embarked on an oration no better understood by Mike than what he saw:

"Even though the boilers were forced to full capacity and pressure, these condensers working together were able to condense low-pressure steam back into water fast enough to fulfill the demands of the boiler feed pumps. But once the safety pressure relief valves started to blow, and steam was being lost, additional fresh water was needed or the feed pumps would starve. So, if it were not for what you see here, (now pointing to a steam-fired vessel alongside the condensers) working in conjunction with the condensers to convert sea water to fresh water, the boilers would have melted down and exploded," said Swede, purposely directing the comment towards Mike.

"And what do you call that?" asked Mike.

This now was Swede's cue to inject his true thoughts into the conversation:

"That's called a 'still'. Much the same as is used for making 'alcohol', only this one makes fresh water from sea water."

The two words "still" and "alcohol" hit Mike like a thunderbolt. The rest of what Swede had said meant little to him, but this last comment hit a nerve. "You mean this ship works like a distillery?" he asked excitedly.

"Well, just about," answered Swede. "All it needs is fermentation tanks to be a distillery; however, it being a seagoing ship, it is allowed to move about."

To Pucci's horror, the conversation was now completely switched from the functioning of a ship to a full-scale distillery.

Sven's desire was to reach out and punch Swede in the nose, for he knew that he had purposely injected the distillery idea into the conversation. The more he tried to suppress it, the deeper it got. In a matter of minutes, the words like "corn mash, brewing vats, fermentation, distillation, alcohol vapors condensed into alcohol," and the horde of brown sugar and its importance in the making of high proof alcohol were thoroughly discussed.

Mike's thoughts were running wild. In his mind, he could picture this whole ship as a floating distillery cruising up and down the coast, stopping off at major ports to unload its cargo of alcohol in exchange for hard cash that he would collect in his ever-present little money sacks.

Swede was in his glory too. This would be his finest hour, the captain of a floating distillery making money, and a generous supply of good drinking whisky on hand at all times. Other than an occasional fight, there was little more to ask for.

As for Sven and Pucci, they, too, had thoughts. They could envision the "Skipjack" bearing down on them with Captain Terranova standing on its bridge shouting instructions to his gunner. They pictured themselves in handcuffs standing on the bow of a police boat being escorted across the Bay waters heading for their new residence, Alcatraz, "The Rock," while their two companions that were so busy masterminding this caper were being carted off in straight jackets to the insane asylum at Napa.

Pucci shattered everybody's thoughts by looking at his watch and announcing the need to pick up Primo who, by now, was standing on the pier waiting for one of the tugs to come and pick him up as promised.

"Oh, that's good. You go pick up the little fella with Sven," said Swede. "I have something else to show Mike. Hurry back."

Hurry back they did. The tug charged across the channel at full speed, swung around churning up a mass of sea water in a tight turn in front of Primo standing at the pier. Pucci all but jerked

Primo on board as he yelled out to the skipper to "Go!"

Primo asked: "What the hell's the matter?" He grabbed onto rigging with one hand and hung onto his hat with the other as the tug churned up the Bay water in its mad dash back to the ship.

"That big jerk, Swede, and that uncle of yours have practically converted the ship into a distillery," answered Pucci disgustedly. "If we don't hurry up and get back there and jar their minds loose of those kinds of ideas, we're all going to end up over there," he said jerking his head towards Alcatraz.

As they approached the ship, Mike, in a complete trance, was standing on the bow gazing out towards San Francisco. This was big business, he thought, as he searched his vest pocket for a cigar butt. He came up with two fair-sized ones, looked at them, then threw them overboard. "By God, from now on I'll smoke only fresh cigars," he mumbled. The thought crossed his mind to throw the old worn-out vest overboard as well. But on second thought, the vest was just too dear to him.

"Look at him!" said Pucci pointing at Mike up on the bow. "He thinks he's Julius Caesar about to capture the world and make San Francisco its capital."

Pucci's disgruntled comments about his uncle caused Primo to chuckle with pride.

"Damn it! This is not funny," snapped Pucci. "Now when we get on board, they're going to go to work on you. And for Christ's sake, don't side in with them, whatever you do."

"Okay! If you say so, buddy, that's the way it will be."

Swede reached over the side with his huge right hand, grabbed Primo by the wrist, and helped him over and onto the deck. Now that he was standing this close to him, Swede looked even bigger than ever. The big grin on that square-jawed face of his was a sure indication that he and Mike had hit it off well. The first place they headed for was the hold. Primo was just as amazed as the others to see all those barrels of wine and 100-pound sacks of sugar labeled "product of Hawaii" neatly stacked and secured, ready for the long trip East that never came about.

Swede then headed for the engine and boiler room with the intent of indoctrinating Primo such as he did Mike. But Primo resisted.

"You know, Swede," he said, "you're wasting a lot of time

277

showing me something I understand nothing about. Why don't we get with the purpose we came for? Let's get that over with first. We can always do that later if we have time."

This made real sense. First things first. So they followed Sven to the galley and dining area for a conference regarding a very serious matter — Money! Mike was in favor of hanging on to the sugar and giving them the money now to repair the ship, but Pucci insisted on selling the sugar to raise the cash. It was obvious, Mike was willing to risk hard cash in favor of hanging onto all the sugar while Pucci was trying to reduce the inventory of sugar. As for the two skippers, they were keeping their mouths shut. Either way, they would benefit.

Primo broke the deadlock. It was, therefore, agreed that enough sugar would be sold to pay for the cost of repairs which would proceed immediately. Also, once the ship was tied up at the pier for repairs, the unloading of wine would proceed. The big question now was how to get it transferred off the ship without being too conspicuous. All kinds of ideas were kicked around. It seems it was easier to hijack the wine than to simply transfer it from ship to shore, at least from a detection standpoint anyway. The two skippers had the best idea: leave it on the ship, and unload it as needed. They weren't about to put the ship in service just yet anyway. They also adopted Sven's idea of stencilling all the barrels in big letters "Molasses" since this is what it was purported to be in the first place (at least to the knowledge of the media and the general public).

"All right," said Pucci. "We're in agreement. No more talk about making moonshine until the wine is all gone and the ship repaired." To his satisfaction, he did manage to, at least temporarily, put down the bootlegging idea. The ship was therefore moored in Central Basin at a pier near the foot of 19th Street in preparation for unloading its cargo.

CHAPTER 37

Mike wasted no time. He immediately contacted his cousin, Terso, so named for the third one born to the family. These two men originated from the same clan on their father's side. Not only did they have a strong resemblance, but they even thought alike. About the only real pronounced difference in them were their voices. Mike's voice was sharper and more commanding, whereas Terso's voice resembled a man with an acute case of laryngitis, more so pronounced after he'd been drinking his own moonshine. Also because of the fact that he was a few years older and experience was in his favor, Mike always assumed that he was also smarter, but such was not necessarily the case.

Terso was, indeed, a tough one to do business with. As a matter of fact, before leaving Italy as a young man, he had already earned the nickname "Veleno," Italian for poison. Thus, the nickname stuck with him at least among his friends. He was already engaged in the bootlegging business operating in the city of Alameda where he lived.

He didn't own or operate a still. His activities comprised of buying high-proof alcohol, then cut, color, and break it down into small lots like quarts and gallons. He'd developed a thriving business selling direct to household consumers. The availability of sugar at the right price, plus the fact it was coming from an untraceable source, interested him no end. The fact that he could now supply sugar to the still operators ensured his supply of alcohol.

As for Mike, he didn't mind selling the sugar to his cousin since it was keeping it in the family. In this manner, he could expect to receive a kickback in the form of cash, or at least in some sort of family favors. Needless to say, he was pleased with the arrangement. The first sale of 200 sacks was scheduled for delivery. It would be transported across the Bay by the tugs to a predetermined pier on the Alameda side of the Oakland-Alameda Estuary.

The tug skippers, Swede and Sven, were delighted. At $5.00 per sack, this first shipment alone would generate $1,000 in cash to apply to the ship repairs. Besides, this would be one step closer to proving themselves to their Italian friends that they, indeed, had much to offer.

Mike went along on the first trip since he had made the arrangements. It would be up to him to also collect the cash upon delivery. His cousin was there to receive the sugar as preplanned. It was transferred in the darkness from the tugs to a waiting truck without a hitch. Money exchanged hands in the dim light of the tug's wheelhouse. It was all there as promised. After the first lot was delivered, it was to become a regular routine on a semi-weekly basis. Yes, indeed, moving the sugar across the Bay with the tugs was the way to do it.

The schedule for payment for the hauling of subsequent lots that would follow was arranged to the satisfaction of everyone. Now everybody was making money. Since Al lived on the Oakland side of the Estuary not too far from the Fruitvale Avenue Bridge and the pier, Mike commissioned him to collect the cash upon each delivery. Not that he didn't trust his cousin, but in this shady business, the cash must exchange hands at the instant of delivery. The cash in Al's hands was secure and the same as being in Mike's.

Dealing with Mike's cousin was indeed an interesting experience for Al. No sooner the collections were shifted to Al, problems developed in the matter of cash collections. Terso attempted to shortchange Al with the excuse that the previous load was short on count.

Al had been pre-warned. He wasted no time nor did he mince words. He walked over to the loaded truck. And to the astonishment of the driver, jerked the keys out of the ignition, signaled the tugs to hold fast, and ordered the load to be transferred back to the tugs. Terso panicked. He immediately came up with the difference. When it came to collections, there would be no nonsense with Al.

Payment for the following load of sugar to Alameda was disputed again. Only this time, the excuse was that the sugar was not 100% pure. Terso pleaded that impurities and sediment were excessive, therefore top price could not be paid because the still operators were refusing to pay full price. The truth of the matter was that they were already paying his jacked-up price and would even pay more if pushed. The still operators wanted all they could get, regardless. Rightfully so, Al would not buy this argument.

"Terso," he would say, "if you want the sugar, then pay the price, or it goes back on the tugs."

Although Swede couldn't understand what the two were always bickering about in their native tongue, he did admire Al's spunky manner.

"You know, Sven," he said, while the two skippers were standing by one night, "I like that stocky little Italian. He's a fighter."

Compared to Swede, Al was a small man, especially noticeable when the two would stand side by side. Swede's massive shoulders towered over these short Italians like a giant. The skippers were instructed to never leave the scene until Al got into his car and was on his way. Once behind the wheel, any danger of being mugged for the money would be minimized for he was one hell of a driver, and he knew all the alleys and streets like the back of his hand. Any attempt to catch or trap him would be futile.

Al made it a point to report to Mike his cousin's constant attempts to cut him short on the cash.

"Too much sediment, you say. What do you know about that?" commented Mike in a thoughtful, amused manner. An idea had struck him like a thunderbolt. He grumbled in disgust because he hadn't thought of it sooner. He was remembering the constant bickering that used to take place back in Italy between the housewives' and the bread bakers.

The bakers would mix up heavy, finely-ground marble dust along with the bread flour in order to increase the weight of the bread, therefore short changing the already financially strapped housewives. Cheating, you might say, in a heavy way. And all for the purpose of raising extra cash in order to support a mistress or pay gambling debts; and, in most cases, both.

Smart cousin, or no smart cousin, by God, Mike would teach him a thing or two about business tactics the old-fashioned way. He immediately instructed Julio to take the Graham truck along with two men equipped with shovels and burlap sacks, and head out to the ocean beach. From the sand drifts they were to fill the sacks with good clean sand and haul the load directly to the ship where Mike would be waiting for them. They carried out his orders to the letter. They hand trucked the sacks of sand directly into the hold of the ship. With the help of others, Mike had already removed the sack bindings from that night's load of sugar, along with 20 pounds of sugar from each sack. As they brought in the sand, he weighed out 10 pounds of sand and dumped it into the sugar sacks, then added back enough sugar to bring the weight back up to 100 pounds. As men sewed the sacks back up again, they, too, joined Mike in singing and humming the old Italian favorite, "O'Sole Mio."

A sudden thought flashed across Mike's mind causing him to cut the singing short. His father's comment came to mind. "Don't be greedy, leave some for others."

"Why, that bugger's been doing the very same thing, sure as hell. I'd bet on it!" he swore. Needless to say, he would have won his bet. He now added his own lyrics to this beautiful song he was so gleefully singing:

"How beautiful it is to have,
Such lovely sand so close at hand,
To fill the needs of those who pride,
In besting others on their side,
But if it were not for their greed,
Our inventive minds would have no need,
So let us say before we part,
That we have bested our Mr. Smart."

CHAPTER 38

Pucci was pleased with Mike's attitude towards the sale of the sugar rather than pursuing the bootlegging idea. However, he knew him well enough to know that in some way he was benefiting by this arrangement and, therefore, the reason for being so content. However, Pucci was unconcerned because this was the lesser of the two evils. But the idea of getting into the bootlegging business was still hot on Mike's mind. He was not about to sit around idle while bootleggers were making their fortune in this illicit, but exciting, business and using his sugar to boot.

He was now pushing wine on a much faster and larger scale. In addition to maintaining his regular customers, he was selling in truckload lots direct from the ship. No longer was he bothering to cut and dilute the wine. His idea now was to move it all out as fast as he could. The sooner the wine was gone, the sooner the bootlegging could start.

Pucci realized this. He and Primo were constantly working on Mike trying to slow him down. He wouldn't argue the point with them but, nevertheless, he was determined to get into it with or without them. His cousin, Terso, in Alameda, was certainly not helping matters much, for he kept urging him to get out of the vegetable business altogether and set himself up a still.

Mike was now busier than ever away from the ranch most of the day and, occasionally, at night. This concerned Livia no end. A family man belongs home with his family after the day's work is done, she reasoned. Besides, the vegetable operation was being neglected to some extent and this, too, was of concern.

The paesani were being pushed, working harder than ever as

the wine operation increased. At the same time, nighttime sugar deliveries demanded the handling of heavy sugar sacks far into the night. The activities around the docked ship were noticed and being watched closely by envious eyes. During these times, sugar didn't attract only flies, it was to also attract at least one unscrupulous bootlegging still operator, who was eager to get his hands on some of this horde of sugar; however, without paying for it. His intent was to hijack it.

The bootlegger had been carefully studying the ship operation from different undetected locations in and around the dock area. Once he had their schedules and method of operations down pat, it would then be only a matter of being ready to move in at the right instant and hijack a load of sugar.

This sinister person was now ready. Each night he would be there with his men and a good-sized truck ready to move in. They stationed themselves unnoticed a short distance away waiting for the perfect situation to occur. Finally, as it is with a patient hunter, his quarry was about to be taken with a fast and decisive blow. On this particular foggy Friday night, both tugs were loaded with sugar ready to pull out. Mike had already left with his men heading back to the ranch at San Bruno.

"Well, Swede, we better get going. We're shorthanded tonight," said Sven to his partner.

Swede's response was a concerned question: "Do you think it'll be all right to leave only one man on watch tonight?"

"Oh, I think maybe this once won't hurt any. We'll only be gone a couple of hours at most," answered Sven in a confident manner.

No sooner had the two tugs faded in the gathering fog, two men came running up to the ship. Keeping to the shadows, they made their way up to the deck. Once on deck, again keeping to the shadows, they silently worked their way down to the hold in search of the man left on watch. They caught up to him as he was making his way up forward through the dimly lit hold to secure the bulkhead door leading to the unloading ramp out the side of the ship.

The watchman was unaware of the unsuspected company until it was too late to put up much of a defense against the leather garrote that flipped over his head and around his neck. The scuffle of feet did cause him to whirl around and get a fair look at his two attackers

284

before losing consciousness. It was no doubt this split-second maneuver that saved his life. For the second man, not being sure whether the garrotter had succeeded in securing a grip on the watchman's throat, proceeded to sap him with his blackjack, therefore knocking him unconscious and down to the floor. The sapper instantly tied the watchman's hands behind his back and left him lay there unconscious off to one side while they proceeded to swing the heavy door open.

This was the cue for the truck driver to pull up alongside the ship and prepare for loading. The driver, along with two more men, joined their two cohorts and hurriedly started hand-trucking sacks of sugar from the ship's hold past the fallen watchman. He remained unconscious during most of the loading. Fortunately for him, the dim lighting and shadows shielded his twitching as he started to regain consciousness. His faint mumbling went unnoticed, overpowered by the constant chatter amongst these Italian-speaking hijackers.

He regained his senses enough to realize what had taken place. The throbbing in his head reminded him to stay silent and keep his eyes closed. The last he heard was the laboring sound of the hijacker's truck as it pulled out. Not caring to attempt to stand, he lay there in a semi-conscious condition in the silence of the hold until he heard Sven's unmistakable voice as he stepped through the bulkhead door, followed by Swede. His faint call to Sven was indicative of an injured man. In sizing up the situation, it was obvious that a load of sugar had been hijacked.

They comforted their man while assessing his injuries. Swede was well experienced in such matters since he had survived many knocked-down, dragged-out fights when, in some instances, pick handles were used against him. Once satisfied that the injured man was not suffering from a severe skull fracture, Swede picked him up gently like cradling a baby, and carried him up the ladders to his bunk. He would stay with him throughout the night. Sven would check back first thing in the morning after reporting the incident to Pucci.

"How is our man doing this morning?" asked Sven as he and Pucci made their way into the crew's quarters.

"He's doing fine," answered Swede. "He ate a good breakfast and held it down. I consider that good. Oh, he has a good welt on the side of his head all right. That's what knocked him out. But what I find somewhat scary is the narrow rope-like burns on his neck, like someone tried to strangle him first."

"Does he remember much of what happened?" asked Pucci.

"Yes, he does. Come, let's go talk to him."

The man was resting back on his bunk as he repeated what he already had told Swede, but now his mind was clearer and could supply more detail.

"You say this one man had a gouged-out eye of sorts?" asked Pucci with interest as he viewed the unmistakable garrote marks on the man's neck.

"Well, what I mean is, it's cockeyed and starry, somewhat frightening. A gruesome scar under it extends down and back towards the side of his face as if cut by a knife. Like maybe his eye had been gouged out and replaced again. He's the one that tried to strangle me with the garrote."

"You say they did a lot of talking amongst themselves during the hijacking?"

"Yes, I'm sure it was in Italian, but it didn't sound anything like Mike's paesani. It was more like what I've heard down around Fisherman's Wharf."

With that comment Pucci straightened up. His face took on a serious expression as if a deputy sheriff had just put a hand on his shoulder.

"Sicilians," he half muttered to himself while deep in thought. "Impossible!" he mumbled as he pondered the thought. Could it be that a group of local Sicilians have organized a hijacking ring or even maybe set up a bootlegging operation in the city? No, he thought, not local. They're doing well enough without this. Someone has moved in from the outside, maybe even the Mafia or, at least, with Mafia connections.

"Were there any names mentioned that you can recall, like maybe addressing the head of the group?"

"No. I never heard any names mentioned although there was a couple of words they repeated several times."

"Like what?" asked Pucci.

"Well, once in a while, they would say something like 'oke-yo' like they were addressing an Okie, but I'm almost sure none of them were Okies."

Now Pucci was really concentrating. "Could it have been a word like 'Occhio'? All one word instead of two words?"

"Give me that again," asked the watchman, pulling himself up, now resting on his elbows as if to better grasp the pronunciation of the word.

"Occhio," repeated Pucci with more emphasis on the pronunciation.

"Hey, yeah! That's it! Oke-yo," he again mispronounced the Italian word "Occhio" for eye.

"Good enough," said Pucci with a grin. "You'll probably never learn to pronounce it right, but 'Occhio' is the Italian word for eye and that fits. The man with the gouged eye is the Capo, as we would call the leader. And Occhio, is his nickname obviously because of his bad eye. Listen, fella, you've been one hell of a great help. Now take it easy for a few days; however, stay out of sight. Someone will be with you at all times."

"Sven," said Pucci, "let's lay low for a while. I'll pass the word on to Mike and Primo that the sugar shipments are being curtailed. You fellows watch your step, at least until we find out what we're dealing with here."

Pucci knew where to find his buddy on a Saturday afternoon. But just to be sure, he first stopped at his house on Lombard Street to inquire of Primo's whereabouts. He hurried up the flight of terrazzo steps to the front porch and rang the doorbell. A moment went by, then the door opened. He stepped in, looked up the full flight of steps to see Primo's stocky, but short, mother, Rosina, at the head of the carpeted steps looking down at him from the flat above. While still gripping the decorative metal lever that opened the front door at the base of the stairwell, she answered his question before he had a chance to ask it.

"He's over at the cheese fields," she said in a disgruntled frame of mind. With that, she swung her left arm across the front of her pointing in the direction of the Marina District up Lombard and off to the right towards the bay. "And tell him to send that good-for-nothing, lazy bum of a father of his home. I want him here, now!" She was obviously mad. No doubt such as was his habit on a Saturday, her husband Teodoro would sneak out to avoid doing the chores she designated.

Pucci stepped back out the door as she leaned back on the

fancy metal lever that would slam the door back shut. To get caught half in and half out the doorway once everything was in motion, could cause injury.

It was a short drive to the so-called cheese fields. Sure enough, both father and son were there engaged in betting. And in the case of the father, he had entered the tournament and was about to take his turn at cheese rolling. The field is the length of a football field with several well-worn paths or avenues approximately three yards wide and ten yards apart for the full length of the field. At the throwing end of the avenues, there is a scrimmage line that must not be stepped over, at least not until the cheese has left the hand. To do so will disqualify the throw.

Perfectly round, dry, grating-type cheeses weighing some 6 to 8 pounds are selected for this sporting event. Their approximate 12- to 14-inch diameter and 2-inch thickness are just right to fit the hand of a good size man. The wood ashes, black pepper and olive oil used to cure the cheeses gives them a firm black crust that holds them together when rolled. They're thrown much like a bowling ball except, in this case, distance is the target and not pins.

Pucci walked up and interrupted Primo from his betting frenzy. He was busy placing two-bit and four-bit bets with any and all takers. At the closest avenue to them, his father Teodoro was about to throw. This, then, would end the frame. His throw now would be crucial.

He was a big, heavyset man, a good foot taller than little Primo. He had removed his coat, rolled up the sleeves of his collarless shirt, and pulled his hat down firmly on his pumpkin-like head. His strong, wide suspenders were pulled up tight, firming his pants up against his hog-like buttocks. He had a firm right-hand grip on the cheese he was cradling in his palm, swinging back and forth like the pendulum of a grandfather clock. All betting activities had now stopped as the men waited tensely for the throw. He had pre-gauged the distance to the scrimmage line so as to start with a left-foot-forward prancing run and end up with his right foot firmly planted in a depression just short of the line as he would let go of the cheese.

"You got your money riding on the old man?" asked Pucci, serious like.

"Yeah," answered Primo.

"I've got a dollar that says he'll blow it."

"I'll take that bet. Do you have any more of that kind of money?"

"No, just a dollar," stated Pucci.

"You're on, buddy!"

No sooner these words were spoken, Primo's father leaped forward in heavy, prancing strides. He came to an abrupt halt at the scrimmage line, sending forward a splattering of dirt, much like a bull pulling up short from his headlong charge. The cheese shot forward in a fast-spinning parallel flight to the ground, not touching down for at least some five yards or so. The fast spinning cheese kicked back a spurt of dirt as it touched down, picking up more speed as it rolled on past the spectators gathered on either side of the avenue.

"Well, buddy, I think you've lost your bet. That roll will take it well past the needed distance," said Primo.

"Another buck, the cheese blows apart," answered Pucci hurriedly and confidently.

"I'll take it," snapped Primo.

Within seconds of the statement, chunks of cheese went flying through the air as the fast-rolling cheese literally exploded from the outward thrust of its internal forces.

"Damn it!" swore Primo. "How the hell did you know that would happen?"

"It was obvious. Your old man was too eager. He was putting too much power behind the throw. You owe me two bucks, Shorty," said Pucci, followed by a good belly laugh. "By the way, your mother wants him home right now. Shall we give him a lift?"

Primo glanced over at his dad still waving his arms around arguing defensively against his angry, voracious, losing supporters. He turned to Pucci. "Come on, let's go. Let him walk. He'll be there for another hour at least. Besides, either way, he's going to catch hell at home, regardless," he stated in a disgusting manner.

"Okay. I'll follow you over to your place. Leave your car there. We're going to take a ride," said Pucci.

CHAPTER 39

"Well, where are we going?" asked Primo as he made himself comfortable.

"San Bruno to see your Uncle Mike," answered Pucci. As they drove through town, he brought Primo up to date on the latest events–the sugar hijack.

"Well, I'll be damned! Sugar hijackers! And you think they're operating a still somewhere close by?" asked Primo.

"Yes, I do. For one thing, they had to be casing our operation for quite some time in order to time and pick the perfect moment to pull it off. Secondly, they were able to bring in the truck on short notice. Last night, being foggy, they moved in quick, which means they had to be close by. We can expect them to strike again, and maybe hurt someone else. They're pretty rough."

"Do you have a plan in mind?" asked Primo.

"For one thing, stay healthy and out of jail."

"That's fine. But are we going to just let them take what they want and walk all over us?"

"That's just it. Until we find out more about these hijackers, bootleggers, or whatever they are, we're going to have to lay low or risk bringing the authorities down us. They're liable to associate us with their operations, whatever it is, and haul us all in. After all, it is our sugar they're using," answered Pucci.

As they neared the ranch, they agreed on one thing for sure, and that was to convince Mike to back down on his endeavor to start bootlegging even on his own.

At the ranch they were greeted by Livia with open arms. "You will stay for supper. I have planned corned beef and cabbage for dinner. Made just like Sheriff Kelly's wife taught me. Mike likes it and so will you. We'll have plenty."

"Sure, Aunt Livia, we'd be delighted. But tell me, where is Uncle Mike?" asked Primo.

"Oh, he went to town to bring the Sheriff some winter cabbage," answered Livia. "Oh, by the way, make sure you take some cabbage home to your mother, she'll enjoy it."

"Fine, I'll do that. In the meantime, we'll take a walk over to the paesani and see how they're doing."

Primo watched her retreat back up the back stairs and disappear back through the screen door. Does she have any idea what this is all about? Probably not, he thought. Still, she must know something is afoot. She greeted them wholeheartedly with an expression of gladness, but her eyes betrayed her true inner feelings. It was there that he sensed the feeling of fear that she so graciously tried to disguise. Was she afraid that their presence was intended to further embroil the father of her children even deeper into this illegitimate business that she so strongly feared and despised? He dwelled on the thought as he started out across the yard in a slow casual walk–wondering: "How can I possibly understand a mother's feelings towards matters such as this. Even being married to a woman doesn't necessarily qualify a man to really understand the deep inner feelings of a mother, and a wife that must look to her husband for support and care of her children. No man, even if he has fathered a number of children, can possibly understand the feelings of a mother towards her children: the motherly love, the concern for their well being, the happiness and gladness when they're well, and the rendering heartaches when they're not or one is lost. Any man that says he fully understands a mother's inner feelings has got to be the first cousin to a jackass."

Primo walked a little fast in order to catch up to Pucci now heading into the field. He's right, he thought. We must convince Uncle Mike that he's moving too fast. He must weigh the consequences or his family could suffer for it.

The two buddies walked across the vegetable patch towards the paesani's house. Pucci spoke first: "Sheriff Kelly? Jesus Christ! Here I am worrying about the authorities, and your Uncle Mike socializes with the Sheriff and thinks nothing of it. He's in and out of your uncle's wine cellar like a pesky, unemployed brother-in-law. Boy, I hope it continues that way, but I doubt it."

Primo got a kick out of his buddy's statement. "You see, that's what I've been trying to tell you right along. Don't be so concerned, relax. Take it easy."

"Oh, yeah. You just wait until moonshine gets into the picture, then we'll see just how friendly Mr. Sheriff Kelly will be towards your uncle. Your Aunt Livia will also be in for one hell of a letdown, believe me."

Julio saw his two friends coming. He walked out meeting them part way. The meeting was pleasant, all smiles and grins. They were indeed happy to see each other. "Come on out back. I want to show you something," suggested Julio.

The three friends walked out around the barn. Off to one side the paesani had constructed a charcoal kiln, and near it was a pile of broken-down oak barrel staves ready for making into charcoal.

"What the hell's all this about?" asked Primo inquisitively.

"We're going to make a batch of charcoal from some of the empty barrels," answered Julio.

"That's a damned good idea. Why not use them all up that way?" suggested Primo.

"Oh, no! Not all of them," answered Julio. "We're going to take the ends out of the thicker, French barrels and char the insides and save them for future use. They'll make fine aging barrels."

"Oh, Jesus Christ!" exclaimed Pucci with a heart-sinking feeling of despair. "Whiskey-aging barrels, complete with an abundance of filtering charcoal. God help us! Oh Christ, God help us! Julio, we came here today to tell Mike that the ship was hijacked last night by a tough bunch of bootleggers. They made off with a good size truckload of sugar and damned near killed one of Sven's men in the process. You have to keep this charcoal business and bootlegging idea undercover. Whatever you do, don't do anything, at least not for a while."

This was unpleasant news to Julio, especially the fact that there was violence involved. "Do you have any idea who these hijackers might be?" he asked.

"No, I don't. Only that they were Sicilians with a head man nicknamed Occhio for his bad eye. And you can be sure they will do it again, and maybe even attract others, if not the authorities themselves."

Julio was not a man of many words. He preferred to listen rather than talk, but this time he found the need to interrupt Pucci:

"Excuse the interruption," he said in an almost whisper, then continued cautiously as if he might be overheard: "You think it was a man with a bad eye, a Sicilian, maybe even a mafioso?"

"I don't think it, that's who it was for sure. Why? Do you know him?"

"No, I don't, but one of our men might know him. Come, let's go talk to him."

They followed Julio around the side of the barn and over to the tool shed where his friend Salvatore Di Cultiliari was busy making a new handle for his cauliflower knife.

"Sal," called out Julio as the three stepped into the shop. "Pucci here has something that might interest you. Can you spare a minute?"

"Sure! Hello, Pucci . . . Primo. I haven't seen you two fellows for a while. How're things going with the ship?"

"That's what we come to talk to you about," said Pucci. "It seems the word got out to the wrong people and so the ship was hijacked, resulting in the loss of a good-size load of sugar and a hurt man. The man responsible or, I should say, the head Capo goes by the nickname 'Occhio,' no doubt because of his gruesome, gouged eye. Do you know anything about this man?"

Pucci knew instantly that he had hit pay dirt. The expression on Sal's face changed instantly from a pleasant greeting to a fierce penetrating look you would expect to see on a man about to carry out a vendetta, to settle an old score. He came down hard with his cauliflower knife, deeply penetrating the wood stump he was using as a workbench. He let go of the handle and walked around the stump in order to shorten the distance between him and his three friends standing just inside the door.

"Where's the man you talk about?" he asked in a demanding manner.

"Then you do know him?" asked Primo calmly so as not to antagonize him.

Sal's black curly hair and piercing dark-brown eyes and deep olive complexion were typical features of the men of Southern Italy. They, along with their women, could express strong, unbelievable passionate love, and even stronger feelings to satisfy a vendetta. This time, love was not on Sal's mind.

"Yes, I do know him," he admitted. It was obvious that he wasn't proud of it.

"We're convinced that he's operating a still somewhere near the Central Basin," said Pucci. "But what concerns us is that he may be a Mafioso operating a still for the Mafia syndicate. If that is the case, then he could be a real threat to us, especially Mike."

Pucci made it a point to emphasize Mike's well-being because he knew that Sal had befriended him and, therefore, his strong Sicilian loyalty would put Mike's best interest ahead of his own, if not his very life.

"This man is extremely dangerous," said Sal. "He was a Mafioso back in Sicily, but he became a renegade. He was greedy beyond reason, to the extent that he ruined my father, causing the family to lose most of their land. For this, the mafia organization of Sicily disowned him. He fled Italy with a price on his head."

Sal stopped talking for a moment. The expressions on the faces of his three friends indicated they were sympathetic towards his reason for hating this man. After several years of searching and being alone, it was now obvious to him that these were true friends standing before him, and they now had a common enemy. Working together now, more than ever, was paramount. He continued:

"No, he's no longer a Mafioso. He has no friends. I'm sure he would be working alone." Hesitating momentarily, he added, "I will help you find him."

Julio put his arm around Sal in a firm embrace. "Come, my friend," he said softly, "let's go into the basement and have a glass of wine. When Mike gets here, we'll talk some more."

CHAPTER 40

"Wasn't the corned beef good?" asked Primo of his buddy as they pulled out of the ranch heading back to the city.

"You bet. It's one of the few dinners that pasta doesn't fit," answered Pucci. Then continuing on another subject: "Your uncle is a riot. 'Why, that's illegal. They're a bunch of crooks,' he said of the hijacking. Look who's calling the frying pan black. He was actually delighted when I told him we curtailed all further shipments of sugar like . . . as if he wanted to keep it all for himself. However, losing the sugar to the hijackers really threw him out of gear, and I can't blame him. And of course, Swede doesn't help matters much. He's always pushing your uncle. Planting ideas in his mind, and I mean, real wild ones."

"Yeah, I didn't get all the details about their latest brainstorm. What's the deal on that one?" asked Primo.

"Swede has convinced your uncle that the ship could be converted to a floating distillery. And I suppose it could. They have the nutty idea that once out on open seas, no one can touch them so they're free to operate a still without interference. Well, it does have some merit because at least you would be able to dispose of the distillation residue and that can be a problem in a populated area. It stinks to high heaven; a dead giveaway."

"Hey, you know, that's not a bad idea," said Primo.

"Now, wait a minute. There's more. They picture themselves cruising across the Pacific Ocean making moonshine, aging it in charcoal barrels by the rocking motion of the ship, then selling it to the Hawaiians. They would then take on a load of sugar and do the same thing on the way back."

296

"Terrific!" said Primo. "That would make one hell of a good whiskey."

"Damn it! Don't interrupt!" snapped Pucci. He was getting annoyed with Primo's positive attitude. He'd rather that he take an adverse position to the idea. He continued: "Anyway, on the way back, they would head for Seattle and sell a batch there. At Portland, the same thing; then work their way down along the coast all the way down to San Diego. By that time, they would be low on sugar so they would head across the Pacific back to Hawaii, and so on, and so forth."

"What the hell makes you think that it would be such a bad idea? Sounds great to me," insisted Primo.

"The Coast Guard and the Navy, that's what makes it a bad idea. They'd like nothing better than to take potshots at that ship every time it came near land, especially the Navy. Since the war ended (referring to World War I), they have been having a problem justifying their very existence. Why, the Admirals themselves would take direct command. They'd have a field day especially knowing there was aged whiskey on board. They'd hound and chase that ship all over the seas like a pack of horny dogs after a bitch in heat. There'd be so damned many battleships out there trying to overtake her, they'd be running into each other in the process. Can you imagine a shipload of whiskey exposed to a bunch of sailors? With the blessing or, I should say, orders from the high command of the United States Government to take control of it? No, my good buddy, we're doing fine just as we are. Leave the ocean to the sharks."

"Boy, you're really up tight about . . ."

"I'll even go you one better," interrupted Pucci. "If I thought for a second those sugar hijacking bastards would be satisfied with what they got, I'd be happy to forget the whole affair. But they won't be," he warned. "They're like hornets. They'll keep coming after us until they get it all, or we go in and burn 'em out."

"Hey, wait a minute," put in Primo. "I hope you're not serious about that statement?"

"Maybe not literally. But if by chance their outfit was to catch fire, and I knew for sure it was them, you can be sure our fire units would be damned slow getting there, by God."

Their thoughts shifted to Sal, Julio's friend, who was determined to go it alone in the endeavor to locate the bootlegging operation headed up by the man Occhio. If, in fact, the location was somewhere in the vicinity that Pucci thought it might be, Sal was confident he could find it. He had at one time spent a number of months working in the Central Basin area near where the ship was moored. At the time he was living in a boardinghouse near 19th and Mississippi, just a few blocks up from 3rd Street. The district overlooking the Basin was known as "Potrero Hill." There was a small colony of Sicilians scattered throughout the area which led Sal to believe that Occhio, also being a Sicilian, would settle there. It made sense.

Mike was to drop Sal off at 19th Street on the following Monday morning while on his way to the produce market. With a bundle of extra clothing and sufficient cash in his pockets, Sal would seek out the same boardinghouse under the pretense of being unemployed and looking for a job. No one would know what his true purpose was except for the man Occhio, who would no doubt remember him from old Sicily. This didn't concern Sal one bit. As a matter of fact, an encounter was what he'd hoped for. In any event, he would see to it that he wasn't caught off guard. At least the element of surprise would be in his favor, for Occhio had no idea that Sal would be looking for him and/or his bootlegging operation here in San Francisco.

"I really think Sal will locate them," said Primo.

"Probably," answered Pucci in a thoughtful manner. "I just hope to Christ it doesn't end up like the Benicia carnage masterminded by Al. By the way, don't forget to tell Al about the curtailment of sugar shipments."

"Yeah, that's right. I'll tell him first thing Monday."

"I wish we could locate a warehouse convenient to the ranch so we could at least get the rest of the wine off the ship," said Pucci.

"Yeah, that is something to think about. I'm surprised that those bootleggers haven't attempted to hijack Uncle Mike's Graham since the barrels are marked molasses."

"That'll never happen because an Italian knows, at a glance, the difference between a wine barrel and a molasses barrel."

"I never thought of that," said Primo. "So why the urgency to move the wine?"

"Well, if it wasn't for the daily need to get to it, I would have Sven move the ship out in the Bay and anchor it. That would certainly throw a curve at this Occhio character." Pucci thought for a second, then added: "He's not going to take much of a risk for wine. It's the sugar he's after. For that, he'll play rough."

"God, I hope to Christ he doesn't get the jump on Sal. That garrote could do him in but quick!" said Primo with great concern.

"Yes it can," confirmed Pucci, "especially on a man that doesn't know how to defend himself against it. In this case, he would be dealing with an experienced knife man. There's a difference."

"In what way?" asked Primo curiously.

"Well, I've obviously never seen it done, but I've heard about the method, assuming the garroter comes up from behind. What the knife man does is reach for his knife rather than fight the garrote. He does have a minute or so before losing his strength or consciousness. The garroter must use both hands and pull the victim towards himself to apply full pressure for a quick kill. This puts their heads close together. Close enough that the knifer gripping his knife blade edge up, swings his arm back close to the back of his head and in a downward direction behind him such as he would do to scratch his back, catching the garroter in the face with the knife or slashing his arms."

"God damned!" exclaimed Primo. "I'll bet that's how this guy got his eye gouged out."

"No doubt about it. And I'll bet you he has a fair-size scar across his belly as well, left there when the knifer broke free, turned, and came up and across with the blade still in the same position in an attempt to gut him."

"Do you suppose Sal has a knife on him?"

"You damned well better believe it. And a good razor-sharp one, at that. He comes from a clan of cutters."

Primo took a deep breath and let it out slowly, relieved to know that at least Sal was prepared to defend himself if need be. This talk about garrotting and gutting unnerved him. He had little to say for the rest of the trip home, until they turned off Van Ness and onto Lombard.

"Hey, hold it a minute! What's that newspaper kid yelling about? It's an extra for some reason. Pull over to the curb. If it's what I thought I heard, it may be worth reading."

Primo stepped out of the car and started back as the kid ran up to him. "Newspaper, Mister?" he asked.

"Yeah, kid. Here's a quarter. Keep the change."

He started to read the big headlines, then the large print directly beneath. He backed up a few steps in order to get the benefit of the overhead street lamp, then read the first couple of paragraphs before re-entering the car.

"What's it all about?" asked Pucci inquisitively.

"Two high-ranking Treasury officials have been found murdered in a gangland-style killing back East."

"You don't say? What the . . . ?"

"And that ain't all," interrupted Primo. "There's speculation that it may be connected to four other federal agents murdered in like fashion just out of St. Louis back in late July. They were driving a car with California license plates. I guess you know who they might have been, don't you?"

"Is there any mention about Benicia?" asked Pucci eagerly.

"None that I can see. Turn on the dome light. Let's see what else it might say."

Pucci switched on the dome light and waited anxiously as Primo scanned through the fine print of the front-page article searching for information that he hoped was not there.

"Listen to this," said Primo. Then read out loud: "It's believed that the Treasury officials were connected to the mob in illicit rum-running, bootlegging, and to some extent, narcotics. The vengeful killings were, no doubt, connected to the late discovery of three half-crazed, believed to be gangsters, found in a shipping container originating in San Francisco. As of this writing, the only audible understandable words they seem to utter, do implicate Federal agents at various levels of authority."

"Holy Christ!" said Pucci unbelievably. "The bastards survived all this time. No wonder they're half crazed."

"Hey, that's good, don't you think?" asked Primo somewhat delighted by the news.

"Yeah, I guess you're right. The mob is blaming the crooked Feds for the loss of the ship. I'll bet anything that those two Benicia men in the Essex were Federal agents. And not having any identification because of their undercover operation, nobody really knew who they were. Hopefully, they still don't know and never will know."

With that, Pucci switched off the dome light as Primo folded the newspaper and stuffed it in his pocket, lit a cigarette, and took a long, deep drag to satisfy his nicotine hunger.

"Drop me off short of the flat. The folks are probably asleep. No need to disturb them," said Primo considerately.

If his parents were fully aware of his activities and the full extent of his involvement in the Benicia incident, you can be sure they would have been a lot more than just "disturbed." Even his father would join his mother in saying the "Rosary" over and over again.

CHAPTER 41

Monday morning Mike pulled out of the ranch with the Model-T Ford loaded with fresh vegetables and wine in the usual manner. What was not so usual was his passenger, Sal, with his bundle of clothes tucked between them on the seat.

"This early October air is quite brisk," said Mike, "especially this early in the morning."

"Yes," answered Sal, "but that's what winter vegetables like, nice crisp air. Makes them crunchy and firm. The change in weather will help you; it will slow the cabbage down. They're coming in a little too early. But the cauliflower will be just right, don't you think?"

"Yes, it seems you can never outguess the weather. But what must be, must be."

This was to be the extent of the type of conversation this early morning as they made their way along the nearly deserted Bayshore Highway, then onto 3rd Street. Mike was now watching for street signs in the dim lighting along the way. He knew pretty much where he was since he made this trip several days a week on the way to the produce market.

"I think that's 19th Street up ahead there, Sal."

"Regardless, Mike, you can let me off there anyway. It's still early. I can walk an extra block or so. I have plenty of time."

The farm truck pulled up to the curb of the lonely semi-dark industrial area to let Sal off. As Sal reached for his bundle and was about to disembark, Mike asked him to wait a minute. Without explaining why, he reached into his coat pocket and came up with a fresh, full-length Toscanello cigar. He then reached into his pants' pocket and retrieved his folding knife. Holding the cigar up to what little lighting there was, he was able to distinguish its mid-point, then rolled it back and forth against the knife blade until it severed in half with a snap. The pocket knife went back into the same pocket as he handed Sal a half cigar keeping one half for himself.

"Let's have a smoke, Sal," he said as he struck a match and lit Sal's first, then his own. "We have plenty of time." He then added: "Besides, there's something I want to say to you before you leave. Sal, I know you have intentions of returning to Italy as soon as you finish your business here." Mike had to talk in interrupted delays in order to keep his cigar lit with the required methodical puffing. "But to go back to Italy without first making some money to take back with you might prove to be foolish."

He knew Sal was there listening to what he had to say because he, too, was puffing and popping his lips in order to keep the cigar going. They didn't have to look at each other, only talk and listen.

"You stay with me for a little while longer and you'll have that money I refer to, and you won't be sorry. What I've been paying you is nothing compared to what it will be like once we set up a still and get into production."

"Mike, you have been paying me well enough already. I wouldn't want to take advantage of you. I would stay for a while if you need me, but not because I would expect more from you."

Mike pulled the canvas curtain back in order to let some of the accumulated smoke out. Sal did likewise. The brisk, fresh air was now welcomed. There was one thing for sure, there were no spiders or bugs living in the Model-T. It was impossible for them to survive. Mike then advised:

"Keep in mind — don't leave the area without first coming to see me. You have a bonus coming, and I want to be sure you get it–you're entitled to it."

"Whatever the outcome of this affair before us, I do intend to stay with you until the cauliflower harvest is finished," answered Sal in real sincerity.

"Good. Now, listen to me carefully. A good way to find a still is to be up very early in the morning while the air is crisp and quiet. The reason is that in some manner, the waste from the still must be disposed of. The waste could reveal its location. Search for it."

"How will I know what it is?" asked Sal.

"You'll know it by its smell. You could almost relate it to cooked grains with sugar gone sour; a sickening, putrid fermented smell that even the hogs would refuse. Believe me, you'll know it when you smell it. Now, remember our agreement. Once you find it, report to Pucci, or if need be, to Primo at the paper company garage. We'll handle the matter together," insisted Mike.

"I understand," said Sal as he stepped out of the cab to bid his employer farewell for the moment.

"And for God's sake, be careful. We don't want you hurt. Run if you have to. The hell with valor." Mike was passing on to him what he would do under adverse circumstances. With these parting words, the Model-T pulled away from the curb leaving Sal standing there watching it head down 3rd Street.

The "chit . . . chit . . . chit . . . chit" cricket-like sound echoed amongst the industrial buildings until the little red taillight disappeared in the distance.

"God bless and care for you, my friend," said Sal as he stepped off the curb to cross the street and head up 19th Street to seek out the boardinghouse where he once stayed. Halfway up the steep hill, he looked back over the buildings and to the eastern sky. There was no fog cover this brisk October morning. Daybreak was now evident. He took his time, stopping and looking at each street sign lit up by the corner street lights. They were strange names, at least to him: Tennessee, Minnesota, Indiana, Pennsylvania. Someone once told him these were names of States. He couldn't pronounce them, but didn't really care. Why anyone would want to name a state Mississippi, the street name he was looking for, was beyond him. The only one of the bunch that made any sense to him was Carolina because it was as close to Italian as you could get. This one, being a popular woman's name in Italy, he could pronounce.

Sal didn't have to be able to actually say the street name to know when he found it. The word Mississippi was easily recognized and set apart from all the others. Besides, Sal knew it to be the first cross-street as you topped the hill. The boardinghouse was to the left on Mississippi, south of 19th within sight of the corner. At the boardinghouse, the lights were on and the front door unlocked, so he entered and inquired of a room.

"Yes, we have a room," said the robust woman as she was

preparing breakfast for the early risers. She took a second look at Sal and said: "Oh, it's you. I didn't recognize you at first. You've been gone for some time. Do you have a job?" she inquired.

"Well...no, but I hope to have one soon. Why do you ask?"

"No job, no room. That's why," she said abruptly.

"But I always paid you before, didn't I? And I'll pay you now as well."

She was used to hearing these sorts of promises from unemployed men. But when it came time to pay, they didn't have the money. She didn't even bother to look his way as she said: "Please go. I'm busy." Then added: "Since you were here last, we have raised our rates to $5.00 a week. That does include a lunch. But you can't pay anyway, so . . ." She was implying that this was beyond his means, especially since he was unemployed. There would be no nonsense with her, either pay up or be on your way.

Sal held his ground. Nonsense wasn't his big suit either. He walked over to the table, set down his bundle, counted out $10.00 from a roll of bills he was holding in his left hand, then shoved the rest back in his pocket. The shuffling of money caught the woman's immediate attention. She walked up to the table wiping her hands on her apron as she glanced at the money and then to Sal. Before she could say anything, he cut her short:

"There is two weeks, paid in advance. I'll continue to pay you in advance during my stay. Is that satisfactory with you?"

His intent was to stay at this same boardinghouse in preference to others because she was Italian and so was he. Their dialects were somewhat different but that made no difference to either of them. The important thing was they could communicate.

"Why didn't you tell me you could pay in advance?" she asked while glancing at the slight bulge in his left coat pocket as he retrieved his hand.

"Because you didn't ask me," responded Sal politely.

She reached up and removed a key from a peg on the wall.

"Your room is upstairs to the left. The last one down the hall past the bathroom. Breakfast will be ready shortly. I suppose you're hungry?"

As he reached for his bundle, the front door opened and in walked a fellow Sicilian, however unknown to him. The man walked up and set his lunch bucket on the table, bid the busy woman good morning addressing her by her first name in an informal manner in his native tongue. He turned to Sal with a smile on his face and addressed her again without looking in her direction:

"Fedora, is this a new boarder?"

"Yes," she answered. "Carpo, meet Mr. . . . I'm sorry, I forgot your name."

"Sal," he quickly responded, extending his hand for a friendly handshake. Both men's Sicilian features were apparent.

"Good to meet a fellow Sicilian," said Carpo as he too extended his right hand. This gesture brought the two men almost toe to toe. A few words of welcome and appreciation were exchanged between the two men before Carpo excused himself.

"Fedora, I'll clean up and be back down to breakfast shortly. It's been a long night. I can hardly wait to get to bed." It was apparent that he was working a night-shift job. Sal stepped to one side and let him take the lead up the flight of stairs.

"He works hard and long hours. He needs his rest," commented the woman Fedora as if intended for Sal's ears.

Sal started up the stairs as the man well ahead of him turned left at the top of the stairs heading for his own room.

"Carpo!" called out a voice from the opposite direction of the hall. Another man had stepped into the hall from his room, apparently heading down to breakfast.

"Good morning, Victorio," answered Carpo cheerfully as he turned to face the man addressing him. "I'll join you at breakfast in a few moments."

About this time, Sal reached the top of the stairs as Carpo unlocked the door to his room and called out to his friend:

"Victorio, meet our new boarder, Sal, a fellow Sicilian."

Again Sal extended his hand in a friendly handshake. He excused himself, for he, too, would return shortly to the dining room for breakfast. Sal closed the door to his room behind him, dropped his bundle on the bed, and proceeded to look the room over. As is the habit with a new occupant to a room, he walked over to the window and raised the shade as he pulled back the curtains. It was now daybreak. He glanced out the window. It faced the small rear yard well below and to the east towards Central Basin, its docks across 3rd Street, and the Bay. Since this location was uphill from 3rd Street, he could look over the rooftops of houses and industrial buildings extending a half-dozen blocks below. He liked this room much better than the one he had previously. It reminded him of his room at the family villa back in Sicily. Only there, the view was scenic overlooking tile roofs, flowered balconies, and the azure blue of the Mediterranean Sea.

He took off his hat and set it down alongside his bundle. The mirror above the old dresser reflected his Sicilian features as he brushed his hair back with the palms of both hands. Curly, jet black hair always looked in place in contrast to some types that constantly needed combing. At least until he would be settled in, formality would be in order. He left his coat on and returned to the dining room for breakfast. Victorio was seated talking to still another boarder, non-Sicilian, but also of Italian extraction.

"Come, sit next to me," said his newly made acquaintance. No sooner he was seated, Carpo came in and sat across from him.

"Sal, have you met Gino, here?" said Carpo.

Nodding his head in a manner of acknowledgement, Sal, in a partly rising, crouched position reached across the table and shook the man, Gino's, hand. Again, such as he had noticed previously, Sal was able to detect a strong smell of some sort emitting from the clothing of the first two men he had met. At first meeting, he thought it to be coming from the kitchen. But now, he was sure it was related to the two men's employment. No doubt they both worked for the same employer, probably a food processing operation of some sort in the nearby vicinity.

As breakfast was being consumed in the usual workmanlike manner, Carpo asked Sal where he was employed.

"I'm not employed at the moment," he answered.

"Not employed?" said Victorio in surprise without looking in his direction. There was silence for a moment as they wondered how this newcomer, unemployed, could meet the steep tariff of this particular boardinghouse. Why didn't he pick a cheaper one? By the same token, Sal wondered how these men could afford it and be so cheerful about it. The food processing industry was known to pay the least of all for common labor, or any other employer for that matter, other than the highly-skilled mechanical trades.

"Are you seeking employment?" asked Carpo curiously.

"Yes, I seek employment, but in the mechanical field," answered Sal.

"Oh, you're a mechanic?" said Carpo, expressing surprise.

"Metal is my trade. I work with metals, not automobiles. I'm sorry, I should have been more specific," answered Sal.

"Ah, yes, those are good-paying jobs. I do wish you success." As he said that, Carpo was studying Sal. To him, Sal didn't really look the part.

The man Gino was saying nothing. It was apparent that he was not employed in the same manner or line of work as the other two so he, therefore, had less in common. Nevertheless, Victorio held out a pack of cigarettes with the accompanying offer to the others to take one. A wooden match was struck, providing a light for all four cigarettes. As they smoked and chatted for a few moments after breakfast while still seated, Sal glanced around for an ashtray. There were none, so he shook the ashes in the cuff of his pants. The others chose to dispose of their ashes in the traditional manner so common in Italy; they simply reached back and aside with their cigarette, shaking the ashes onto the floor of the room. It was the same with the particles of tobacco caught between their lips; they simply spat them in any which way except in the faces of each other.

Well, Sal had learned to do otherwise, for Livia didn't adhere to the Italian tradition in reference to smoking and, therefore, would not permit this sort of conduct, not even for an instant. To shake ashes on her kitchen or dining room floor meant you found yourself crawling on your hands and knees until you had gathered it all up, and that went for Mike as well.

The lady Fedora came in with two lunch buckets and set them in front of Gino and Victorio with the comment: "I pray you will enjoy last night's leftovers."

The comment was made more for the benefit of Sal to let him know that this is what he could expect for lunch every day except Sunday. The others were already well aware of it. The two men with the lunch buckets were the first to rise from the table. They bid each other good day with the statement: "We'll see you at supper this evening."

It was now definitely apparent to Sal that Gino didn't work with the other two men, and neither did he work as long a shift. Carpo excused himself with a yawn along with a stretching motion as he headed for the stairs and up to his room. He was ready to sack in for the day.

"Will you be needing a lunch bucket today?" asked Fedora of Sal.

"No, that won't be necessary," he answered. "I can do without lunch today." Sal thought for a moment. Do Carpo and Victorio work for a bakery? The yeasty smell about them could easily be related to baking bread.

Sal rose from his chair, thanked the landlady for breakfast, and headed up to his room. He undid his bundle of extra clothes and hung them up in the closet. The sheathed, long-bladed knife that was wrapped amongst them lay on the bed, along with the special, thin leather belt. He removed his coat, slipped the suspenders off his shoulders, and pulled his shirttails up under his armpits. As if he had done it a thousand times before, he expertly picked up knife, sheath, and belt, then slipped it around his waist and buckled it in place, tucked in the shirttails over the sheathed knife, and with his thumbs, snapped his suspenders back in place. The knife was so situated that he could reach across with his right hand through his shirt, grab the already slanted handle in a right-hand retrieving position, and have it ready for action — all within the blink of an eye. Although it was always his hope to never have to use it, he would if need be. It was bred into him.

With his coat on, and hat in hand, he walked out the front door, stood there in the early morning sun for a moment while he adjusted his hat, then briskly made his way down the street on his way to seek out his enemy for his own satisfaction as well as to remove the threat to his newfound friends, the paesani.

CHAPTER 42

For the next several days, Sal walked the streets between China Basin and Central Basin, and south to the Islais Creek channel. He would pass the ship berthed opposite Pier 64 but pretended he had nothing to do with it, never stopping to give it a second glance or talk to anyone. Somewhere in this industrial complex, there was a still operating. He must find it. The heavy industrial area between 3rd and the Bay was finally ruled out. If anything, he reasoned, it would be in the lighter industrial area west of 3rd Street where there were many old smaller buildings, some appearing to be vacant. He made it a point, however, to stop in here and there and ask for a job, always being careful to state his qualifications as the opposite of what they were seeking so as not to get the job. Each day during supper or at times during breakfast, the same questions were asked of him:

"Have you had any luck?"

"No," he would answer.

On this one particular evening, Carpo once again posed the question to Sal:

"No luck today either?" Then added: "Maybe you're not going about it right. Be specific and to the point; cite your qualifications before they get a chance to turn you away."

"Each time I explain my qualifications, no one believes me. Apparently, to them I don't look the part."

"You'll find that to be true amongst all the new immigrants," stated Carpo. "All they want you for is cheap, common labor. They don't appreciate our skills. And they're hard to fool; they can tell we're foreigners."

"Don't give up," stated Gino. "I too thought the same, but then one day, this particular machine shop needed someone and there were no others available. Fortunately, I happened by again for the third time, and as you can see, I'm still there. They are pleased with my work."

A machine shop, thought Sal. Yes, he does smell of a machine shop, unlike the others that smell more like bakers or brewers. Brewers! Yes, that's what they smell like. A yeasty brewer's smell. I wonder . . . .

That night he lay in bed thinking. Mike was on his mind. He remembered what he had told him. Early in the morning when the air is crisp and quiet, you'll smell it. He was thinking of the old brewery down on Arkansas Street.

Next morning, he was up earlier than usual. When he reached the bottom of the stairs, the lady Fedora had just entered the kitchen.

"My, you're up early this morning. It'll be another hour before breakfast is ready," she said after bidding him a good morning.

"Oh, I realize that! But I had such a good night's rest that I felt like getting up early and catch a breath of crisp, fresh morning air." His coat on and hat in hand indicated that he was about to leave.

"Will you be having breakfast?" she asked.

"Oh, yes. Of course. I'll only take a short walk and be back." Without further comment, he made his way to the door, stepped into the brisk morning air and gently closed the door behind him.

He strolled casually down Mississippi, crossed 19th and 18th, then left on the next street, Mariposa. Continued west a few blocks until he reached Arkansas, then left again, sniffing the air as he walked along. The old brewery was still there all right, but it was obvious that it had been shut down for some time. There were no smells emitting from it. They certainly don't work there, he thought.

Making his way back to the boardinghouse, he crossed 18th Street as a bread truck passed him on its way to drop off its early morning deliveries at the close-by businesses. The smell of fresh bread emitting from it was overpowering. Fresh baked bread, he thought to himself as he inhaled the inviting aroma. "No, it's not the same as their smell. They're not bakers either," he mumbled.

Walking east along 18th Street, he reached Mississippi and headed back up the hill towards the boardinghouse. As he crossed

19th, Carpo appeared walking from the opposite direction, also heading for the boardinghouse. The two men arrived at the front entrance at the same time.

"Well, good morning," said Carpo puffing somewhat, for it was a steep hike from either side. "Out for some early morning fresh air?" he asked.

"Yes," answered Sal. "Since I was awake earlier than usual, I thought I'd take advantage of it."

Sal followed Carpo through the front door. The peculiar smell about him was as strong as ever. Only this time he also smelled of soot, like being caught in a tunnel when a train's coming through.

They walked in. Gino was already seated so Sal took his place at the table and poured himself a cup of coffee as Carpo started up the stairs meeting Victorio starting down. He heard the two men greet each other. "So, you got caught in the tunnel again!" he heard Victorio say laughingly.

"Yes, I miscalculated the locomotive's speed. I saw it coming but I thought I could make it through that short tunnel before it came through."

Now, this was of interest to Sal. These two men never once talked about where they worked or what they worked at. As a matter of fact, they never talked about their employment at all. And still, they obviously worked at the same trade because they smelled alike. One, days, and one, nights, and walking the same route. This is unusual, thought Sal. They have so much in common, but never talk about it, at least not in the presence of others. Questions crossed Sal's mind; they could be working a still. Maybe Occhio's? Feelings of anxiety quivered throughout his body. He finished his breakfast, excused himself, picked up his hat, and retreated to his room.

As he did so, Gino commented to the others: "Sal seems to be somewhat concerned about not having found employment."

"Finding a specialty job such as he prefers isn't an easy task," answered Victorio as if he too had previously tried. "But sooner or later, he'll succeed," he added.

"If his money holds out long enough," added Carpo with a chuckle. "Fedora will throw him out before long."

Little did they know that if Sal was to so much as indicate to Mike that the boardinghouse should be bought, they would find Sal to be their landlord instead of a fellow tenant.

Sal was sitting at his bedroom window looking out towards the Bay. The crisp morning air was clear as a bell. He could clearly see the ship berthed down at Central Basin opposite Pier 64 just off of China Basin Boulevard.

The two tugs were tied up, one alongside, and one at the pier itself. Several men, along with the two skippers, Sven and Swede, could be seen plainly as they moved about the ship. He thought for a moment, then raised the bottom half of the window, leaned out and looked to his right. Carpo's room just across the hall had the same window and therefore the same view of the ship. The haunting thought that Carpo and Victorio were connected with Occhio's still was now being viewed as reality.

"Now, this is beginning to make some sense. From this vantage point, every move on or about the ship can be observed," he mumbled, as he retreated from the window. With a thoughtful expression on his face, he pursed his lips while shaking his head up and down as if giving a positive "yes" answer to his own questions. Were they casing the ship from here? Was Carpo the lookout?

It was no doubt a coincidence that the ship was berthed such as it was just below the hill. However, this fact was exploited and used to an incredible advantage by the bootleggers that, no doubt, had heard of its salvage and load of sugar. Sal was now convinced that these two fellow Sicilians were employees of the man called Occhio. No doubt about it.

Sal was pleased with himself. "Today I shall walk the tracks," he murmured softly in delight. No, maybe that would not be wise, he thought. It would be best to avoid being seen along the tracks. He was now talking to himself softly with great eagerness. "Take it easy," he was telling himself. "Instead of walking the tracks, I'll study them from different vantage points, as they have done with the ship. Better still, I'll make it a point each morning and evening to be at different concealed locations and let them lead me undetected to the still."

This was Friday morning. Hopefully, this day and the next would be somewhat more productive than the previous four days of scouting. Since they're walking through tunnels, I'll explore them first, thought Sal. He immediately ruled out the Western Pacific Railroad branch that tunneled from 22nd Street and Mariposa under Arkansas because Carpo had come from the opposite direction.

Besides, if he had come through that tunnel, Sal probably would have seen him; and there was no point in using it anyway since either direction would take him out of his way. The same thing applied to the longer Southern Pacific Railroad tunnel that ran parallel to Pennsylvania and Indiana. He did recall the sound of the train on the Southern Pacific Railroad branch some minutes before he met Carpo that morning. Sal remembered Carpo's mention of a short tunnel, so he reasoned that he must have got caught in the short Southern Pacific Tunnel that runs under 25th Street.

"Yes," he whispered as if being careful of being overheard. Since they appear to be walking on the tracks to and from the still, that puts it somewhere south of Army Street, and maybe not too far south at that. Tomorrow morning I'll learn even more, he confidently thought.

He picked up his hat with his left hand, and with his right hand checked the position of his concealed knife as he headed for the door of his room. Instinct played a major part in this constant checking of one's weapon before taking up the trail of his quarry. Any sign of excitement or anxiety was avoided as he reached the bottom of the stairs.

"Good luck to you today!" called out Gino. "You're about to connect. At least I hope you do," he added.

"Maybe you should try the district further south. What they call Bayshore," put in Carpo in real sincerity. This one time, they had both hit the nail on the head because that's exactly what he was about to do.

"That's a good suggestion; I believe I will," answered Sal, agreeably. With that comment, he started out the front door. It was his intention to at least get out on the street before Victorio did, who was picking up his lunch bucket about the time Sal cleared the front door. Sal casually strolled down Mississippi towards 19th, then turned to wave to Victorio who was walking towards the direction that Carpo had come. Sal then turned east on 19th Street putting himself completely out of sight of Victorio, who would also turn east on 22nd as he dropped down on the opposite side of the hill. The downhill hike speeded Sal up almost to a run. At Indiana he turned right, now heading south at a very fast walk. He had purposely gone past Pennsylvania for fear of running into Victorio who would be coming in that direction and crossing it in order to pick up the railroad tracks, hopefully heading south. By the time he reached 23rd Street where the entrance was to the short tunnel, he figured Victorio (having the much shorter distance to travel) was probably already going through the tunnel. So he hurried along Indiana at a run until he reached Army. The fast pace over the short hump was causing him to breathe hard. It made sense for them to use the tunnel instead of hiking over the hill such as he did. He could now see the railroad crossing at Army Street two blocks up. It wasn't a minute until he saw Victorio up on the trestle still walking the tracks heading south at a leisurely pace.

Now I'm screwed, thought Sal. He would now have to go three blocks east to 3rd Street and cross the bridge at Islais Creek channel in order to keep up the intermittent surveillance. No point, thought Sal. He was too out of breath. Besides, it would be taking him well away from his quarry. So he did the next best thing — waited a few minutes until he caught his breath, then walked up to the crossing. He made his way up the embankment and onto the trestle over Army Street where he could now see Victorio still walking south down the tracks.

Standing off to one side of the tracks somewhat obscured, Sal watched him until the sound of an approaching switch engine pulling a dozen or so cars came clanking and puffing out the tunnel just behind him. Of the two sets of tracks, the train was on the side furthest from him. As it passed by heading south, Victorio disappeared from view. Rather than step over to the other set of tracks and let the train go by, Victorio chose to leave the track bed entirely. From where Sal was standing, it was close to a half mile to where he saw Victorio leave the tracks. A quarter of a mile further down the tracks, the train continued past Oakdale Avenue, then disappeared through the next tunnel under Palou Ave. This tunnel ran for approximately a half mile emerging at Williams Avenue. Oakdale Avenue and Williams Avenue both were bridged over the tracks at the crossings. He expected to see Victorio step back up on the railroad bed and proceed through this tunnel as well. But that was not the case. Somewhere west of the railroad tracks, in one of the many industrial buildings, Victorio was at work. Sal thought it best not to walk the tracks in search of him for fear of exposing himself.

He spent the better part of the rest of the day walking the

315

various streets on both sides of the tracks in the general area between Army Street and Palou Avenue, but came up with nothing positive. At one point, he seemed to get a faint whiff of the same related smell on the two men's clothing. However, he was not able to pinpoint it. His thoughts turned back to the morning that Mike had let him off at 3rd Street, and the advice that was offered:

"The best time to find it is early morning when the air is brisk. Search for it. You'll know when you've found it." Mike's words weighed heavily on his mind. No question now; the still is somewhere close by.

CHAPTER 43

It was early afternoon when Sal arrived back at the boardinghouse. He planned to clean up before going out for the evening. As he was about to ascend the stairs, a bundle of clothing came tumbling down towards him. Sal stepped aside, then proceeded up the stairs. The lingering yeasty fermentation smell indicated the clothing needed washing. It was obvious the clothing belonged to Carpo and Victorio.

Fedora, up at the head of the stairs, didn't bother to apologize for her actions but instead said: "You're back early. Did you find a job today?"

"No," answered Sal as he climbed the stairs. "I'm going out for the evening, so I thought I'd take a bath. You needn't plan supper for me."

She waited until he cleared the stairway then descended while advising him that the next day was wash day.

After his bath, Sal encountered Carpo in the hallway. Sal's neat shaven appearance drew comment from Carpo:

"Ah, I see you're going out tonight," he said. "I wish I was going with you. Give my regards to the Madame down at the mansion. Tell her you want Loleta. She's a good one, if you can get her of course." The remark drew chuckles and laughter. It wasn't a bad thought, but Sal had previously arranged to meet Pucci down at the Southern Pacific Railroad Depot. Loleta, the olive-skinned Armenian lust quencher, would have to wait.

Parked on 3rd Street just north of Townsend, Pucci and Primo waited for Sal. "I guess we have our time right," said Primo as he sat behind the wheel of his Hudson Sedan.

"There's still time. It's only 5:30. He'll show up pretty soon now," answered Pucci as he glanced at his watch. The time was decided to purposely coincide with the increased evening commuter activity in and around the train depot. They were scanning the area between the depot and the 3rd Street bridge where it crossed the China Basin Channel when Pucci saw Sal walking towards the depot on their side of the street.

"That's him all right," said Primo as he was about to open the door and walk down to meet him.

"Hold it a minute, let him keep coming. Let's be sure he's not being followed," stated Pucci cautiously.

Sal had seen the Hudson before when Primo visited the ranch. He was sure it was them. Except for his hat, Primo's head could barely be seen, in contrast to Pucci sitting in full view, head and shoulders looming up behind the windshield. He stopped in front of the depot entrance. He, too, looking back and across the street. There was no sense in trying to be coy. If in fact he was being followed, his intention would be to confront the person direct and head-on, keeping his friends' presence concealed. Satisfied, he stepped into the train depot and disappeared from view.

"Okay, drive up to the front entrance. I'm sure he spotted us," said Pucci.

As soon as the car stopped, Sal came out the door and let himself into the back seat of the sedan. Greetings were exchanged as they drove off. Primo made a left just short of the bridge, headed down Berry Street, and onto the Embarcadero.

"We're going over to a fish restaurant just off the Embarcadero," announced Pucci to Sal's delight.

"That's good. Fish is my favorite. Can we talk there?"

"That's another good reason for going there. We can have privacy."

Pucci was walking at a brisk pace from the parked car to the restaurant entrance. He was eager to hear what Sal had to report. By what Sal had already indicated, there was no question that he was definitely onto something.

The restaurant owner was well known to Pucci. "Can we have a table with privacy?" asked Pucci.

"Yes, definitely! Follow me." The owner led them to an alcove to the rear somewhat out of view of the rest of the patrons.

"Would you care to have some wine with your dinner tonight, Mr. Puccinelli?" inquired the owner.

"Why, yes. Providing, of course, that it's good wine."

"Trust me. It's the very best of wines, direct from the northern counties. I now get it by the barrel delivered to me here at the restaurant."

"Yes, I believe you," answered Pucci. "It comes in a barrel marked 'Molasses,' and it's delivered in a farm truck by a pleasant little Italian, always smiling but always demanding payment just the same," added Pucci with a big grin on his face.

The restaurant owner abruptly stepped back and with raised eyebrows asked the question with extreme surprise: "How did you know that?" The reaction and expression of surprise on the owner's face caused the three men to burst out laughing. It took a minute to regain their composure. No explanation was given, but to the owner's delight, Pucci suggested that he best bring at least two carafes of wine, not one as he had suggested.

Sal had much to talk about. As they ate their dinner and enjoyed their wine, he covered his days of vigilance and searching in every detail. Since Pucci referred to Julio's wine deliveries, he also pointed out that from the window of the boardinghouse, he could see the stepped up unloading of wine barrels from the ship.

"Is Mike worried about the wine being hijacked?" asked Sal, somewhat curiously.

"No, not really. We decided to get it off the ship as soon as possible," answered Pucci. "That way, we can move the ship away from the dock and anchor it out in the bay. Mike's filling the barns and basements with as much as he can in anticipation of this. Just being smart, that's all."

"That sounds like him all right," said Sal with a respectful grin, followed by a chuckle.

Pucci directed the conversation back to the issue at hand:

"No question, you're right," he said. "Those two men at the boardinghouse are working at the still. And, no doubt, it's located in the Bayshore District in one of those old industrial buildings close to the tracks. All we have to do now is find out which one and get some idea of how they operate, like schedules in and out, whatever."

Primo suggested what had already crossed his friends' minds: "It'll be dark by the time we leave here, so why not take a ride out there and look things over?"

"Good idea," answered Pucci as Sal set his wine glass down long enough to nod his approval as well. This was the first wine he'd tasted since he'd left the ranch some five days before. He hadn't realized how important it was to have a glass of wine to enhance the meal until he found himself without it. He let the others know of this discovery as well.

"You mean they don't serve paesano wine at the boardinghouse?" inquired Primo.

"No, I'm afraid not," answered Sal.

"Now, there's a prospective customer for your Uncle Mike. Why not suggest it to him?" offered Pucci somewhat jokingly.

"By God, I'll do that," retorted Primo with a chuckle. "And I'll bet he'll make them a paying customer."

"No bet," said Pucci. "Chances are I'd lose it."

As they walked out the restaurant, Pucci made a comment to the owner that the wine was "superb." Little did the owner know that he was talking to the key man who was responsible for making these fine wines available to his gratified patrons.

Primo sat down behind the wheel of the Hudson. His short frame disappeared from view. You could see more of his hat than his head as he peered over the steering wheel of the big car. His sight of vision ran along the long shiny black hood as if he was aiming a short barreled cannon. Anything crossing the street within a half block in front of him that was shorter than the top of the radiator was sure to get run over.

In contrast, Pucci, being the much larger man, always drove around in the little Reo runabout. All he had to do is lean slightly forward and he could just about see the crank hanging on its leather strap out front.

"What the hell did you buy such a big car for?" remarked Pucci somewhat seriously.

"Why, what's the matter with it?" snorted Primo.

"For one thing, the damned hood is as long as the rest of the car. How can you see where you're going? You're liable to hit somebody."

"What's there to see? If people want to crawl on their hands and knees and get run over, that's their tough luck."

There was one thing for sure, no sane person dare step out in front of that big Hudson. Especially at night, the two big washtub-size head lamps resembled two locomotives coming down the street side by side; and the smoke belching out the exhaust pipe gave it even more of a locomotive appearance. The shadow of the two-piece bar-type bumper being cast on the street just ahead of it gave the appearance of a cow catcher. No, there was no need to worry. Primo was right. No one would be fool enough to step out in front of this seemingly driverless vehicle. To do so would be outright suicide.

The two carafes of wine consumed by the trio were having an effect. They laughed and horsed around in a relaxed mood. Even Sal, as serious and quiet as he was, was now joining in with comments and horseplay. He was among good friends. It was a good feeling to let loose a little.

The Hudson reached the end of the Embarcadero and swung right on Berry Street, then left on 3rd, rattled across the steel bridge at the China Basin channel, and headed south.

"Okay, where do you want to go first?" asked Primo.

"Up to the boardinghouse," answered Pucci. "That is, if you can find it."

"Sal, how do you get there?" asked Primo.

"Go right on 19th, then turn left on Mis—esi—epi. . ." That's about as far as Sal got with the pronunciation of "Mississippi" before Primo cracked up, followed by Pucci, then Sal joining in on the laughter.

The ensuing laughter was broken up by Pucci's question to Primo: "Do you think you can see the street sign?" asked Pucci with a questionable expression.

"No, just tell me which corner the light pole is on, and I'll show you how to take a corner by dead reckoning." With that, the Hudson sped into the turn. Primo cut the corner at high speed knowing he had the hill to climb up ahead.

"For Christ's sake, take it easy! You jump the curb and you'll roll it over sure as hell," advised Pucci.

It was Primo's intent to show his buddies what this big Hudson had under its strapped-down hood. It had enough momentum to carry it roaring up the hill in high gear. It wasn't until the car was to make the left turn on Mississippi that the second gear was brought into play. Primo let up on the accelerator.

Now moving at a slower sensible speed, they cruised past the boardinghouse. Once it was pointed out, Sal instructed Primo to make a slow turn at the next intersection and come back the same way. The Hudson came to a momentary stop at the intersection while facing the Bay.

"Damn. What a view!" exclaimed Pucci. "Look at that. There's the ship and the two tugs. No obstructions whatever. What a coincidence to have berthed it there. How convenient for those goddamned bootleggers. "

"From the rear windows of the boardinghouse, it's even better. You can watch the tugs make their trips all the way across the bay and back," remarked Sal.

Sal instructed Primo to head back down 19th Street, then right on Indiana, following the same route he had taken that morning. From Army Street, he pointed out where he had last seen the man called Victorio leave the tracks. However, the darkness created a problem in pinpointing the exact location.

Retracing Sal's route, they proceeded to cruise around within several blocks of Palou Street between 3rd Street and the railroad tracks. The dimly lit industrial area was devoid of traffic or activity at this time of night.

"Pull over and stop at the corner of the next block," instructed Sal. The three men stepped out of the car. Sal took the lead strolling slowly along sniffing the air as he walked along. "There it is, I can smell it again. Just as Mike had said."

Primo was smoking a cigarette so he couldn't smell anything but tobacco smoke. Pucci walked back and away from his companions and into the center of the intersection. They watched him get down on his hands and knees. In the dim light, he looked like he was praying Arabic fashion, head down facing east.

"What's he doing?" inquired Sal.

"Well, if he was an Arab, I'd say he was praying to Mecca. But since he's an Italian and Catholic at that, I'd say he lost his marbles," answered Primo chuckling in disbelief at his buddy's conduct.

If the lighting had been any better, they would have noticed that Pucci had that splendid Roman nose of his stuck into one of the sewer manhole-cover holes, drawing up sewer gasses into his nostrils and past his odor-sensing membrane like a bloodhound on scent.

Standing back on his feet, he announced:

"That's it all right! Distillation residue waste from the still is being run out into the sewer system, sure as hell," announced Pucci as he approached his two surprised companions.

"Well, I'll be damned! What do you know about that?" said Primo. "You could tell all that by just sticking your nose in a hole. Imagine what you could find out if you stuck your whole head in there."

"You're damned right! And I'll tell you something else. Since the Bay is in that direction (pointing east) and sewage runs downhill, I'd say the still is somewhere in the opposite direction and across the tracks not too far from here. So cut the clowning and let's try to find it."

They walked up past a row of industrial buildings that backed up to the railroad right-of-way, then turned right at the first alley they came to. The alley crossed the tracks on an angle, indicating that the streets didn't run parallel to the railroad either. This made for odd-shaped buildings on both sides of the tracks along the right-of-way. They had just passed the end of a building as they approached the right-of-way. They were now debating whether or not Primo should go back for the car rather than continue on foot. Because it's a truck driver's habit to cautiously look in both directions when approaching railroad tracks, Primo was doing just that when a flashing, small light attracted his attention.

"Hey, look at that over to your right," said Primo in an almost whisper.

Some distance away a train whistle could also be heard in the still of the night. It was obviously coming down the track and would pass by them shortly. However, it was also obvious that the flashing signal light had nothing to do with the approaching train. They stepped up to get a better idea of the exact location and distance the flashing signal was coming from.

To their left, some two blocks or so down the track, at the entrance to the tunnel that runs under Palou Street between Williams Avenue on the far end and Oakdale Avenue closest to them, another signal flash was detected. With the approaching train, the signaling had stopped. The three men stepped in the shadows and alongside the closest building as the train came by. It was a fast-moving passenger train heading south towards San Jose. No sooner had it passed, they stepped back alongside the tracks. To their right, the equivalent of two city blocks, the flashing signal resumed. To their left, looking in the direction of the dark tunnel entrance, again the other flashing signal light could be seen responding from the opposite end of the tunnel.

"Let's stick around a few minutes and see what happens," said Pucci. "It's a cinch. This signalling business means something is about to take place."

Sure enough, off to their right coming from the direction of the signalling, a handcar could be heard coming down the tracks. The positive clatter of pins slapping in the well-worn bushings caused by the pumping action indicated the handcar was loaded. They hurriedly moved back off the right-of-way and to the sanctuary of the shadows. From their position, they could see the handcar pass by the dimly lit intersection. Two men were facing each other, straining as they pumped hard to keep the loaded handcar moving. The muffled sound of full five-gallon cans stacked and held together by canvas was a dead giveaway of its cargo.

"Alcohol," whispered Pucci. "They're taking it out through the tunnel. Damned clever of them. You have to give those bastards credit for having figured that one out. Anyone happening by and seeing them in the handcar would surely mistake them for a railroad maintenance crew."

"They, no doubt, pick it up at the south end where the tunnel comes out at Williams Avenue, and I'll bet you they bring in their supplies the same way," commented Primo.

"You better not take that bet either," said Sal directing his remark to Pucci, then adding: "That tunnel is a good half mile long. No doubt they time their trip through it right after a train comes through, intentionally, so as not to get caught in it regardless of the double track."

"Go get the car," ordered Pucci. Primo headed back to the car eager to carry out Pucci's order.

"Let's walk back down to the corner, Sal, and wait there. No telling who else might be out there along the right-of-way," said Pucci while glancing back down the tracks.

Once on board, the Hudson swung around the next corner to the right, then over and across the railroad tracks below at the Oakdale Avenue bridge past the first close diagonal cross-street that ran back towards the tracks again. The car then turned right at the next corner, moved along and past a long row of buildings, turned right again, and stopped just around the corner facing east towards the bay. This street dead-ended at the railroad tracks, with old wooden industrial buildings on either side that extended to the end of the street less than a half block away. This was about where they figured the signal light had come from.

"You guys wait here. I'm going to take a quick walk down there. In the meantime, get turned around facing out of here," ordered Pucci in his customary no-nonsense manner, then disappeared instantly in the shadows of the buildings.

"Wait a minute!" called Sal. "He didn't say not to get out of the car. You get turned around. I'll wait here for him. That man is a fool to wander off in the darkness without some sort of weapon."

Sal stepped out of the car and gently closed the back door then proceeded to quietly close the front door. It was then that Primo noticed under Sal's unbuttoned coat the partially exposed knife handle glisten in the dim street lighting. Sal had purposely unbuttoned his coat and a shirt button in preparation of dealing with the two bums he'd seen cross the street to their side no sooner Pucci had disappeared. The two bums reached the shadows and started walking towards Pucci, but Sal, also keeping to the shadows, was directly behind them.

Before the bum up front realized what was taking place behind him, Sal had grabbed the closest one to him from behind clamping his hand across his mouth. One quick downward slash of his knife slit the back of the man's pants clear down to his asshole. Then, in three quick movements, the knife slashed his suspenders allowing the bum's pants to fall to his knees. With this, Sal whispered in the bum's ear as he held the point of the knife against his belly. In his broken English, he instructed the horrified bum to keep his mouth shut and to run as fast as he could or get his balls cut off with the next pass of the razor-sharp knife.

The instant he set the bum free, the other one up front turned around to see what was delaying his companion. Seeing his cohort dragging his pants while stumbling out from the shadows led him to believe he was answering nature's call. He turned away from him and proceeded to stalk Pucci, not seeing the shadowed figure that was coming in fast along the building. Before he could react or utter a sound, Sal's open left hand struck him across his Adam's apple leaving him hardly able to breathe, let alone make any sounds other than gasping for air.

Sal grabbed his belt buckle, jerked the bum towards himself, at the same time in a slashing movement came down with the knife, splitting belt, pants, and underwear, along with nicking the bum's pecker. There was no need to instruct him to run, or else! He thoroughly understood the unspoken message.

He didn't hesitate; as he turned to run, Sal grabbed him again by the back of his coat, wiped the blood off the point of the knife on the man's coat, then shoved him away from himself. The bum was still gasping for air as he crawled and stumbled in the direction of his departing cohort. Sal stepped back into the shadows, sheathed his knife, buttoned his shirt and coat, and waited for Pucci now heading back towards him hurriedly.

"What the hell's all that about?" asked Pucci of Sal, as he made out the two figures stumbling and scrambling on the far side of the street.

"Just a couple of bums that had lost their direction," said Sal calmly as they walked across the street and up to the waiting Hudson.

Primo looked at them as they walked up, then back again in time to see the two bums that had just passed by him that were now taking the corner up ahead at a dead run. In the process of getting turned around, he had missed the events that had taken place shortly before.

"What the hell's going on with you two?" he asked mystified. "Did you see those two characters that just ran by?"

"Don't look at me," answered Pucci as he climbed aboard. "They're friends of Sal's."

"They didn't act much like friends to me," snorted Primo as he pulled out and away from the curb leaving behind a cloud of exhaust smoke in the process.

"They're operating the still out of that last building. No question about it. It's completely sealed from the inside, no windows, just a big door facing the street, and a loading ramp on the side along the spur track," announced Pucci with satisfaction.

"How can you be sure?" asked Sal.

"I can smell it. That's one thing they can't seal off. They're in there, all right, making alcohol with our sugar. Those goddamn bastards!" swore Pucci.

Sal was saying nothing. The grin on his face was not one of amusement, it was more like a satisfied expression as if he was about to cut the throat of his and his family's worst enemy.

"Where to now?" asked Primo.

"Get back down on 3rd Street, then head up to Williams Avenue. Let's get a look at the south end of the long tunnel under Palou," instructed Pucci. The Hudson made a right off of 3rd Street onto Williams. "Mostly residential on the hill section, much like the other side," commented Pucci.

The Hudson stopped on the bridge that crossed over the tracks below. It was now being illuminated by a slow-moving switch engine emerging from the tunnel to their right and about to pass under them.

"Hold it here! Let the engine go by," said Pucci. He wanted to take advantage of the lit-up area on both sides of the tracks as it proceeded to move down the right-of-way. "Mostly industrial on your side. They could be using any one of those buildings along there for warehousing."

"Shall we work our way down that area?" asked Primo.

"No, let's call it a night," answered Pucci.

On their way back to drop off Sal at 19th Street, they discussed and agreed to meet again the following evening, only this time after supper and along 3rd Street south of the China Basin channel bridge. Sal was to hang around the boardinghouse during the day such as a man might do on a Saturday while off work. Pucci and Primo would scout the area of the still and both ends of the tunnel during the light hours so as to get a true, firsthand picture of the situation. If they were to be seen or suspected, there would be no indication of a tie-in with Sal.

Sal stepped out of the car, looked skyward and announced the possibility of rain: "Should we meet as agreed if it's raining?" he asked.

Some thought was given to this question before Pucci gave him an answer: "No. In the event of rain, we'll then meet on Sunday, same place, but about ten o'clock in the morning. We'll take no chances of arousing suspicion."

Sal bid them good night, satisfied more than ever that Pucci was a cautious-thinking man. This made him feel comfortable and secure. His father once told him:

"A false friend is more dangerous in broad daylight than your worst enemy in pitch darkness."

CHAPTER 44

The first good October rainstorm of the season turned out to be a real gutter washer. This gave Sal a good excuse to stay indoors as instructed. As for Carpo and Victorio, they bitched about the need to go to work in the rain. But, in their line of work, circumstances demanded they work every day, rain or shine. The still was not to be shut down for their convenience.

The heavy rain that continued throughout this Saturday was also of benefit to Pucci and Primo. They dressed themselves in firemen's water-repellent gear complete with rubber boots, then cruised the area with the little Reo fire truck pretending to be checking out minor flooding conditions.

They parked one block from the suspected still location and brazenly walked the railroad right-of-way studying the building, its loading platform, and its relation to the spur track in which the handcar had departed the night before loaded with alcohol. It was obvious that the one corner of the building closest to the tunnel had been recently modified to accommodate access to the spur track without the need to use the loading platform. The platform itself had been cut off some ten or twelve feet short of the corner. Saw cuts and shiny nail heads driven into the old vertical boards revealed the fact that there now existed a pair of doors hinged from the inside at this location of the building. They kept right on walking until they reached the next block. At this point, they left the right-of-way and made their way back to the Reo.

"Leave your wet gear on," ordered Pucci as he stepped into the Reo. "Let's see what it looks like from Palou Avenue where it crosses over the tunnel entrance."

He parked the Reo where it couldn't be seen from the railroad right-of-way below. They walked through the constant rain and over to the guardrail in full view of the double tracks below the Oakdale Avenue bridge. They were looking north where the tracks went under the bridge just a short distance from the tunnel entrance. The constant rain obscured their view. They couldn't see far enough up the tracks to where they finally disappeared through the next tunnel up at Army Street.

"Now, tell me something," said Pucci. "How do you suppose they managed to get that handcar out of that building onto the spur, load it, and secure it with tarps? All in the space of several minutes after the train went by, and without rattling those noisy five-gallon cans? The light from that train last night showed the area to be clear as it approached it."

"A damned good question," grunted Primo as rainwater dripped off the end of his nose. "There's only one logical answer that I can think of. They had it loaded in the building ready to go."

"Exactly!" exclaimed Pucci, then added: "The bastards have made up a set of wooden rails that they can easily carry out, set in position, roll out the handcar, and take off instantly down the track. Smart buggers, don't you think?"

"You better believe it!" confirmed Primo.

"That means, there are at least four or more men working out of there, at least when the shipment goes out. Two that take off with the handcar, no doubt Occhio is one of them, and two to handle the makeshift tracks after they depart," added Pucci.

"And I'll tell you something else, my friend," said Primo. "They know the schedule of the train so they make their shipment accordingly. No doubt once a night, or every other night at the same time. You want to bet?"

"No, I won't take that bet either. Do you remember what time it was last night when the shipment went out?"

"About 10:30," answered Primo.

"Good. We'll be back here at the same time tonight for another check."

"Come on, let's get over to the south end of the tunnel on the Williams Avenue side and take a look around."

They drove around studying the area making comments as if they would be the ones needing to arrange a pickup, putting

330

themselves in the bootleggers' shoes, so to speak.

"Whatever method they use to transfer the alcohol must be quick and obscured from view. We know that for sure," said Pucci in a thoughtful manner.

"That doesn't mean it has to be in a building, does it?" asked Primo.

"No, maybe not," stated Pucci. "But you can be sure they'll take off onto the closest spur that suits their cause. They're not about to make the transfer out here at the elevated crossing. Besides, they would have a hell of a time carrying those five-gallon cans up the embankment. Did it occur to you last night that they were coming down the same track the train was on?"

"As a matter of fact, I did notice that. What you're saying, then, is, the rendezvous takes place on a spur off the west side, like maybe over there?" Primo was now pointing to the first spur visible, running between two long industrial buildings south of the Williams Avenue Bridge they were parked on.

"That's a starting point." With that, Pucci put the Reo in gear, proceeded up Williams, drove to the first street and turned left. The spur track crossed the street some 400 yards from the corner, again between more industrial buildings, then dead-ending before reaching the next cross-street. Some 600 yards ahead, another spur crossed the street in exactly the same manner.

"This has to be it. If the first spur is occupied with freight cars, they simply signal to come in on the second one or vice versa. Either way, they simply back in off the street between the buildings. The handcar then comes in up to the back end of the truck for unloading. You see, they don't need a warehouse. Neat little set up, I'd say."

Primo was studying Pucci's expressions as he continued to further explain their method of operation. He could see that as much as he detested the thought of getting involved with this bootlegging business, it was obvious that the challenge to match wits with this Occhio fellow was overpowering. It showed in his expressions as well as in his speech. He was enjoying it.

"We've got 'em!" exclaimed Pucci. "Yes, indeed, we've got 'em, dead to rights!"

"What do you mean, 'we've got 'em?' How do you figure it?" questioned Primo.

"Simple, my friend. I'll explain it to you in short. There can't be more than a half dozen of them running this thing. So every time they make a shipment, they're split up. At least one on this end with the truck. I now believe that to be Occhio. He probably wouldn't trust anyone but himself with the finished product to be delivered and collect the cash. Then there are two of them coming through the tunnel losing complete contact with both ends, at least for a short while. While they're on the tracks, I doubt that there's more than two or three, at most, left behind to tend the still."

"I get it!" interrupted Primo. "Take advantage of the fact that they're split up and out of contact with each other."

"Exactly!" snorted Pucci.

"Come on, let's go back up to the crossing and take a better look at that spur from there." As he suspected, the spur came off the main tracks in a northerly approach instead of direct from a southerly approach. "It makes no difference," he announced as if having been asked the question. "They simply go past, then come back up the track onto the spur."

"It's worth the extra effort since they need the easy access from the street and the privacy while loading," added Primo.

Pucci wasted no time in getting under way. The little Reo bounced around as it sped from one location to the other. There was no point in asking the question, for Primo knew by his actions that a plan was being formulated. Finally Pucci stopped the Reo back up on Palou Avenue overlooking the tracks as they emerged from the tunnel below. He was studying the distance from the tunnel face and the Oakdale bridge that crossed over them and the embankments sloping up from the tracks on either side.

"This will work," he announced while bobbing his head up and down as if he was saying "yes" to an asked question. "We'll need four men up here with a few sacks of sand. They shouldn't have any problem scrambling down those embankments once the train goes by."

Primo kept quiet while he studied the expressions on his buddy's face. At times, Pucci would purse his lips, then clench his teeth. His eyes were constantly shifting up the track towards the still as if trying to gauge the distance to the last inch.

"It takes them a few minutes to get the handcar on the main rails and then another few minutes to pick up speed, so there should

332

be plenty of time to carry it out," said Pucci as if Primo was fully aware of the plan as it was being formulated in his mind. "We'll need a half-dozen men to crash the still, demolish it, and take back our sugar, or at least what's left of it. Another four men at the other end covering the spur track to jump Occhio once the signals are completed and the handcar is on its way; kick his ass around but good, and wreck his truck permanent." Pucci thought for a few minutes before making his final comment: "With you and I, plus Mike and the paesani, we'll be just enough, including Sal, of course."

"Don't forget Al. He'll want to be in on this too," added Primo excitedly.

"Yes, that's right. And we can also count on Swede with a few of his men too if we need them. They're anxious to settle a score with that Occhio character and his sidekick, the sapper, that's for damned sure."

"Whether you need them or not, they're going to be here. No way are they going to miss this Halloween party," stated Primo in a positive tone of voice.

The thought of Halloween flashed through Pucci's mind: "Hey buddy, you're a real genius!" exclaimed Pucci. "Halloween night! That's when we'll hit 'em. Perfect! Absolutely perfect! Just what the doctor ordered."

"The doctor is going to order us both in bed for a week if we don't get the hell out of these wet clothes and get warmed up," pleaded Primo.

"Okay, we're leaving. I'll explain the rest on the way out. Damn, this is going to be one hell of a Halloween Party!"

"Halloween Party?" exclaimed Primo still wondering what it was all about.

"That's what I said. Complete with costumes, the works."

"For Christ sake! What are you talking about? And catch that drip off your big nose, it's been hanging there long enough," ordered Primo as he swept across his own nose with the sleeve of his coat.

"Firemen's outfits. That's what I'm talking about, complete with badges and dress caps. Those Sicilian immigrants will think we're cops pulling off a raid, and so will anyone else that happens by. In the moonlight and confusion, no one will know the difference." He finally got around to taking a swipe across his nose sucking in air through his flared nostrils, as he did so. "They'll scatter like a flock of quail when you batter the door down with the old Doane," explained Pucci.

"Batter the door down! What the hell! You're going to put me right up front, aren't you?"

"No. You won't be up front, because you're going to back into that big door facing the street loaded with whistle-blowing, masqueraded paesani hell-bent for destruction."

"You better figure out how to masquerade that famous paesano duck walk if you expect them to look like cops."

The two buddies left the area satisfied that a raid on the man Occhio's still could be pulled off without incident, or at least avoid an all-out gang fight. But they were to underestimate the feelings within some of their own participants, some running deep enough to commit murder. Pucci wasn't so brilliant that he could foresee everything. His next step was to somehow coordinate a bunch of men, some with different objectives, into an efficient striking force, regardless of the mixed feelings. It had to be done. The next day they would head for the ranch.

CHAPTER 45

By Sunday morning the storm had subsided. Billowing white clouds were giving way to warm sunshine. Sal was already at the agreed pickup point when the Hudson pulled up. As Sal stepped in, Pucci stepped out of the front seat and followed him into the back seat, slamming both doors as he did so.

Greetings were exchanged as the seemingly driverless car roared off heading south for the ranch at San Bruno.

"Primo, put your hat back on or someone might think this is a runaway car," suggested Pucci jokingly.

Primo's unprintable remarks drew a roar of laughter from the two chauffeured passengers in the back seat. Nevertheless, he did put his hat back on. Once the horseplay subsided, Pucci proceeded to outline the plan of attack to Sal. He was all ears. This working as a team was intriguing. He liked it, especially the thought that Occhio would be alone at the south end of the long tunnel. Somehow he would manage to get to him before the others. Merely kicking his ass would not suffice as vindication for what Occhio had done to his father and family back in Sicily. There was a score to settle, and he would settle it himself in his own way. Sal kept these thoughts to himself. In no way would he want to disrupt the planned teamwork. By the time they reached the ranch, Pucci had outlined the entire plan to Sal's satisfaction. He wanted Sal present while explaining it to Mike, along with Julio, and some of the other key men. Thus, the reason for driving down to San Bruno on this beautiful early fall day. It reminded Sal of the song "O'Sole Mio" — the part that refers to the sun breaking out after a tempest. Nothing could be more beautiful and pleasant.

As the big Hudson approached the two side-by-side ranches, Pucci and Sal noticed something different about the big barn at the paesani's ranch.

"What the hell!" exclaimed Pucci as he leaned and looked across the front of Sal who was also looking at the odd position of the barn off to his left. "Primo, pull up! Turn into the paesani's driveway. Let's go take a look at that barn."

With that, Primo braked the Hudson, swung across the highway in a left turn, and started down the driveway. He, too, could now see the squatty appearance of the barn. "The damned thing looks like a big setting hen spread out over a clutch of eggs," remarked Primo.

"You mean, wine barrels," responded Sal.

It was now apparent to them that the barn had collapsed over a pyramid stack of barrels, the likes that had never been seen before. The sides had been pushed out in both directions now resting on the barrels that had once made up the base of the pyramid. The total height of the barn had dropped a good ten feet. Except for the crumbled and somewhat splintered boards on the ends, the rest of the barn was still pretty much intact.

"What the hell do you suppose happened?" asked Primo of Pucci, who was studying the situation as Primo swung the Hudson into the wet yard and came to a stop.

"Beats me," answered Pucci as he stepped out to confront Julio who was on his way across the yard to greet them. "Hey, Julio! What's with the barn?" he called out.

Julio's answer was in the form of a wave of the hand and shrug of the shoulders as if to say, let's not talk about that now. Others started to congregate in the yard area greeting the newcomers in their usual fashion. All smiles with hand shakes and back slapping extended even amongst themselves as if they hadn't seen each other in ages, but nevertheless avoiding Pucci's questions.

Primo didn't wait around for explanations. He marched right out to the barn for a firsthand look at this huge stack of barrels being sheltered by a henlike squatting barn. Some of the paesani followed him out back to take a second look for themselves as well. When asked questions, they, too, gave the same answers as Julio: a wave of the hand and a shrug of the shoulders, somewhat noncommittal and reluctant to talk about it. As they walked back to the yard to rejoin the others, Primo became more insistent about getting an answer from these smiling and grinning characters. Seeing the horses missing from their quarters, which were also flattened, he asked:

"Where's the horses? Did they get out?"

"Oh, they sensed it coming so they jumped the corrals and beat it. They're down along the railroad tracks grazing. They're O.K. No need to worry."

"Well, at least they've got some horse sense; that's more than you characters have. Come on, now," coaxed Primo. "Somebody did something wrong here. Who was it? Why, and how did it happen?"

Finally Contini stepped forward prepared to give an explanation. Since he had nothing to do with the planning, engineering, construction, or, for that matter, applying any effort or labor whatsoever in creating this pyramid of barrels within a hay barn, he obviously had nothing to lose. He was clean, so to speak. The others that did have something to do with it at some stage or other, encouraged him to explain the matter because they knew he would anyway. Being a great philosopher such as he was, practical engineering was trivial to such an ingenious mind.

Matteoli, his opponent in such philosophical matters, and having had something to do with the pyramid's construction, moved in closer within earshot, prepared to give counter-argument when the opportunity occurred. Contini, now surrounded by eager listeners, proceeded with his presentation:

"Had the Etruscans joined Caesar on his march into Egypt, they would have learned firsthand how to build pyramids. But no, they chose to remain in Tuscany amongst beautiful olive-skinned women, sexually stimulated by good wine, and where pyramids were never heard of, let alone ever built. When word first came back that such things did exist, they too felt the need to erect towers that would reach to the heavens just in case the good Lord was to forget to reach down and lift their souls into Heaven. However, they were going to go one better and place bells atop these towers so as to arouse the good Lord in event he fell asleep on the job. Even to this day, the continuous bonging of bells throughout the nights, and days as well, not only keeps the good Lord awake at all hours, but everyone else also."

"For God's sake, Contini," interrupted one of the paesani, "get to the point!"

"All right! All right!" answered Contini comfortably. "The paesani of Tuscany couldn't build a bell tower that would stand up straight (referring to the leaning Tower of Pisa), so what makes one think they could build a pyramid that would endure through the ages? As you can see, this one didn't endure through the age of a wine gnat. Why? Because wine barrels are round, not square like the stones of the pyramids."

"Come on, Contini. Give us a break. The roof leaked and softened up the ground. That's why we lost it," put in another paesano. "Besides, if it rained in Egypt like it does in Italy, their pyramids would be cockeyed too."

This now was Matteoli's cue to move in on Contini. Since he made the story so long, he didn't deserve to enjoy the final punch line. He stated:

"Contini has a point there. Tomorrow, we will order square barrels and stack them like a true pyramid. The top one will support a bronze statue of Mr. Contini holding a square glass in his left hand while pouring from a square carafe with his right hand. A fitting tribute to the man that just invented the square wine barrel." Matteoli's timely statement brought about a surge of hilarious laughter.

The three men, followed by Julio, with tears of laughter still streaming down their cheeks, retreated back to the Hudson and bid them all a temporary good day. They were still chuckling when they drove into Mike's yard next door only to start the hilarious laughter all over again.

Mike had spotted the Hudson across the winter cabbage patch and couldn't help but hear the voices and laughter drifting across the field. Livia, too, was standing at the head of the rear steps waiting to greet them upon their arrival. A short ceremonial of friendly greetings took place before Mike, gesturing with his thumb as if hitchhiking, and without looking in the direction of the paesani, asked the question: "What did that bunch of idiots over there tell you? What kind of story did they fabricate in regards to the collapsed barn?"

They didn't get a chance to answer the question, for Livia, from the top of the stair landing, instantly charged into her husband with full fury. She first hurried back into the kitchen in search of a weapon of sorts. The cast-iron skillet that she normally used for such purposes was setting on the stove full of simmering veal stew so, of course, that one would not be available. Reaching up over the stove, she grabbed a long-handled steel frying pan (about the size of a tennis racket) off the wall, and immediately headed back to the head of the stairway whence she had come. Gazing down at Mike in a menacing manner, she started out by saying: "You are the idiot! Not the poor innocent paesani such as you infer. It was your idea. You planned it, you engineered it, you supervised it, and you refused to heed the sound advice of Matteoli. He advised you to fix the roof before stacking the barrels."

By now she was halfway down the back stairs and continuing to lambast Mike with all the accusations she could think of. She reached the bottom of the stairs and walked slowly towards the men with a threatening left-hand finger pointing directly at her husband as she continued the barrage, while holding the frying pan firmly in her right hand like a determined tennis player ready to serve. She'd had enough. She was determined to put an end to this tomfoolery once and for all.

She continued her attack while Pucci and the others started to move away from Mike as if he had just contracted the plague. Getting hit on the head with that frying pan was bad enough, but to get caught in a side-swiping swing and have the edge of it catch you on the side of the head, could mean a severed ear for sure. They wanted her to have plenty of swinging room so they casually moved away from the battle ground.

She now shifted her strategy to center her attack on Mike's ancestors and the city they founded: "Your entire clan were forced out of Pisa and made to settle back into the hills isolated from all others." She was referring to the City of Buti, stuck back in an out-of-the-way ravine at the foot of the mountains that separated her Lucca from the provence of Pisa. She continued:

"For it was your ancestors that were responsible for the construction of the foundation, as well as the rest of the lopsided leaning 'Tower of Pisa.' They, too, ignored the advice of simple peasants that knew better than to build a structure of such magnitude on saturated mud, with an active spring under it at that. And, to make matters even worse, they tried to pass it off as the engineering feat of the century; therefore, leaving it to stay leaning intentionally."

Across the cabbage patch, the paesani were standing at the edge of the yard facing the direction of the battleground. With big grins on their faces, they were taking it all in. This was music to their ears. Contini and Matteoli, the two opposing philosophers, masters of wit, were standing there with an arm over each other's shoulders and waving their hats as encouragement to Livia, who by now had backed Mike clear into the cabbage patch. Her threatening finger was not what he was afraid of or, for that matter, the frying pan either. It was her sharp pointed elbows that were the real devastating weapons. To be flailed with those elbows could result in serious injury. An occasional, unintentional poke in the eye as she rolled over in bed during the night was a constant reminder of the damage that could be done if it were done intentionally during a fit of rage. Her final words before she backed off were several well-chosen, mild swear words that punctuated her final argument. Mike was the last one to join in on the laughter but, nevertheless, he did. He knew when he was beaten, so he might just as well join in on the fun.

Once settled down, Pucci managed to get the key men together and lay out the plan before them. They'd go along with it. Further discussions and rehearsals would follow over the next few days.

CHAPTER 46

Sal insisted on staying on at the boardinghouse. Being fully aware of the plan, he studied and took in all accounts of the bootlegging operation, which he passed on to Pucci. Now the stage was set; Halloween night was only two nights away.

Pucci had no problem gathering up the needed firemen's outfits. His buddies were delighted to contribute to his so-called masquerade party. However, they had no idea of the extent, or the kind of party he was planning. All the participants, including Swede and his men, were thoroughly familiarized with the area and the part they must perform. Pucci saw to that in his meticulous, thorough manner. As much as he detested this business, he was almost glad the sugar hijacking had taken place. He loved and lived the strategy and challenge it provided, like a general about to launch a crusade.

Finally the time had come, this was it, Halloween night; a bright, crisp moonlight night. The plan went into motion. This now was not a rehearsal, it was the real thing.

Primo in the old Doane, with Al sitting alongside, moving south on 3rd Street, pulled up at 19th Street to pick up Sal. He was not to be in a uniform. Neither was Al. Their next stop was just past the bridge where it crosses the Islais Creek channel. Here, he picked up Swede plus five of his men. They had come into the channel with the tug and docked near the bridge, leaving one man behind with the tug. They scrambled aboard the Doane carrying a sizable toolbox consisting of an assortment of tools such as would be used by a pipe fitter.

Sven and his men remained with the ship. Since it was Halloween night, they would take no chances of a hijack raid by other bootleggers that may be hungry for sugar.

They moved down to Palou Avenue where they met Mike with the Model-T parked across the street facing north, loaded with the damnedest looking uniformed men imaginable. They obviously had strict orders to not utter a word as they broke into the building housing the still for fear of giving away their true identity. They wanted the occupants to run, not stay and fight.

Behind Mike was Julio with the Graham truck. Al surrendered his seat to Vosco, then joined three other non-uniformed men. The four boarded the Graham. Julio then took off, made a U-turn, and dropped them back down on Williams, then swung back again to join Mike.

Al, leading his troupe of three men, walked up Williams past the south end of the train tunnel, made a left on the next street (Newhall) to a spot within sight of the spur track, and waited in the shadows for the man Occhio to show up.

Swede and his pipe-fitter crew member stayed with Primo while the other four walked up Palou Avenue where Pucci was waiting with the Reo above the north end of the train tunnel. Four heavy burlap sacks filled with sand were lifted out of the Reo and carried down the slope to the tunnel's face wall that extended some two feet above the ground directly over the southbound tracks. Crouched behind the wall, the men waited while Pucci drove off in the direction of the still.

Sal had disembarked from Primo's Doane, made his way up to the Oakdale Avenue bridge where he then stepped off and down the embankment to the railroad tracks below.

As he walked south towards the tunnel, he glanced up to see the shadowy forms of the four men with the sacks of sand above, at the face of the tunnel. He stepped into the dark tunnel and laid down several yards inside between the wall and the northbound tracks with his head facing north towards the entrance.

The uniformed paesani had now transferred from the Model-T to the back of Primo's truck. They had pulled the row of six-foot stakes off the back of the truck bed plus those extending halfway around both sides. They held them in their hands straight up as they crowded against the bulkhead. In event a section of wall was to break loose above the big door as the old Doane crashed it, they at least had some protection.

The Doane made its way over to where it parked at the corner of the street where the still was located. Behind him was Mike with the Model-T and Julio with the Graham, accompanied by Swede and his man, the pipe fitter. These two men would be indispensable since they knew better than anyone else how to handle hot pipes, vessels, kettles, and the still itself.

Pucci's Reo was already parked ahead and across the intersection while he was down at the end of the dead-end street sticking his head around the corner of the building to be crashed, waiting for the moment to signal Primo and the rest to come in. Pucci heard the door at the other end of the building open up. A figure stepped out onto the main tracks. Presumably, this would be Occhio's right-hand man, the sapper. He held a flashlight in his hand and proceeded to flash a signal in the direction of the tunnel. In the distance, from the south end of the tunnel a signal flashed back, apparently from Occhio. The figure stepped back into the building and pulled the door partially closed behind him. The southbound express passenger train heading this way from San Francisco was now emerging from the south end of the Army Street tunnel at its usual fast pace. It was on schedule.

The clanking sound of the locomotive echoing throughout the buildings, plus its light beam illuminating the track ahead, announced its arrival. The train raced past Pucci and continued into the tunnel where Sal lay. Just as the last car cleared the tunnel opening at Palou Street, the four men above dropped the four sacks of sand onto the tracks, then scrambled down around the slope to the tracks below. Sal jumped up and joined them in moving and adjusting the sacks in position a few yards back inside the tunnel in order to stop the handcar about to come down the track. They quickly laid down flat on their bellies as the second signal now flashed. The handcar then started its run towards the tunnel — they waited.

Pucci struck a match on the side of the wood building. This was Primo's signal to move in quick. The Doane came down the street, swung left, and up to the opposite curb, then reversed with full throttle and crashed the back end of the truck into the large door, knocking it clean into the room in a thoroughly shattered condition. Protruding square nails didn't stop the Doane with its hard rubber tires from continuing on through the opening and over the top of the flattened door.

Pucci, in full uniform, charged on through the opening and took the initiative. He gave several blasts from a genuine police whistle, then yelled at the top of his voice in perfect English:

"You're all under arrest! You're all under arrest! Don't anyone make a move! This is a raid!"

All this yelling was for absolutely nothing; a complete waste of effort. These noncitizen immigrant Sicilians hadn't been in this country long enough to learn to say "Good Morning" let alone understand the spoken English words being yelled out by Pucci. What caught their attention was the blue uniforms sporting fancy silver badges, to say nothing of this group of uniformed men jumping off the trucks wielding six-foot-long hardwood stakes. Every last one of them, however many there were, beat it out the back door and across the railroad tracks before you could say, "Cock Robin."

The handcar by now was about to pass under the Oakdale bridge crossing and into the tunnel under Palou. The two men pumping the handcar expected to enter its darkened shadowed entrance as usual and emerge from the other end such as they had done in the past. However, at the instant the handcar disappeared through the opening, it came to an abrupt halt as it thudded against the heavy sacks of sand placed on the rails. The impact not only derailed it, but it also sent the forward man cartwheeling backwards along with five-gallon cans of alcohol. The man facing the direction of travel did a mid-air flip over the bar as he, too, was catapulted forward.

They were immediately jumped by the tug crew and held firmly to the ground while their pockets were searched for the blackjack. The sapper was the one they really were after. Once it was found, the other man was led to the tunnel entrance, firmly booted in the ass a few times, and set free. The sapper, however, would not have it quite that good.

One of the men gave Sal a hand in getting the now empty car back on the southbound set of rails. Sal waited for no one. He pumped his way down towards the south end of the tunnel as fast as he could while the tug crew went to work on the sapper. The crew men were holding him down on his knees in a prone position with his head down to the ground and his ass pointing upward. They had pulled his pants down to his knees and literally ripped his longjohns open exposing his ass to the elements. They tied his hands firmly behind his back with his own bootlaces. The crewman with the pocket flask poured a generous portion of turpentine in the palm of his hand and forced it up and around the sapper's asshole as a lubricant. He then proceeded to thoroughly soak the blackjack with the rest of the available turpentine and forced it up the sapper's ass as far as his stiff muscular finger could manage.

"So blackjacks are a big thing with you, are they now? Well, let's see how you like it shoved up your ass?" growled the crewman as he wiped his finger and hand on the sapper's longjohns. There was enough turpentine oozing from the jacket of the blackjack to shrink the hemorrhoids of a fair-size buffalo, say nothing of the charge he pre-received for lubricant. They then stood him up on his feet, pulled up his pants, and gave his belt a good tight cinch. Now he was given some sound advice that could barely be heard above his screams and groans of agony as the turpentine singed its way through tender, delicate tissue.

"Run, you son-of-a-bitch, or we'll pull that frigg'n blackjack clean out your throat!"

Whether the sapper understood or was able to comprehend the true meaning of the message was neither here nor there, for run he did. His headlong dash took him away from the tunnel entrance and up the embankment, and onto Oakdale where he chose to run towards the nearby residences. His screams and yells were being heard from the residences above as if the devil himself was skinning a sinner alive. He ran through the streets begging for help, but all he got was slammed doors and doused lights as parents ushered their children off the streets. Those children that were skeptical about goblins on Halloween night became firm believers as they witnessed this screaming, maddened demon who appeared to have just fallen off of "Satan's" cart.

Putting turpentine on a domestic house cat's butt and sending him screaming across rooftops was an old Halloween trick used by ruffian kids to spark some life into the true spirit of Halloween. However, this was the first time ever that it happened to a human being.

At the south end of the tunnel, Sal had brought the handcar to a halt just short of the tunnel entrance. His intention was to let Al and the others work Occhio over, then move in and finish the job. This, of course, was not part of the original plan. Al and his men were to get the jump on him, work him over, and wreck his truck permanently. But the full moon rising from the east was illuminating the shadows the men needed to work their way up along the buildings, so as to get in striking range of Occhio as he was standing ready at the rails to throw the switching mechanism to divert the handcar onto the spur.

The east-west direction of the spur was to Occhio's advantage. His keen senses told him that all wasn't well. The handcar should have been there by now. Instinct caused him to look around in all directions. The men coming in on him along the spur were detected. He had no idea what was going on. But as far as he was concerned, the men moving towards him were after him, possibly for the purpose of hijacking the alcohol, so he thought.

The tracks leading up towards the south end of the tunnel where Sal waited were clear. With a good head start, Occhio no doubt could outrun his pursuers and disappear through the tunnel or in the shadows of the residential area above. He had no other option. It was a split-second decision that sent him running towards the tunnel.

Realizing that they had been detected, Al and his men rushed forward and gave chase, running headlong across moonlit tracks and ties in pursuit of Occhio. Just as he was about to step out of the protective shadows, Sal saw him coming in his direction. He moved back to one side and waited.

Occhio reached the Williams Avenue bridge above, just a few yards from where Sal was waiting at the tunnel. He hesitated for a split second as if trying to decide which way to run. The thought of climbing up the embankment crossed his mind but the steepness made it impractical.

At the same instant, Sal also made a split-second decision by calling out in his native Sicilian tongue: "Occhio, over here." Spoken in his same dialect and calling out his nickname, the call was construed to be from one of his men. Under the circumstances, a helping hand being extended from the shadows was indeed welcomed. A helping hand, indeed!

No sooner had Occhio reached the shadows, Sal's powerful left hand grabbed a handful of clothing at his chest, then while holding him firmly, said:

"Occhio, this is Di Cultilieri from Sicily!" snarled Sal. The short, to the point speech didn't slow down either man's instinctive actions — kill, or be killed.

Occhio's hands came up fast, flipped the loop of his garrote around Sal's neck and pulled up tight. But it wasn't quick enough to stop the plunge of Sal's long-bladed knife from penetrating his belly to the hilt. Sal knew better than to fight the garrote. Instead, he held his left-hand grip firmly while bringing the knife's cutting edge upward and into Occhio's rib cage.

The finely honed, razor-sharp cutting edge sliced through guts, liver, lungs, and heart all in one mighty upward thrust. Sal held his deathlike grip on his opponent as the lack of oxygen to his own brain was starting to render him faint. But the knife remained firmly implanted as the stench of gut gasses commingled with blood, impregnated the brisk night air. The hefty grunt followed by a deathly gasp that omitted from Occhio's mouth as the knife found its mark, was well justified. It was followed by a series of coughs, gurgles, and gasping as blood spurted from his mouth and nose. The instant shock sent surges of tremors throughout his body as he relaxed his grip on the garrote and crumbled to the ground taking Sal in his half-dazed condition along with him. The strong smell of human excrement from the dying man added to the already sickening stench. The shadows prevented the revelation of Occhio's wide-eyed look of death staring in disbelief.

The two men lay there, both gasping for air, as Al and his men approached them cautiously, not being sure what to expect. The reflection of moonlight indicated that there was no one standing. All they could make out was the empty handcar and the two forms lying there alongside.

Al's hand reached in his pocket and came up with a wooden match; all in the same swift motion, like a western gunman drawing and firing his handgun, he struck the match with the nail of his thumb. The instant light revealed that one of the men was Sal. He quickly reached down and removed the already loose garrote from around his neck. He was coming around, breathing in deep gasps. Al doused the match, then knelt down and helped Sal to his knees. His breathing was now taking on the rhythm of normalcy. Al rose and pulled Sal up on his feet. The firmly held knife retracted from the still-quivering body with a suction sound as it followed the bloody fist from within the cavity it had created.

"Sal, are you okay?" asked Al.

"Yes, thank you, Al," came the almost inaudible answer."You must take your men and leave here at once!" added Sal.

"And leave you behind? No way. You come with us," stated Al with a firmness.

Sal took out his handkerchief and tied it tight around his burning, stinging neck. The finely braided leather garrote had left cutting burn bruises that would, no doubt, create scars that would be a constant reminder to Sal of this horrendous ordeal.

"No, Al, I don't wish to drag you into this. This is my doing, so I will have to deal with it," said Sal.

"Sal, listen to me!" pleaded Al. "This is a case of self-defense!" Then striking another match, he looked around in search of the discarded garrote. He picked it up and held it firmly in his hand. "He had this thing around your neck with the intention of killing you. I removed it from around your neck. I, along with these three men, bare witness to it. Ask them," said Al as he doused the match by swinging it back and forth.

The light reflection on Sal's face had revealed teardrops streaming down his cheeks. These were not tears of fear, hurt, or joy. They were tears of relief. He had just unloaded one of the greatest burdens a man can carry. The burden of a young man that must exonerate his obligation to vindicate his elders, which they were not able to do for themselves.

"He's right, Sal, we would testify to that. Please reconsider and come with us," said one of the others.

"Trust me, Sal, leave this mess and come with us now," pleaded Al once more.

"All right, I'll come with you. I trust your judgment."

"Good! Come on, let's get the hell out of here!"

Without saying another word, Sal reached down, grabbed Occhio by the shoulders, and dragged him on and across the tracks just in front of the handcar. Using the dead man's coattails for a towel, he wiped his fist and knife as best he could and shoved the knife back into its sheath.

Al put the garrote in his pocket and walked to the edge of the shadows, peered down the moonlit tracks towards the spur as if contemplating heading back that way.

"How about the truck, Al. What are we going to do about

that?" asked the closest man to him.

"The hell with it! It makes no difference now," was his answer. Then continued: "Now, listen! All of you! If you've never been able to keep your mouth shut before, you damned well better do so now! Do you understand what I mean? We tell no one; not a single person!"

They all acknowledged the importance of his statement and therefore agreed.

"Okay, come on. We're heading down to 3rd Street. Once up on the street, keep to the shadows as much as possible. Move quietly–avoid detection."

The minute the bootleggers had fled, Pucci headed up the street signaling Mike and Julio to pull up to the opening in front of the Doane, then backed his Reo into the intersection blocking all access to the short dead-end street. His job now was to use his authority to keep any and all intruders away from the area. Unbeknownst to him, Mike had made a deal with Swede to save intact as much of the equipment as possible rather than deliberately ripping it apart as Pucci had intended.

Swede was all for the idea. He and his man, along with Taliaferro, worked fast and efficiently in dismantling the still and its related equipment. The still itself, kettles, vats, tanks, burners, condenser, and all its related piping, etc., was loaded on the Graham. Whatever room was left on the Doane after the available sugar, mash, yeast, and other related ingredients were loaded, was also used for the odds and ends that the Graham couldn't handle.

The word went out for everyone to clear out and climb back aboard the trucks. The Halloween masquerade party was over. As the paesani were climbing aboard the Model-T, Mike reached in his coat pocket and came up with a fresh, full-length Toscanello cigar. He rolled it between his thumb and knife blade, then snapped it in half, putting one half between his lips and handing the other to Swede as he walked up to him. Swede took his half in the palm of his hand and crushed it into a gob, proceeded to put the whole of it in his mouth, and started chewing it. He preferred his tobacco in this manner.

Mike, however, struck a match and torched his in the usual manner. The flash of the struck match was an indication to Pucci that Mike was lighting up, satisfied that all had gone well.

Pucci backed away from the crossing and let the caravan go

by. He could hardly believe his eyes when they drove on past him with fully-loaded trucks. Hot distillery equipment was giving off clouds of vapors because of its now coming in contact with brisk, cold damp air. It didn't look demolished to him at all. As a matter of fact, it looked more like it was still in operation.

As usual, the Model-T was taking up the rear. The "chit . . . chit . . . chit . . . chit" of the cricket-like sound could be heard fading away, along with an occasional spitting-spurting sound resembling a barnyard goose, as Swede splattered the street with his chew.

Pucci swung his Reo down the street to the raided building, trained his headlights into the now darkened interior, it was picked clean. He swore out loud: "Those damned characters, they didn't demolish it! They dismantled it! And hauled off the whole damned kit and caboodle! They're crazy! Just plain crazy!"

He backed out hurriedly and headed back out in pursuit of the others. The Reo caught up to the Model-T as it was picking up the tug crew and the full cans of alcohol retrieved from the handcar. The Doane and the Graham had already made a right on 3rd Street, now heading south.

Pucci was about to step out and tell Mike what he thought of the bootlegging business when a police car, with red light on and siren screaming, came around the corner at 3rd Street and headed up in their direction.

"Oh, Christ! They've got us!" exclaimed Pucci out loud.

The police car came roaring up the street and charged right on by not paying much attention to the two trucks stopped at the crossing. The police car contained two police officers. The passenger made comment to the driver:

"Now, what the hell do you suppose that's all about?" referring to the Model-T and the Reo parked just past the bridge.

"The hell with them!" came the comment from his partner at the wheel. "We gotta find that crazed madman that's running around terrorizing the neighborhood. I hope the bastard isn't armed!"

They were referring to the sapper who wasn't armed per se, but he was well-fueled. The strike of a match close to his butt would send him up into the clouds like a rocket.

Pucci, not knowing for sure of the police car's purpose for being here at this hour of night, decided to stick around a few minutes. After all, he too could be there on official business as far as anyone would know. If they come back this way, I'll give them the red light and stop them. At least delay them long enough for the paesani to beat it across the city limits, he thought. The more he thought about it, the better the idea sounded.

In the meantime, Mike took off with his load of men not looking back to see who was coming. When he reached the corner, he stopped only long enough to let the tug crew scramble off, along with Swede and the pipe fitter. They would make it back to the tug on foot carrying a couple of five-gallon cans of alcohol they had grabbed off the Model-T as they parted. Mike now headed south for one more stop, to pick up Al and the others, then head for the ranch at San Bruno.

Pucci waited a few minutes until the thought occurred to him that maybe the Police Department had received a call related to Al and his men demolishing Occhio's truck or whatever may have taken place at the south end of the tunnel. "That's it," he told himself. "They came up on the wrong end of the tunnel. I better get over there before they do."

As he headed down 3rd Street, he heard the whistle of another southbound commuter passenger train also heading south. Although it was scheduled to make stops at each town as it proceeded down the Peninsula, it was travelling at a fair rate of speed, and on the same track as where the "handcar" rested.

"Oh, Christ!" swore Pucci. "I better get up to the bridge crossing at Williams before that train gets there. It will, no doubt, light up everything around there."

He was almost too late. By the time he made it around, the train was about to emerge from the tunnel. He looked to his right to see the lit-up tunnel entrance below as the locomotive was about to come through.

The sight of the handcar just inside the tunnel setting on the tracks directly in the path of the oncoming locomotive caused him to wince before exclaiming in a somewhat disturbed and mystified manner: "What the hell's that thing doing there? Jesus Christ, it's on the southbound track!" The handcar with the lighting coming from the opposite side was shadowing the body of the man, Occhio. This Pucci didn't see.

As far as the engineer on the locomotive was concerned, the track should be clear. Nevertheless, he was keeping an eye on the

351

track up ahead as was his custom. The wisps of smoke and steam vapors that drifted back and around the cab as it sped through the tunnel impaired his vision to the extent that he didn't see the low handcar on the rails up ahead until it was too late to brake and avoid hitting it.

"Those stupid work crews!" swore the Engineer catching the attention of his firebox tender as he went about his chores. Instinct told him to brake, but in the few seconds that he had time to think, it occurred to him that the safety of his passengers should prevail.

"We're not going to scatter passengers all through the aisles for a damned handcar that's been abandoned by some stupid work crew!" he yelled out. With that, he reached up and grabbed the whistle cord and pulled on it firmly. The train came roaring out of the tunnel with steam whistle screaming. It's big head lamp lit up whatever of the night that the full moon didn't.

The crushing, crashing sound of impact of the massive cast iron fender against the handcar added to the clanking and clattering sound of the locomotive and its hissing steam.

The mangled, twisted frame of the handcar was bouncing out in front of the locomotive like a country lad kicking a tin can while walking along a gravel road. Gravel was flying in all directions like grapeshot fired from a cannon. The handcar in its battered condition finally bounced away and against the side of a metal building with a rattling blast of noise that surely sent surges of fear through the hearts of children that did believe in Halloween goblins and demons.

As for the corpse of the hapless man called Occhio — if one was to try hard enough, no doubt some evidence of a human being could have been found amongst the shreds of clothing strewn along the right of way.

"Jesus Christ!" exclaimed Pucci. "I don't remember Halloween nights ever being anything like this when I was a kid!"

He drove across the bridge and over to the spur where he expected to see a somewhat demolished truck. The truck was there all right, but it was intact. No sign of damage and no sign of anyone around.

"What the hell?" he mumbled. "Why didn't they wreck the damned thing?"

Now the disturbing thought occurred to him: "It's possible

353

that Al may have kicked that Occhio character once too often. Or, maybe somehow Sal got to him first? And why was the handcar left on the southbound track just inside the tunnel, minus the alcohol? Sal was supposed to continue the journey and take it all the way down and join Al, leaving the handcar on the side spur. If Sal did get to him first, why isn't the body lying around there?" He shuddered at the possible answers to his own questions.

Stepping out of the Reo with flashlight in hand, he walked around to the rear of the truck pulling back the canvas cautiously while flashing the light into the empty truck. He actually expected to see the alcohol loaded in the back end thinking that maybe Al intended to steal it, along with the truck, although this was not part of the plan. There was no point in walking up the spur track. The bright moonlight showed the area to be clear between the buildings. The flooding light of the locomotive shown the right-of-way from the bridge down past the spur to be clear also.

"The buggers must of had a plan of their own and said nothing about it. At least not to me," mumbled Pucci. The thought of the undamaged still, along with all the rest of the moonshine-making paraphernalia, loaded and hauled off with the Graham and the Doane, also crossed his mind: "Mike, too, had made different plans as well, no doubt."

He drove back onto Williams and headed back down to 3rd Street arriving at the corner in time to see the police car with its bright red light once again coming his way like a bat out of hell.

"Oh, Christ! Here they come again, no doubt looking for the Doane and the Graham," he said, talking to himself. "They'll overtake them sure as hell!"

He quickly reached over and snapped on the switch to his own red light. The driver of the police car saw the red light come on at the corner. This time seeing and recognizing the official fire truck, the police car pulled alongside facing the opposite direction and stopped. Through the rolled-down window the policeman asked the question:

"Have you seen anything of any half-crazed lunatics running around out here scaring the hell out of people?"

The question caught Pucci by surprise. "No. Not really!" he answered. He would have liked to have answered: "Yes, there's quite a bunch of them heading south," but he chose the more

354

appropriate answer instead.

By now the caravan of trucks loaded with all sorts of dripping equipment had reached the Bayshore Highway rattling and bouncing along, leaving behind a trail of smelly distillery juice.

The conversation continued for a few minutes when Pucci added the comment:

"You shouldn't have any trouble finding a few lunatics on a night like this. What do you intend to do with them once you catch up to them?"

"Damned good question," answered the policeman laughingly, then said: "I think we'll give it up and get the hell out of here. We've got better things to do."

"Amen," put in Pucci with relief.

The police car then headed on up Williams Street in the direction that Pucci had come. He watched them long enough to see them disappear, then made a left turn onto 3rd Street and headed north instead of south as preplanned. Since the caravan could still be overtaken, he would take no chances. If anything, he would direct the police away from the caravan, in the event they were to intercept him again. Besides he'd about had his fill of this bootlegging related affair.

Pucci then spoke softly as if talking to his paesano buddies:

"Good night, my fellow paesani. I'd like to join you, but bootlegging is not for me."

END

To the Reader

Thank you for sharing my fond memories of the old folks and the times gone by. Hopefully you have enjoyed reading this story as much as I have enjoyed writing it.

But wait, there's more. There's a sequel to this story, titled: "Jackass Brandy", also a must read. Watch for and ask for it at your favorite bookstore. The illustration on the back cover of this book is the front cover of "Jackass Brandy". It will help you identify it.

In this second story, Mike and his countrymen's wine hijacking venture gives way to the more sophisticated and riskier business of bootlegging; namely, cranking out alcohol, and converting it into what was then referred to as "Jackass Brandy", as well as other identifying names such as "Moonshine".

Mike Buti, the "Capo", sets up his operation in Crow Canyon on the outskirts of Hayward, Alameda County, California, on a chicken ranch that becomes the front for the bootlegging enterprise. He gradually transforms into a tough, domineering boss with a short fuse, especially when dealing with tainted lawmen.

Julio Matteoli, second in command, ramrods production at the stills. His loyalty to Mike holds firm even to the day he enters San Quentin prison, successfully posing as the "Capo" using the name of "Gelio Rossi", an alias, in order to protect Mike. His ever pleasant disposition finally hardens.

Al Giovanetti, the driver, enforcer and henchman of sorts, sets out to destroy the crooked Federal agents that constantly hound the operation. But, in his reckless ways with cars and trucks, comes within a whisker of being destroyed himself. The gun-toting Federal agents didn't appreciate his sometimes fatal car dueling tactics.

Joseph P. Lacey, Mike's legal counsel, a crook in his own right, to protect himself attempts to sell Mike out, but instead, ends up being sentenced to two consecutive five year terms in San Quentin. This delighted Mike to no end.

Honorable Earl Warren, late governor of the state of California and Chief Justice of the United States, the then District Attorney of Alameda County, successfully breaks up Mike's gang, but to his disappointment, the ones he was really after, the two Buti cousins, "Mike and Terso", slipped through his fingers. They were just plain too smart for him.

Be sure to read it; I promise, you'll not be disappointed. *Bruno*